THE LITURGY DOCUMENTS

A PARISH RESOURCE

Revised Edition

Constitution on the Sacred Liturgy

General Instruction on the Roman Missal

*Appendix to the General Instruction
  for the Dioceses of the United States*

Lectionary for Mass: Introduction

*General Norms for the Liturgical Year
  and Calendar*

Directory for Masses with Children

Music in Catholic Worship

Liturgical Music Today

Environment and Art in Catholic Worship

THE
LITURGY
DOCUMENTS

A PARISH RESOURCE

Revised Edition

Edited by
Mary Ann Simcoe

LITURGY TRAINING
PUBLICATIONS

WITH GRATEFUL ACKNOWLEDGMENT:

The English translation of the Introduction from the *Lectionary for Mass* (Second *Editio Typica)* © 1981, International Committee on English in the Liturgy, Inc. (ICEL); the English translation of the Constitution on the Liturgy, the General Instruction of the Roman Missal, the Directory for Masses with Children, the General Norms for the Liturgical Year and Calendar from *Documents on the Liturgy, 1963–1979: Conciliar, Papal, and Curial Texts* © 1982, ICEL; the English translation of *Emendations in the Liturgical Books following upon the New Code of Canon Law* © 1984, ICEL. All rights reserved.

Music in Catholic Worship, Revised Edition © 1983; Liturgical Music Today © 1982; Environment and Art in Catholic Worship © 1978; Appendix to the General Instruction for the Dioceses of the United States of America from the General Instruction of the Roman Missal © 1982, United States Catholic Conference. All rights reserved.

Printed in the United States of America.

Library of Congress Catalog Card Number: 84–82155

ISBN 0–930467–03–5

CONTENTS

FOREWORD

Since the first edition of *The Liturgy Documents: A Parish Resource* was published, the twentieth anniversary of the *Constitution on the Sacred Liturgy*, the document which mandated the liturgical renewal, has come and gone. With that anniversary came the proliferation of more documents and statements that size up and celebrate how far Roman Catholics have come as we enter the third decade of liturgical renewal.

From these many words Liturgy Training Publications once again presents a few basic documents—including the groundbreaking *Constitution*—from Rome and the United States Bishops' Committee on the Liturgy. We are ever convinced that these, more than any other wise words, are central sources for those who have responsibility for the liturgical life of a parish. Such words must be kept close—not just within arm's reach of the desk as a handy reference—but to us. The process of making them our own and applying their insight to living worship has not stopped after 20 years. We are still taking in the revised rites and the principles that drive them. We are just beginning to learn them by heart.

Only one of the documents which appeared in the first edition of *The Liturgy Documents* is omitted in this edition, the excerpts from the 1967 *Instruction on Eucharistic Worship*. Although the instruction is still useful and timely, it has been dropped in favor of adding the following to this collection of basic documents: the full text of *General Norms for the Liturgical Year*, the revised *Lectionary for Mass: Introduction*, and *Liturgical Music Today*. All selections are presented in their most recent editions or translations, and the emendations in the liturgical books following upon the 1983 Code of Canon Law which apply to these documents have been made.

This edition of *The Liturgy Documents* includes background notes for each document which have been prepared by Gabe Huck. The supremely useful index which Father Edmund Siedlecki created for the first edition has been updated by James Bradley Burke. To these contributors thanks are due. The outline of each document is presented as a "table of contents" to help readers find information they are looking for. Finally, a list of abbreviations is given for those documents which are frequently referred to in the footnotes.

The best future I can think of for this book is that you who use it will—in spite of its good paper and binding—wear it out in the process of learning and returning to the sources.

Mary Ann Simcoe

FOREWORD to the First Edition

Over the past three decades, a lengthy series of documents has been promulgated by both the Holy See and the American bishops concerning liturgical reforms in the Roman Catholic church. In the ten years between 1963 and 1973 alone, over 90 official documents were issued to reshape liturgical attitudes and practices. These pronouncements have been significant not only in terms of the actual changes of ritual they initiated, but also in terms of the wealth of wise insights, solid principles and long-range vision they offer. Taken in their entirety, these statements provide an incomparable sense of liturgy, a refined sense of church and a keen sense of future direction—for anyone capable of digesting such a mountain of documentation.

The practical problem is that the majority of those charged with pastoral responsibility for liturgical celebrations at the local level have neither the time nor the background to process all the data. Somewhere, however, a start must be made.

For this reason, the staffs of the Office for Divine Worship and Liturgy Training Publications have collaborated to produce this primer of liturgical documentation. The contents of this book are obviously far from being comprehensive, but they do provide a substantive beginning for the parish liturgical minister. In addition, we have included something very special—an index where all important terms are listed together with references to any of the documents in which they are discussed. This feature should be a tool constantly used by liturgy teams and ministers.

Where to Begin

This present resource book is intended to provide parish personnel with a handy copy of the most basic post-Vatican II documents on liturgy. These texts were selected not for their canonical or rubrical interest, but because of their long-range importance and parish usefulness.

There can be no substitute for a personal reading and rereading through these fundamental documents with careful reflection. They can and should be marked up according to the reader's perception of their practical and pastoral implications. Only by personal familiarity with these primary sources of renewal can a minister gradually grow into an informed sense of good liturgy.

With a Little Bit of Help from My Friends

As a helpful guide (but not substitute) for individual and group study of these basic documents, the actual texts found in this book are previewed by a thumbnail synthesis. This gives the reader an overview of the contents of the documents, highlighting the most salient points to be found in each. With such assistance, hopefully the reader will come to a better grasp of the deeper rationales underlying specific ritual changes. The lessons to be learned from this documentation are many, but the reader is encouraged to be attentive to some of the most basic.

The Basic Lessons

All of the post–Vatican II liturgical reforms have been based upon the first document reprinted here, the *Constitution on the Sacred Liturgy* (1963). From the outset, the criteria of simplicity and clarity are established as the guiding principles for liturgical renewal. The *Constitution* also provides the plan of action for the reform: the revision of the liturgical books and the clarification of the structure of the basic rituals will yield the firm foundation for pastoral adaptation and the interior renewal of our worshiping assemblies at a later date. The fundamental premises, both theological and pastoral, are here established for the universal church. This compendium of the "basic truths" of contemporary liturgical renewal is the indispensable bedrock upon which everything else will be built. As any constitution of an institutional community, this first decree of the Second Vatican Council offers the "new school of thought," the "new spirit," to direct all that will come after.

In the very first place, these principles were then brought to bear upon the renewal of the eucharistic liturgy. Although the Mass has never been intended to exhaust the liturgical life of the church, as our preeminent celebration it serves as the exemplar of how the *Constitution's* basic principles are to be applied. *The General Instruction of the Roman*

Missal (1969) revised eucharistic celebration in light of the historical genesis and development of this Judaeo-Christian ritual of praise prayer, and in the revision attempts to emphasize the integrity of a single, flowing eucharistic action by highlighting the relationship of parts to the whole. Exterior participation of those who are the body of Christ, the church, is intended to facilitate their interior participation since the assembly is the true subject of this liturgical activity. The legitimate variety of options within a basic structural framework enables the living body of Christ to make this integral prayer ritual an authentic expression of their deepest identity in Christ. . . .

All of these new directives, however, are to be understood according to a new philosophy of liturgical law. So that we might learn Rome's way of viewing the new Mass rubrics, the *Directory for Masses with Children* was promulgated (1973) to demonstrate how the standard shape of eucharistic celebration might be adapted pastorally to the human situation of real people. Just as people are not made for the Sabbath, but the Sabbath for people (Mark 2:27), so also people are not made for the sacraments, but sacraments are for living people. In this *Directory* (as also in the new *Order of Penance* and the *Rite of Anointing and Pastoral Care of the Sick)* we have a clear lesson in viewing liturgical ritual as a ministerial response to an existential situation. Our principles, structures and laws must be accommodated to meet the pastoral needs of our people, since our liturgy is divine worship only when it is an exercise of genuine love. Intelligent creativity and prudent flexibility in adapting ritual texts and actions to the local community do not deteriorate the unity of the church; rather, by enhancing the spiritual quality of liturgical celebration, they can stimulate us to deeper bonds of union in Christ.

These renewed attitudes about our eucharistic liturgy might possibly be misunderstood as applying only to verbal elements. As a matter of fact, in some places liturgical renewal has implied little more than a movement from the priest "reading the Mass" to the laity "writing the Mass." Keenly aware that liturgy consists more in nonverbal interaction than in verbal communication, the American bishops wisely delineated their concern for the sights, sounds and movements of our worship by issuing two critically important national documents, *Music in Catholic Worship* (1972) and *Environment and Art in Catholic Worship* (1978). Their emphasis on the primary significance of the nonverbal elements involved in eucharistic celebration must still filter down to those who continue to labor under the misconception of an exaggerated didactic and verbose approach to pastoral adaptation. We can be justly proud of the leadership shown by our American hierarchy in these two documents, keeping our vision and practice on target toward the goals of authentic liturgical renewal.

This book focuses the reader's attention almost exclusively on eucharistic celebrations, because if we are to begin somewhere, we might as well begin with the prayer form which consumes the most time and talent on the parish scene. We hope that the basic principles illustrated by the documents contained here, particularly the final ones on music, and environment and art, will be brought to bear upon our renewal of our sacramental celebrations and moments of communal prayer. The eucharist will always remain our paramount way of observing the Lord's Day, but its authentic interiorization on the part of our people will gradually lead us to reawaken communal partication in the liturgy of the hours as our daily prayer and to relocate our sacramental moments within the framework of the liturgical feasts and seasons according to individual and communal cycles of human life. We still have a long road to travel; may the use of this book by many parish ministers of liturgy assure firm ground for a solid beginning.

Gerard Broccolo

ABBREVIATIONS

AAS *Acta Apostolicae Sedis*

AG *Ad gentes,* Vatican Council II, *Decree on the Missionary Activity of the Church*

AP Congregation for Divine Worship, instruction *Actio pastoralis,* Instruction on Masses for Special Gatherings, 15 May 1969, AAS 61 (1969) 806–811

Baptism Roman Ritual, Rite of Baptism for Children

BCL Bishops' Committee on the Liturgy

BCLN *Bishops' Committee on the Liturgy Newsletter: 1965–1975* (Washington: United States Catholic Conference, 1977)

CCL Code of Canon Law, 1983

CDW Congregation for Divine Worship

CR Congregation of Rites

CSDW Congregation for the Sacraments and Divine Worship

CSL *Constitution on the Sacred Liturgy (Sacrosanctum Concilium),* Vatican Council II

CTr John Paul II, apostolic exhortation *Catechesis tradendae,* 16 Oct 1979: AAS 71 (1979) 1277–1340

DC John Paul II, epistle *Dominicae Cenae,* 24 Feb 1980: AAS 72 (1980)

DMC Congregation for Divine Worship, *Directory for Masses with Children (Pueros baptizatos),* AAS 66 (1974) 30–46

DV *Dei Verbum,* Vatican Council II, *Dogmatic Constitution on Divine Revelation*

EAW *Environment and Art in Catholic Worship*

EM Congregation of Rites, *Eucharisticum mysterium* (on Worship of the Eucharist), 25 May 1967: AAS 59 (1967) 539–573

EN Paul VI, apostolic exhortation *Evangelii nuntiandi,* 8 Dec 1975: AAS 68 (1976) 5–76

GCD *General Catechetical Directory*

GI *General Instruction of the Roman Missal*

GIapp Appendix to the *General Instruction* for the Dioceses of the United States

GNLY Congregation of Rites, *General Norms for the Liturgical Year and the Calendar*

ID Congregation for the Sacraments and Divine Worship, instruction *Inaestimabile Donum*, 3 April 1980: AAS 72 (1980)

IOe Congregation of Rites, instruction *Inter Oecumenici*, 26 Sept 1964: AAS 56 (1964) 877–900

LG *Lumen Gentium*, Vatican Council II, *Dogmatic Constitution on the Church*

LI Congregation for Divine Worship, instruction *Liturgicae instaurationes*, 5 Sept 1970: AAS 62 (1970) 692–704

LMIn Lectionary for Mass: Introduction, second *editio typica* (1981)

LMT *Liturgical Music Today*

MCW *Music in Catholic Worship*

MQ Paul VI, Motu Proprio *Ministeria quaedam*, 15 Aug 1972: AAS 64 (1972) 529–534

MS Congregation of Rites, instruction *Musicam sacram*, Instruction on Music in the Sacred Liturgy, 5 March 1967: AAS 59 (1967) 87–105

PG *Patrologiae cursus completus: Series graeca* (ed. Migne)

PL *Patrologiae cursus completus: Series latina* (ed. Migne)

PO *Presbyterorum Ordinis*, Vatican Council II, *Decree on the Ministry and Life of Priests*

RCIA Rite of Christian Initiation of Adults

RM Roman Missal *(Missale Romanum)*

RR Roman Ritual *(Rituale Romanum)*

CONSTITUTION
ON THE
SACRED LITURGY

SACROSANCTUM CONCILIUM

December 1963

BACKGROUND

This document is prologue not only to the several documents which follow in this book, but to the revisions of all our rites, and the pastoral introductions to these. It was completed by the Second Vatican Council in 1963. After more than 20 years we still sense, reading the *Constitution*, that the task it set for the church is hardly begun.

We must not think that the *Constitution* came from nowhere. For a century the work had been underway: scholarly research, pastoral experimentation, national and international liturgical conferences. But few foresaw how eagerly, critically and completely the world's bishops would embrace this work.

Certain directions in the *Constitution* caught people's attention from the start: the introduction of vernacular languages, concelebration, stress on active participation, the expanded role of scripture reading. Time would show how profound were other aspects little noticed at first: the restoration of the catechumentate, for example, and with it the recognition of the true character of Lent, the Triduum and Eastertime. The document freely ranges from general observation and sweeping reform (#30, for example, says that "the people should be encouraged to take part by means of acclamations, responses, psalmody, antiphons, and songs, as well as by actions, gestures, and bodily attitudes") to rather small details (see some of the notes on the liturgy of the hours or on books of Gregorian chant).

The *Constitution*, in hindsight, has its faults. There is a marvelous and constant demand for active participation, but little recognition of how deep was the division in practice between "attending the liturgy" and the rites and prayers that truly belonged to the people. There is an open acknowledgment that cultural adaptation is necessary, but some hesitation to recognize all that this might mean. There is no statement about the life of justice that is expressed in and fostered by the liturgy. These are not small omissions, but there is so much else to be grateful for in the *Constitution*.

The *Constitution* should be read as a foundation for the generations-long work in which we are engaged. Its enthusiasm, its dedication and its great openness are contagious yet.

OUTLINE

CONSTITUTION ON THE SACRED LITURGY

1.   This Sacred Council has several aims in view: it desires to impart an ever increasing vigor to the Christian life of the faithful; to adapt more suitably to the needs of our own times those institutions that are subject to change; to foster whatever can promote union among all who believe in Christ; to strengthen whatever can help to call the whole of humanity into the household of the Church. The council therefore sees particularly cogent reasons for undertaking the reform and promotion of the liturgy.

2.   For the liturgy, "making the work of our redemption a present actuality,"[1] most of all in the divine sacrifice of the eucharist, is the outstanding means whereby the faithful may express in their lives and manifest to others the mystery of Christ and the real nature of the true Church. It is of the essence of the Church to be both human and divine, visible yet endowed with invisible resources, eager to act yet intent on contemplation, present in this world yet not at home in it; and the Church is all these things in such wise that in it the human is directed and subordinated to the divine, the visible likewise to the invisible, action to contemplation, and this present world to that city yet to come which we seek.[2] While the liturgy daily builds up those who are within into a holy temple of the Lord, into a dwelling place for God in the Spirit,[3] to the mature measure of the fullness of Christ,[4] at the same time it marvelously strengthens their power to preach Christ and thus shows forth the Church to those who are outside as a sign lifted up among the nations,[5] under which the scatttered children of God may be gathered together,[6] until there is one sheepfold and one shepherd.[7]

3.   Wherefore the Council judges that the following principles concerning the promotion and reform of the liturgy should be called to mind and practical norms established.

Among these principles and norms there are some that can and should be applied both to the Roman Rite and also to all the other rites. The practical norms that follow, however, should be taken as applying only to the Roman Rite, except for those that, in the very nature of things, affect other rites as well.

4.   Lastly, in faithful obedience to tradition, the Council declares that

the Church holds all lawfully acknowledged rites to be of equal right and dignity and wishes to preserve them in the future and to foster them in every way. The Council also desires that, where necessary, the rites be revised carefully in the light of sound tradition and that they be given new vigor to meet the circumstances and needs of modern times.

CHAPTER I

GENERAL PRINCIPLES FOR THE REFORM AND PROMOTION OF THE SACRED LITURGY

I. NATURE OF THE LITURGY AND ITS IMPORTANCE IN THE CHURCH'S LIFE

5.   God who "wills that all be saved and come to the knowledge of the truth" (1 Tm 2:4), "who in many and various ways spoke in times past to the fathers by the prophets" (Heb 1:1), when the fullness of time had come sent his Son, the Word made flesh, anointed by the Holy Spirit, to preach the Gospel to the poor, to heal the contrite of heart;[8] he is "the physician, being both flesh and of the Spirit,"[9] the mediator between God and us.[10] For his humanity, united with the person of the Word, was the instrument of our salvation. Therefore in Christ "the perfect achievement of our reconciliation came forth and the fullness of divine worship was given to us."[11]

The wonderful works of God among the people of the Old Testament were a prelude to the work of Christ the Lord. He achieved his task of redeeming humanity and giving perfect glory to God, principally by the paschal mystery of his blessed passion, resurrection from the dead, and glorious ascension, whereby "dying, he destroyed our death and, rising, he restored our life."[12] For it was from the side of Christ as he slept the sleep of death upon the cross that there came forth the sublime sacrament of the whole Church.[13]

6.   As Christ was sent by the Father, he himself also sent the apostles, filled with the Holy Spirit. Their mission was, first, by preaching the Gospel to every creature,[14] to proclaim that by his death and resurrection Christ has freed us from Satan's grip[15] and brought us into the Father's kingdom. But the work they preached they were also to bring into effect through the sacrifice and the sacraments, the center of the whole liturgical life. Thus by baptism all are plunged into the paschal mystery of Christ: they die with him, are buried with him, and rise with him;[16] they receive the spirit of adoption as children "in which we cry: Abba, Father" (Rom 8:15), and thus become true adorers whom the Father seeks.[17] In like manner, as often as they eat the supper of the Lord they proclaim the death of the Lord until he comes.[18] For that reason, on the very day of

Pentecost when the Church appeared before the world, "those who received the word" of Peter "were baptized." And "they continued steadfastly in the teaching of the apostles and in the communion of the breaking of bread and in prayers . . . praising God and being in favor with all the people" (Acts 2:41–47). From that time onward the Church has never failed to come together to celebrate the paschal mystery: reading those things "which were in all the Scriptures concerning him" (Lk 24:27); celebrating the eucharist, in which "the victory and triumph of his death are again made present";[19] and at the same time giving thanks "to God for his inexpressible gift" (2 Cor 9:15) in Christ Jesus, "in praise of his glory" (Eph 1:12), through the power of the Holy Spirit.

7.   To accomplish so great a work, Christ is always present in his Church, especially in its liturgical celebrations. He is present in the sacrifice of the Mass, not only in the person of his minister, "the same now offering, through the ministry of priests, who formerly offered himself on the cross,"[20] but especially under the eucharistic elements. By his power he is present in the sacraments, so that when a man baptizes it is really Christ himself who baptizes.[21] He is present in his word, since it is he himself who speaks when the holy Scriptures are read in the Church. He is present, lastly, when the Church prays and sings, for he promised: "Where two or three are gathered together in my name, there am I in the midst of them" (Mt 18:20).

Christ always truly associates the Church with himself in this great work wherein God is perfectly glorified and the recipients made holy. The Church is the Lord's beloved Bride who calls to him and through him offers worship to the eternal Father.

Rightly, then, the liturgy is considered as an exercise of the priestly office of Jesus Christ. In the liturgy, by means of signs perceptible to the senses, human sanctification is signified and brought about in ways proper to each of these signs; in the liturgy the whole public worship is performed by the Mystical Body of Jesus Christ, that is, by the Head and his members.

From this it follows that every liturgical celebration, because it is an action of Christ the Priest and of his Body which is the Church, is a sacred action surpassing all others; no other action of the Church can equal its effectiveness by the same title and to the same degree.

8.   In the earthly liturgy we take part in a foretaste of that heavenly liturgy celebrated in the holy city of Jerusalem toward which we journey as pilgrims, where Christ is sitting at the right hand of God, a minister of the holies and of the true tabernacle;[22] we sing a hymn to the Lord's glory with the whole company of heaven; venerating the memory of the saints, we hope for some part and fellowship with them; we eagerly await the

Savior, our Lord Jesus Christ, until he, our life, shall appear and we too will appear with him in glory.[23]

9.   The liturgy does not exhaust the entire activity of the Church. Before people can come to the liturgy they must be called to faith and to conversion: "How then are they to call upon him in whom they have not yet believed? But how are they to believe him whom they have not heard? And how are they to hear if no one preaches? And how are men to preach unless they be sent?" (Rom 10:14–15).

Therefore the Church announces the good tidings of salvation to those who do not believe, so that all may know the true God and Jesus Christ whom he has sent and may be converted from their ways, doing penance.[24] To believers, also, the Church must ever preach faith and penance, prepare them for the sacraments, teach them to observe all that Christ has commanded,[25] and invite them to all the works of charity, worship, and the apostolate. For all these works make it clear that Christ's faithful, though not of this world, are to be the light of the world and to glorify the Father in the eyes of all.

10.   Still, the liturgy is the summit toward which the activity of the Church is directed; at the same time it is the fount from which all the Church's power flows. For the aim and object of apostolic works is that all who are made children of God by faith and baptism should come together to praise God in the midst of his Church, to take part in the sacrifice, and to eat the Lord's Supper.

The liturgy in its turn moves the faithful, filled with "the paschal sacraments," to be "one in holiness";[26] it prays that "they may hold fast in their lives to what they have grasped by their faith";[27] the renewal in the eucharist of the covenant between the Lord and his people draws the faithful into the compelling love of Christ and sets them on fire. From the liturgy, therefore, particularly the eucharist, grace is poured forth upon us as from a fountain; the liturgy is the source for achieving in the most effective way possible human sanctification and God's glorification, the end to which all the Church's other activities are directed.

11.   But in order that the liturgy may possess its full effectiveness, it is necessary that the faithful come to it with proper dispositions, that their minds be attuned to their voices, and that they cooperate with divine grace, lest they receive it in vain.[28] Pastors must therefore realize that when the liturgy is celebrated something more is required than the mere observance of the laws governing valid and lawful celebration; it is also their duty to ensure that the faithful take part fully aware of what they are doing, actively engaged in the rite, and enriched by its effects.

12.   The spiritual life, however, is not limited solely to participation in

the liturgy. Christians are indeed called to pray in union with each other, but they must also enter into their chamber to pray to the Father in secret;[29] further, according to the teaching of the Apostle, they should pray without ceasing.[30] We learn from the same Apostle that we must always bear about in our body the dying of Jesus, so that the life also of Jesus may be made manifest in our bodily frame.[31] This is why we ask the Lord in the sacrifice of the Mass that "receiving the offering of the spiritual victim," he may fashion us for himself "as an eternal gift."[32]

13.   Popular devotions of the Christian people are to be highly endorsed, provided they accord with the laws and norms of the Church, above all when they are ordered by the Apostolic See.

Devotions proper to particular Churches also have a special dignity if they are undertaken by mandate of the bishops according to customs or books lawfully approved.

But these devotions should be so fashioned that they harmonize with the liturgical seasons, accord with the sacred liturgy, are in some way derived from it, and lead the people to it, since, in fact, the liturgy, by its very nature far surpasses any of them.

II. PROMOTION OF LITURGICAL INSTRUCTION
AND ACTIVE PARTICIPATION

14.   The Church earnestly desires that all the faithful be led to that full, conscious, and active participation in liturgical celebrations called for by the very nature of the liturgy. Such participation by the Christian people as "a chosen race, a royal priesthood, a holy nation, God's own people" (1 Pt 2:9; see 2:4–5) is their right and duty by reason of their baptism.

In the reform and promotion of the liturgy, this full and active participation by all the people is the aim to be considered before all else. For it is the primary and indispensable source from which the faithful are to derive the true Christian spirit and therefore pastors must zealously strive in all their pastoral work to achieve such participation by means of the necessary instruction.

Yet it would be futile to entertain any hopes of realizing this unless, in the first place, the pastors themselves become thoroughly imbued with the spirit and power of the liturgy and make themselves its teachers. A prime need, therefore, is that attention be directed, first of all, to the liturgical formation of the clergy. Wherefore the Council has decided to enact what follows.

15.   Professors appointed to teach liturgy in seminaries, religious houses

of study, and theological faculties must be thoroughly trained for their work in institutes specializing in this subject.

16. The study of liturgy is to be ranked among the compulsory and major courses in seminaries and religious houses of studies; in theological faculties it is to rank among the principal courses. It is to be taught under its theological, historical, spiritual, pastoral, and canonical aspects. Moreover, other professors, while striving to expound the mystery of Christ and the history of salvation from the angle proper to each of their own subjects, must nevertheless do so in a way that will clearly bring out the connection between their subjects and the liturgy, as also the underlying unity of all priestly training. This consideration is especially important for professors of dogmatic, spiritual, and pastoral theology and for professors of holy Scripture.

17. In seminaries and houses of religious, clerics shall be given a liturgical formation in their spiritual life. The means for this are: proper guidance so that they may be able to understand the sacred rites and take part in them wholeheartedly; the actual celebration of the sacred mysteries and of other, popular devotions imbued with the spirit of the liturgy. In addition they must learn how to observe the liturgical laws, so that life in seminaries and houses of religious may be thoroughly permeated by the spirit of the liturgy.

18. Priests, both secular and religious, who are already working in the Lord's vineyard are to be helped by every suitable means to understand ever more fully what it is they are doing in their liturgical functions; they are to be aided to live the liturgical life and to share it with the faithful entrusted to their care.

19. With zeal and patience pastors must promote the liturgical instruction of the faithful and also their active participation in the liturgy both internally and externally, taking into account their age and condition, their way of life, and their stage of religious development. By doing so, pastors will be fulfilling one of their chief duties as faithful stewards of the mysteries of God; and in this matter they must lead their flock not only by word but also by example.

20. Radio and television broadcasts of sacred rites must be marked by discretion and dignity, under the leadership and direction of a competent person appointed for this office by the bishops. This is especially important when the service to be broadcast is the Mass.

III. THE REFORM OF THE SACRED LITURGY

21. In order that the Christian people may more surely derive an abundance of graces from the liturgy, the Church desires to undertake with great care a general reform of the liturgy itself. For the liturgy is made up of immutable elements, divinely instituted, and of elements subject to change. These not only may but ought to be changed with the passage of time if they have suffered from the intrusion of anything out of harmony with the inner nature of the liturgy or have become pointless.

In this reform both texts and rites should be so drawn up that they express clearly the holy things they signify and that the Christian people, as far as possible, are able to understand them with ease and to take part in the rites fully, actively, and as befits a community.

Wherefore the Council establishes the general norms that follow.

A. General Norms

22. § 1. Regulation of the liturgy depends solely on the authority of the Church, that is, on the Apostolic See and, accordingly as the law determines, on the bishop.

§ 2. In virtue of power conceded by the law, the regulation of the liturgy within certain defined limits belongs also to various kinds of competent territorial bodies of bishops lawfully established.

§ 3. Therefore, no other person, not even if he is a priest, may on his own add, remove, or change anything in the liturgy.

23. That sound tradition may be retained and yet the way remain open to legitimate progress, a careful investigation is always to be made into each part of the liturgy to be revised. This investigation should be theological, historical, and pastoral. Also the general laws governing the structure and meaning of the liturgy must be studied in conjunction with the experience derived from recent liturgical reforms and from the indults conceded to various places. Finally, there must be no innovations unless the good of the Church genuinely and certainly requires them; care must be taken that any new forms adopted should in some way grow organically from forms already existing.

As far as possible, marked differences between the rites used in neighboring regions must be carefully avoided.

24. Sacred Scripture is of the greatest importance in the celebration of the liturgy. For it is from Scripture that the readings are given and explained in the homily and that psalms are sung; the prayers, collects,

and liturgical songs are scriptural in their inspiration; it is from the Scriptures that actions and signs derive their meaning. Thus to achieve the reform, progress, and adaptation of the liturgy, it is essential to promote that warm and living love for Scripture to which the venerable tradition of both Eastern and Western rites gives testimony.

25.   The liturgical books are to be revised as soon as possible; experts are to be employed in this task and bishops from various parts of the world are to be consulted.

B. Norms Drawn from the Hierarchic and
Communal Nature of the Liturgy

26.   Liturgical services are not private functions, but are celebrations belonging to the Church, which is the "sacrament of unity," namely, the holy people united and ordered under their bishops.[33]

Therefore liturgical services involve the whole Body of the Church; they manifest it and have effects upon it; but they also concern the individual members of the Church in different ways, according to their different orders, offices, and actual participation.

27.   Whenever rites, according to their specific nature, make provision for communal celebration involving the presence and active participation of the faithful, it is to be stressed that this way of celebrating them is to be preferred, as far as possible, to a celebration that is individual and, so to speak, private.

This applies with special force to the celebration of Mass and the administration of the sacraments, even though every Mass has of itself a public and social character.

28.   In liturgical celebrations each one, minister or layperson, who has an office to perform, should do all of, but only, those parts which pertain to that office by the nature of the rite and the principles of liturgy.

29.   Servers, readers, commentators, and members of the choir also exercise a genuine liturgical function. They ought to discharge their office, therefore, with the sincere devotion and decorum demanded by so exalted a ministry and rightly expected of them by God's people.

Consequently, they must all be deeply imbued with the spirit of the liturgy, in the measure proper to each one, and they must be trained to perform their functions in a correct and orderly manner.

30.   To promote active participation, the people should be encouraged to take part by means of acclamations, responses, psalmody, antiphons, and songs, as well as by actions, gestures, and bearing. And at the proper times all should observe a reverent silence.

31.   The revision of the liturgical books must ensure that the rubrics make provision for the parts belonging to the people.

32.   The liturgy makes distinctions between persons according to their liturgical function and sacred orders and there are liturgical laws providing for due honors to be given to civil authorities. Apart from these instances, no special honors are to be paid in the liturgy to any private persons or classes of persons, whether in the ceremonies or by external display.

C. Norms Based on the Teaching and
Pastoral Character of the Liturgy

33.   Although the liturgy is above all things the worship of the divine majesty, it likewise contains rich instruction for the faithful.[34] For in the liturgy God is speaking to his people and Christ is still proclaiming his gospel. And the people are responding to God by both song and prayer.

Moreover, the prayers addressed to God by the priest, who presides over the assembly in the person of Christ, are said in the name of the entire holy people and of all present. And the visible signs used by the liturgy to signify invisible divine realities have been chosen by Christ or the Church. Thus not only when things are read "that were written for our instruction" (Rom 15:4), but also when the Church prays or sings or acts, the faith of those taking part is nourished and their minds are raised to God, so that they may offer him their worship as intelligent beings and receive his grace more abundantly.

In the reform of the liturgy, therefore, the following general norms are to be observed.

34.   The rites should be marked by a noble simplicity; they should be short, clear, and unencumbered by useless repetitions; they should be within the people's powers of comprehension and as a rule not require much explanation.

35.   That the intimate connection between words and rites may stand out clearly in the liturgy:

1.   In sacred celebrations there is to be more reading from holy Scripture and it is to be more varied and apposite.

2.   Because the spoken word is part of the liturgical service, the best place for it, consistent with the nature of the rite, is to be indicated even in the rubrics; the ministry of preaching is to be fulfilled with exactitude and fidelity. Preaching should draw its content mainly from scriptural and liturgical sources, being a proclamation of God's wonderful works in the history of salvation, the mystery of Christ, ever present and active within us, especially in the celebration of the liturgy.

3. A more explicitly liturgical catechesis should also be given in a variety of ways. Within the rites themselves provision is to be made for brief comments, when needed by the priest or a qualified minister; they should occur only at the more suitable moments and use a set formula or something similar.

4. Bible services should be encouraged, especially on the vigils of the more solemn feasts, on some weekdays in Advent and Lent, and on Sundays and holy days. They are particularly to be recommended in places where no priest is available; when this is the case, a deacon or some other person authorized by the bishop is to preside over the celebration.

36. § 1. Particular law remaining in force, the use of the Latin language is to be preserved in the Latin rites.

§ 2. But since the use of the mother tongue, whether in the Mass, the administration of the sacraments, or other parts of the liturgy, frequently may be of great advantage to the people, the limits of its use may be extended. This will apply in the first place to the readings and instructions and to some prayers and chants, according to the regulations on this matter to be laid down for each case in subsequent chapters.

§ 3. Respecting such norms and also, where applicable, consulting the bishops of nearby territories of the same language, the competent, territorial ecclesiastical authority mentioned in art. 22, § 2 is empowered to decide whether and to what extent the vernacular is to be used. The enactments of the competent authority are to be approved, that is, confirmed by the Holy See.

§ 4. Translations from the Latin text into the mother tongue intended for use in the liturgy must be approved by the competent, territorial ecclesiastical authority already mentioned.

D. Norms for Adapting the Liturgy to the Culture and Traditions of Peoples

37. Even in the liturgy the Church has no wish to impose a rigid uniformity in matters that do not affect the faith or the good of the whole community; rather, the Church respects and fosters the genius and talents of the various races and peoples. The Church considers with sympathy and, if possible, preserves intact the elements in these peoples' way of life that are not indissolubly bound up with superstition and error. Sometimes in fact the Church admits such elements into the liturgy itself, provided they are in keeping with the true and authentic spirit of the liturgy.

38. Provisions shall also be made, even in the revision of liturgical books, for legitimate variations and adaptations to different groups, regions, and peoples, especially in mission lands, provided the substantial unity of the

Roman Rite is preserved; this should be borne in mind when rites are drawn up and rubrics devised.

39.   Within the limits set by the *editio typica* of the liturgical books, it shall be for the competent, territorial ecclesiastical authority mentioned in art. 22, § 2 to specify adaptations, especially in the case of the administration of the sacraments, the sacramentals, processions, liturgical language, sacred music, and the arts. This, however, is to be done in accord with the fundamental norms laid down in this Constitution.

40.   In some places and circumstances, however, an even more radical adaptation of the liturgy is needed and this entails greater difficulties. Wherefore:

   1. The competent, territorial ecclesiastical authority mentioned in art. 22, § 2, must, in this matter, carefully and prudently weigh what elements from the traditions and culture of individual peoples may be appropriately admitted into divine worship. They are to propose to the Apostolic See adaptations considered useful or necessary that will be introduced with its consent.

   2. To ensure that adaptations are made with all the circumspection they demand, the Apostolic See will grant power to this same territorial ecclesiastical authority to permit and to direct, as the case requires, the necessary preliminary experiments within certain groups suited for the purpose and for a fixed time.

   3. Because liturgical laws often involve special difficulties with respect to adaptation, particularly in mission lands, experts in these matters must be employed to formulate them.

IV. PROMOTION OF LITURGICAL LIFE IN DIOCESE AND PARISH

41.   The bishop is to be looked on as the high priest of his flock, the faithful's life in Christ in some way deriving from and depending on him.

   Therefore all should hold in great esteem the liturgical life of the diocese centered around the bishop, especially in his cathedral church; they must be convinced that the preeminent manifestation of the Church is present in the full, active participation of all God's holy people in these liturgical celebrations, especially in the same eucharist, in a single prayer, at one altar at which the bishop presides, surrounded by his college of priests and by his ministers.[35]

42.   But because it is impossible for the bishop always and everywhere to preside over the whole flock in his Church, he cannot do otherwise than establish lesser groupings of the faithful. Among these the parishes, set up locally under a pastor taking the place of the bishop, are most important:

in some manner they represent the visible Church established throughout the world.

And therefore both in attitude and in practice the liturgical life of the parish and its relationship to the bishop must be fostered among the faithful and clergy; efforts must also be made toward a lively sense of community within the parish, above all in the shared celebration of the Sunday Mass.

V. PROMOTION OF PASTORAL-LITURGICAL ACTION

43.   Zeal for the promotion and restoration of the liturgy is rightly held to be a sign of the providential dispositions of God in our time, a movement of the Holy Spirit in his Church. Today it is a distinguishing mark of the Church's life, indeed of the whole tenor of contemporary religious thought and action.

So that this pastoral-liturgical action may become even more vigorous in the Church, the Council decrees what follows.

44.   It is advisable that the competent, territorial ecclesiastical authority mentioned in art. 22, § 2 set up a liturgical commission, to be assisted by experts in liturgical science, music, art, and pastoral practice. As far as possible the commission should be aided by some kind of institute for pastoral liturgy, consisting of persons eminent in these matters and including the laity as circumstances suggest. Under the direction of the aforementioned territorial ecclesiastical authority, the commission is to regulate pastoral-liturgical action throughout the territory and to promote studies and necessary experiments whenever there is question of adaptations to be proposed to the Apostolic See.

45.   For the same reason every diocese is to have a commission on the liturgy, under the direction of the bishop, for promoting the liturgical apostolate.

Sometimes it may be advisable for several dioceses to form among themselves one single commission, in order to promote the liturgy by means of shared consultation.

46.   Besides the commission on the liturgy, every diocese, as far as possible, should have commissions for music and art.

These three commissions must work in closest collaboration; indeed it will often be best to fuse the three of them into one single commission.

CHAPTER II
THE MOST SACRED MYSTERY OF THE EUCHARIST

47.   At the Last Supper, on the night he was betrayed, our Savior instituted the eucharistic sacrifice of his body and blood. He did this in order to perpetuate the sacrifice of the cross throughout the centuries until he should come again, and in this way to entrust to his beloved Bride, the Church, a memorial of his death and resurrection: a sacrament of love, a sign of unity, a bond of charity,[36] a paschal banquet "in which Christ is eaten, the heart is filled with grace, and a pledge of future glory given to us."[37]

48.   The Church, therefore, earnestly desires that Christ's faithful, when present at this mystery of faith, should not be there as strangers or silent spectators; on the contrary, through a good understanding of the rites and prayers they should take part in the sacred service conscious of what they are doing, with devotion and full involvement. They should be instructed by God's word and be nourished at the table of the Lord's body; they should give thanks to God; by offering the immaculate Victim, not only through the hands of the priest, but also with him, they should learn to offer themselves as well; through Christ the Mediator,[38] they should be formed day by day into an ever more perfect unity with God and with each other, so that finally God may be all in all.

49.   Thus, mindful of those Masses celebrated with assistance of the faithful, especially on Sundays and holy days of obligation, the Council makes the following decrees in order that the sacrifice of the Mass, even in its ritual forms, may become pastorally effective to the utmost degree.

50.   The Order of Mass is to be revised in a way that will bring out more clearly the intrinsic nature and purpose of its several parts, as also the connection between them, and will more readily achieve the devout, active participation of the faithful.

For this purpose the rites are to be simplified, due care being taken to preserve their substance; elements that, with the passage of time, came to be duplicated or were added with but little advantage are now to be discarded; other elements that have suffered injury through accident of history are now, as may seem useful or necessary, to be restored to the vigor they had in the traditions of the Fathers.

51.   The treasures of the Bible are to be opened up more lavishly, so that a richer share in God's word may be provided for the faithful. In this way a more representative portion of holy Scripture will be read to the people in

the course of a prescribed number of years.

52.   By means of the homily the mysteries of the faith and the guiding principles of the Christian life are expounded from the sacred text during the course of the liturgical year; as part of the liturgy itself therefore, the homily is strongly recommended; in fact, at Masses celebrated with the assistance of the people on Sundays and holy days of obligation it is not to be omitted except for a serious reason.

53.   Especially on Sundays and holy days of obligation there is to be restored, after the gospel and the homily, "the universal prayer" or "the prayer of the faithful." By this prayer, in which the people are to take part, intercession shall be made for holy Church, for the civil authorities, for those oppressed by various needs, for all people, and for the salvation of the entire world.[39]

54.   With art. 36 of this Constitution as the norm, in Masses celebrated with the people a suitable place may be allotted to their mother tongue. This is to apply in the first place to the readings and "the universal prayer," but also, as local conditions may warrant, to those parts belonging to the people.

Nevertheless steps should be taken enabling the faithful to say or to sing together in Latin those parts of the Ordinary of the Mass belonging to them.

Wherever a more extended use of the mother tongue within the Mass appears desirable, the regulation laid down in art. 40 of this Constitution is to be observed.

55.   That more complete form of participation in the Mass by which the faithful, after the priest's communion, receive the Lord's body from the sacrifice, is strongly endorsed.

The dogmatic principles laid down by the Council of Trent remain intact.[40] In instances to be specified by the Apostolic See, however, communion under both kinds may be granted both to clerics and religious and to the laity at the discretion of the bishops, for example, to the ordained at the Mass of their ordination, to the professed at the Mass of their religious profession, to the newly baptized at the Mass following their baptism.

56.   The two parts that, in a certain sense, go to make up the Mass, namely, the liturgy of the word and the liturgy of the eucharist, are so closely connected with each other that they form but one single act of worship. Accordingly this Council strongly urges pastors that in their catechesis they insistently teach the faithful to take part in the entire Mass, especially on Sundays and holy days of obligation.

57.   §1. Concelebration, which aptly expresses the unity of the priesthood, has continued to this day as a practice in the Church of both East and West. For this reason it has seemed good to the Council to extend permission for concelebration to the following cases: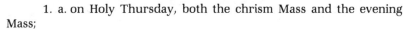

    1. a. on Holy Thursday, both the chrism Mass and the evening Mass;

      b. Masses during councils, bishops' conferences, and synods;

      c. the Mass at the blessing of an abbot.

    2. Also, with permission of the Ordinary, who is the one to decide whether concelebration is opportune, to:

      a. the conventual Mass and the principal Mass in churches, when the needs of the faithful do not require that all the priests on hand celebrate individually;

      b. Masses celebrated at any kind of meeting of priests, whether the priests be secular or religious.

    §2. 1. The regulation, however, of the discipline of concelebration in the diocese pertains to the bishop.

    2. This, however, does not take away the option of every priest to celebrate Mass individually, not, however, at the same time and in the same church as a concelebrated Mass or on Holy Thursday.

58.   A new rite for concelebration is to be drawn up and inserted into the Roman Pontifical and Roman Missal.

CHAPTER III
THE OTHER SACRAMENTS AND THE SACRAMENTALS

59.   The purpose of the sacraments is to make people holy, to build up the Body of Christ, and, finally, to give worship to God; but being signs they also have a teaching function. They not only presuppose faith, but by words and objects they also nourish, strengthen, and express it; that is why they are called "sacraments of faith." They do indeed impart grace, but, in addition, the very act of celebrating them disposes the faithful most effectively to receive this grace in a fruitful manner, to worship God rightly, and to practice charity.

It is therefore of the highest importance that the faithful should really understand the sacramental signs and should with great eagerness frequent those sacraments that were instituted to nourish the Christian life.

60.   The Church has, in addition, instituted sacramentals. These are

sacred signs bearing a kind of resemblance to the sacraments: they signify effects, particularly of a spiritual kind, that are obtained through the Church's intercession. They dispose people to receive the chief effect of the sacraments and they make holy various occasions in human life.

61. Thus, for well-disposed members of the faithful, the effect of the liturgy of the sacraments and sacramentals is that almost every event in their lives is made holy by divine grace that flows from the paschal mystery of Christ's passion, death, and resurrection, the fount from which all sacraments and sacramentals draw their power. The liturgy means also that there is hardly any proper use of material things that cannot thus be directed toward human sanctification and the praise of God.

62. With the passage of time, however, certain features have crept into the rites of the sacraments and sacramentals that have made their nature and purpose less clear to the people of today; hence some changes have become necessary as adaptations to the needs of our own times. For this reason the Council decrees what follows concerning the revision of these rites.

63. Because the use of the mother tongue in the administration of the sacraments and sacramentals can often be of considerable help for the people, this use is to be extended according to the following norms:

a. With art. 36 as the norm, the vernacular may be used in administering the sacraments and sacramentals.

b. Particular rituals in harmony with the new edition of the Roman Ritual shall be prepared without delay by the competent, territorial ecclesiastical authority mentioned in art. 22, § 2 of this Constitution. These rituals are to be adapted, even in regard to the language employed, to the needs of the different regions. Once they have been reviewed by the Apostolic See, they are to be used in the regions for which they have been prepared. But those who draw up these rituals or particular collections of rites must not leave out the prefatory instructions for the individual rites in the Roman Ritual, whether the instructions are pastoral and rubrical or have some special social bearing.

64. The catechumenate for adults, divided into several stages, is to be restored and put into use at the discretion of the local Ordinary. By this means the time of the catechumentate, which is intended as a period of well-suited instruction, may be sanctified by sacred rites to be celebrated at successive intervals of time.

65. With art. 37–40 of this Constitution as the norm, it is lawful in mission lands to allow, besides what is part of Christian tradition, those

initiation elements in use among individual peoples, to the extent that such elements are compatible with the Christian rite of initiation.

66.   Both of the rites for the baptism of adults are to be revised: not only the simpler rite, but also the more solemn one, with proper attention to the restored catechumenate. A special Mass "On the Occasion of a Baptism" is to be incorporated into the Roman Missal.

67.   The rite for the baptism of infants is to be revised and it should be suited to the fact that those to be baptized are infants. The roles as well as the obligations of parents and godparents should be brought out more clearly in the rite itself.

68.   The baptismal rite should contain alternatives, to be used at the discretion of the local Ordinary, for occasions when a very large number are to be baptized together. Moreover, a shorter rite is to be drawn up, especially in mission lands, for use by catechists, but also by the faithful in general, when there is danger of death and neither a priest nor a deacon is available.

69.   In place of the rite called the "Order of Supplying What Was Omitted in the Baptism of an Infant," a new rite is to be drawn up. This should manifest more clearly and fittingly that an infant who was baptized by the short rite has already been received into the Church.

    Similarly, a new rite is to be drawn up for converts who have already been validly baptized; it should express that they are being received into the communion of the Church.

70.   Except during the Easter season, baptismal water may be blessed within the rite of baptism itself by use of an approved, shorter formulary.

71.   The rite of confirmation is also to be revised in order that the intimate connection of this sacrament with the whole of Christian initiation may stand out more clearly; for this reason it is fitting for candidates to renew their baptismal promises just before they are confirmed.

    Confirmation may be conferred within Mass when convenient; as for the rite outside Mass, a formulary is to be composed for use as an introduction.

72.   The rite and formularies for the sacrament of penance are to be revised so that they more clearly express both the nature and effect of the sacrament.

73.   "Extreme unction," which may also and more properly be called "anointing of the sick," is not a sacrament for those only who are at the

point of death. Hence, as soon as any one of the faithful begins to be in danger of death from sickness or old age, the fitting time for that person to receive this sacrament has certainly already arrived.

74.   In addition to the separate rites for anointing of the sick and for viaticum, a continuous rite shall be drawn up, structured so that the sick person is anointed after confessing and before receiving viaticum.

75.   The number of the anointings is to be adapted to the circumstances; the prayers that belong to the rite of anointing are to be so revised that they correspond to the varying conditions of the sick who receive the sacrament.

76.   Both the ceremonies and texts of the ordination rites are to be revised. The address given by the bishop at the beginning of each ordination or consecration may be in the vernacular.

When a bishop is consecrated, all the bishops present may take part in the laying on of hands.

77.   The marriage rite now found in the Roman Ritual is to be revised and enriched in such a way that it more clearly signifies the grace of the sacrament and imparts a knowledge of the obligation of spouses.

"If any regions follow other praiseworthy customs and ceremonies when celebrating the sacrament of marriage, the Council earnestly desires that by all means these be retained."[41]

Moreover, the competent, territorial ecclesiastical authority mentioned in art. 22, § 2 of this Constitution is free to draw up, in accord with art. 63, its own rite, suited to the usages of place and people. But the rite must always conform to the law that the priest assisting at the marriage must ask for and obtain the consent of the contracting parties.

78.   Marriage is normally to be celebrated within Mass, after the reading of the gospel and the homily and before "the prayer of the faithful." The prayer for the bride, duly emended to remind both spouses of their equal obligation to remain faithful to each other, may be said in the vernacular.

But if the sacrament of marriage is celebrated apart from Mass, the epistle and gospel from the nuptial Mass are to be read at the beginning of the rite and the blessing is always to be given to the spouses.

79.   The sacramentals are to be reviewed in the light of the primary criterion that the faithful participate intelligently, actively, and easily; the conditions of our own days must also be considered. When rituals are revised, in accord with art. 63, new sacramentals may also be added as the need for them becomes apparent.

Reserved blessings shall be very few; reservations shall be in favor only of bishops and Ordinaries.

Let provision be made that some sacramentals, at least in special circumstances and at the discretion of the Ordinary, may be administered by qualified laypersons.

80. The rite for the consecration to a life of virginity as it exists in the Roman Pontifical is to be revised.

A rite of religious profession and renewal of vows shall be drawn up with a view to achieving greater unity, simplicity, and dignity. Apart from exceptions in particular law, this rite should be adopted by those who make their profession or renewal of vows within Mass.

Religious profession should preferably be made within Mass.

81. The rite of funerals should express more clearly the paschal character of Christian death and should correspond more closely to the circumstances and traditions of various regions. This applies also to the liturgical color to be used.

82. The rite for the burial of infants is to be revised and a special Mass for the occasion provided.

CHAPTER IV
DIVINE OFFICE

83. Christ Jesus, High Priest of the new and eternal covenant, taking human nature, introduced into this earthly exile the hymn that is sung throughout all ages in the halls of heaven. He joins the entire human community to himself, associating it with his own singing of this canticle of divine praise.

For he continues his priestly work through the agency of his Church, which is unceasingly engaged in praising the Lord and interceding for the salvation of the whole world. The Church does this not only by celebrating the eucharist, but also in other ways, especially by praying the divine office.

84. By tradition going back to early Christian times, the divine office is so arranged that the whole course of the day and night is made holy by the praises of God. Therefore, when this wonderful song of praise is rightly performed by priests and others who are deputed for this purpose by the Church's ordinance or by the faithful praying together with the priest in the approved form, then it is truly the voice of a bride addressing her bridegroom; it is the very prayer that Christ himself, together with his Body, addresses to the Father.

85.   Hence all who render this service are not only fulfilling a duty of the Church, but also are sharing in the greatest honor of Christ's Bride, for by offering these praises to God they are standing before God's throne in the name of the Church, their Mother.

86.   Priests engaged in the sacred pastoral ministry will offer the praises of the hours with greater fervor the more vividly they realize that they must heed St. Paul's exhortation: "Pray without ceasing" (1 Thes 5:17). For the work in which they labor will effect nothing and bring forth no fruit except by the power of the Lord who said: "Without me you can do nothing" (Jn 15:5). That is why the apostles, instituting deacons, said: "We will devote ourselves to prayer and to the ministry of the word" (Acts 6:4).

87.   In order that the divine office may be better and more completely carried out in existing circumstances, whether by priests or by other members of the Church, the Council, carrying further the restoration already so happily begun by the Apostolic See, has seen fit to decree what follows concerning the office of the Roman Rite.

88.   Because the purpose of the office is to sanctify the day, the traditional sequence of the hours is to be restored so that once again they may be genuinely related to the hour of the day when they are prayed, as far as it is possible. Moreover, it will be necessary to take into account the modern conditions in which daily life has to be lived, especially by those who are called to labor in apostolic works.

89.   Therefore, when the office is revised, these norms are to be observed:

a.   By the venerable tradition of the universal Church, lauds as morning prayer and vespers as evening prayer are the two hinges on which the daily office turns; hence they are to be considered as the chief hours and celebrated as such.

b.   Compline is to be so composed that it will be a suitable prayer for the end of the day.

c.   The hour known as matins, although it should retain the character of nocturnal praise when celebrated in choir, shall be adapted so that it may be recited at any hour of the day; it shall be made up of fewer psalms and longer readings.

d.   The hour of prime is to be suppressed.

e.   In choir the minor hours of terce, sext, and none are to be observed. But outside choir it will be lawful to choose whichever of the three best suits the hour of the day.

90.   The divine office, because it is the public prayer of the Church, is a

source of devotion and nourishment also for personal prayer. Therefore priests and all others who take part in the divine office are earnestly exhorted in the Lord to attune their minds to their voices when praying it. The better to achieve this, let them take steps to improve their understanding of the liturgy and of the Bible, especially the psalms.

In revising the Roman office, its ancient and venerable treasures are to be so adapted that all those to whom they are handed on may more fully and readily draw profit from them.

91.   So that it may really be possible in practice to observe the course of the hours proposed in art. 89, the psalms are no longer to be distributed over just one week, but over some longer period of time.

The work of revising the psalter, already happily begun, is to be finished as soon as possible and is to take into account the style of Christian Latin, the liturgical use of psalms, including their being sung, and the entire tradition of the Latin Church.

92.   As regards the readings, the following shall be observed:

a.   Readings from sacred Scripture shall be arranged so that the riches of God's word may be easily accessible in more abundant measure.

b.   Readings excerpted from the works of the Fathers, doctors, and ecclesiastical writers shall be better selected.

c.   The accounts of the martyrdom or lives of the saints are to be made to accord with the historical facts.

93.   To whatever extent may seem advisable, hymns are to be restored to their original form and any allusion to mythology or anything that conflicts with Christian piety is to be dropped or changed. Also, as occasion arises, let other selections from the treasury of hymns be incorporated.

94.   That the day may be truly sanctified and the hours themselves recited with spiritual advantage, it is best that each of them be prayed at a time most closely corresponding to the true time of each canonical hour.

95.   In addition to the conventual Mass, communities obliged to choral office are bound to celebrate the office in choir every day. In particular:

a.   Orders of canons, of monks and of nuns, and of other regulars bound by law or constitutions to choral office must celebrate the entire office.

b.   Cathedral or collegiate chapters are bound to recite those parts of the office imposed on them by general or particular law.

c.   All members of the above communities who are in major orders or are solemnly professed, except for lay brothers, are bound individually to recite those canonical hours which they do not pray in choir.

96. Clerics not bound to office in choir, if they are in major orders, are bound to pray the entire office every day, either in common or individually, following the norms in art. 89.

97. Appropriate instances are to be defined by the rubrics in which a liturgical service may be substituted for the divine office.

In particular cases and for just a reason Ordinaries may dispense their subjects wholly or in part from the obligation of reciting the divine office or may commute it.

98. Members of any institute dedicated to acquiring perfection who, according to their constitutions, are to recite any parts of the divine office are thereby performing the public prayer of the Church.

They too perform the public prayer of the Church who, in virtue of their constitutions, recite any little office, provided this has been drawn up after the pattern of the divine office and duly approved.

99. Since the divine office is the voice of the Church, that is, of the whole Mystical Body publicly praising God, those clerics who are not obligated to office in choir, epsecially priests who live together or who meet together for any purpose, are urged to pray at least some part of the divine office in common.

All who pray the divine office, whether in choir or in common, should fulfill the task entrusted to them as perfectly as possible: this refers not only to the internal devotion of their minds but also to their external manner of celebration.

It is advantageous, moreover, that the office in choir and in common be sung when there is an opportunity to do so.

100. Pastors should see to it that the chief hours, especially vespers, are celebrated in common in church on Sundays and the more solemn feasts. The laity, too, are encouraged to recite the divine office either with the priests, or among themselves, or even individually.

101. § 1. In accordance with the centuries-old tradition of the Latin rite, clerics are to retain the Latin language in the divine office. But in individual cases the Ordinary has the power of granting the use of a vernacular translation, prepared in accord with art. 36, to those clerics for whom the use of Latin constitutes a grave obstacle to their praying the office properly.

§ 2. The competent superior has the power to grant the use of the vernacular in the celebration of the divine office, even in choir, to nuns and to members of institutes dedicated to acquiring perfection, both men who are not clerics and women. The version, however, must be one that has been approved.

§ 3. Any cleric bound to the divine office fulfills his obligation if he prays the office in the vernacular together with a group of the faithful or with those mentioned in § 2, provided the text of the translation has been approved.

CHAPTER V
THE LITURGICAL YEAR

102. The Church is conscious that it must celebrate the saving work of the divine Bridegroom by devoutly recalling it on certain days throughout the course of the year. Every week, on the day which the Church has called the Lord's Day, it keeps the memory of the Lord's resurrection, which it also celebrates once in the year, together with his blessed passion, in the most solemn festival of Easter.

Within the cycle of a year, moreover, the Church unfolds the whole mystery of Christ, from his incarnation and birth until his ascension, the day of Pentecost, and the expectation of blessed hope and of the Lord's return.

Recalling thus the mysteries of redemption, the Church opens to the faithful the riches of the Lord's powers and merits, so that these are in some way made present in every age in order that the faithful may lay hold on them and be filled with saving grace.

103. In celebrating this annual cycle of Christ's mysteries, the Church honors with special love Mary, the Mother of God, who is joined by an inseparable bond to the saving work of her Son. In her the Church holds up and admires the most excellent effect of the redemption and joyfully contemplates, as in a flawless image, that which the Church itself desires and hopes wholly to be.

104. The Church has also included in the annual cycle days devoted to the memory of the martyrs and the other saints. Raised up to perfection by the manifold grace of God and already in possession of eternal salvation, they sing God's perfect praise in heaven and offer prayers for us. By celebrating their passage from earth to heaven the Church proclaims the paschal mystery achieved in the saints, who have suffered and been glorified with Christ; it proposes them to the faithful as examples drawing all to the Father through Christ and pleads through their merits for God's favors.

105. Finally, in the various seasons of the year and according to its traditional discipline, the Church completes the formation of the faithful by means of devout practices for soul and body, by instruction, prayer, and works of penance and of mercy.

Accordingly the sacred Council has seen fit to decree what follows.

106. By a tradition handed down from the apostles and having its origin from the very day of Christ's resurrection, the Church celebrates the paschal mystery every eighth day, which, with good reason, bears the name of the Lord's Day or Sunday. For on this day Christ's faithful must gather together so that, by hearing the word of God and taking part in the eucharist, they may call to mind the passion, the resurrection, and the glorification of the Lord Jesus and may thank God, who "has begotten them again unto a living hope through the resurrection of Jesus Christ from the dead" (1 Pt 1:3). Hence the Lord's Day is the first holy day of all and should be proposed to the devotion of the faithful and taught to them in such a way that it may become in fact a day of joy and of freedom from work. Other celebrations, unless they be truly of greatest importance, shall not have precedence over the Sunday, the foundation and core of the whole liturgical year.

107. The liturgical year is to be so revised that the traditional customs and usages of the sacred seasons are preserved or restored to suit the conditions of modern times; their specific character is to be retained, so that they duly nourish the devotion of the faithful who celebrate the mysteries of Christian redemption and above all the paschal mystery. If certain adaptations are considered necessary on account of local conditions, they are to be made in accordance with the provisions of art. 39 and 40.

108. The minds of the faithful must be directed primarily toward those feasts of the Lord on which the mysteries of salvation are celebrated in the course of the year. Therefore, the Proper of Seasons shall be given the precedence due to it over the feasts of the saints, in order that the entire cycle of the mysteries of salvation may be celebrated in the measure due to them.

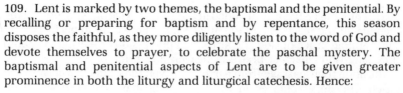

109. Lent is marked by two themes, the baptismal and the penitential. By recalling or preparing for baptism and by repentance, this season disposes the faithful, as they more diligently listen to the word of God and devote themselves to prayer, to celebrate the paschal mystery. The baptismal and penitential aspects of Lent are to be given greater prominence in both the liturgy and liturgical catechesis. Hence:

a. More use is to be made of the baptismal features proper to the Lenten liturgy; some of those from an earlier era are to be restored as may seem advisable.

b. The same is to apply to the penitential elements. As regards catechesis, it is important to impress on the minds of the faithful not only the social consequences of sin but also the essence of the virtue of penance, namely, detestation of sin as an offense against God; the role of the Church in penitential practices is not to be neglected and the people are to be exhorted to pray for sinners.

110. During Lent penance should be not only inward and individual, but also outward and social. The practice of penance should be fostered, however, in ways that are possible in our own times and in different regions and according to the circumstances of the faithful; it should be encouraged by the authorities mentioned in art. 22.

Nevertheless, let the paschal fast be kept sacred. Let it be observed everywhere on Good Friday and, where possible, prolonged throughout Holy Saturday, as a way of coming to the joys of the Sunday of the resurrection with uplifted and welcoming heart.

111. The saints have been traditionally honored in the Church and their authentic relics and images held in veneration. For the feasts of the saints proclaim the wonderful works of Christ in his servants and display to the faithful fitting examples for their imitation.

Lest the feasts of the saints take precedence over the feasts commemorating the very mysteries of salvation, many of them should be left to be celebrated by a particular Church or nation or religious family; those only should be extended to the universal Church that commemorate saints of truly universal significance.

CHAPTER VI
SACRED MUSIC

112. The musical tradition of the universal Church is a treasure of inestimable value, greater even than that of any other art. The main reason for this preeminence is that, as sacred song closely bound to the text, it forms a necessary or integral part of the solemn liturgy.

Holy Scripture itself has bestowed praise upon sacred song[42] and the same may be said of the Fathers of the Church and of the Roman pontiffs, who in recent times, led by St. Pius X, have explained more precisely the ministerial function supplied by sacred music in the service of the Lord.

Therefore sacred music will be the more holy the more closely it is joined to the liturgical rite, whether by adding delight to prayer, fostering oneness of spirit, or investing the rites with greater solemnity. But the Church approves of all forms of genuine art possessing the qualities required and admits them into divine worship.

Accordingly, the Council, keeping the norms and precepts of ecclesiastical tradition and discipline and having regard to the purpose of sacred music, which is the glory of God and the sanctification of the faithful, decrees what follows.

113. A liturgical service takes on a nobler aspect when the rites are celebrated with singing, the sacred ministers take their parts in them, and the faithful actively participate.

As regards the language to be used, the provisions of art. 36 are to be observed; for the Mass, those of art. 54; for the sacraments, those of art. 63; for the divine office those of art. 101.

114. The treasure of sacred music is to be preserved and fostered with great care. Choirs must be diligently developed, especially in cathedral churches; but bishops and other pastors of souls must be at pains to ensure that whenever a liturgical service is to be celebrated with song, the whole assembly of the faithful is enabled, in keeping with art. 28 and 30, to contribute the active participation that rightly belongs to it.

115. Great importance is to be attached to the teaching and practice of music in seminaries, in the novitiates and houses of study of religious of both sexes, and also in other Catholic institutions and schools. To impart this instruction, those in charge of teaching sacred music are to receive thorough training.

It is recommended also that higher institutes of sacred music be established whenever possible.

Musicians and singers, especially young boys, must also be given a genuine liturgical training.

116. The Church acknowledges Gregorian chant as distinctive of the Roman liturgy; therefore, other things being equal, it should be given pride of place in liturgical services.

But other kinds of sacred music, especially polyphony, are by no means excluded from liturgical celebrations, provided they accord with the spirit of the liturgical service, in the way laid down in art. 30.

117. The *editio typica* of the books of Gregorian chant is to be completed and a more critical edition is to be prepared of those books already published since the reform of St. Pius X.

It is desirable also that an edition be prepared containing the simpler melodies for use in small churches.

118. The people's own religious songs are to be encouraged with care so that in sacred devotions as well as during services of the liturgy itself, in

keeping with rubrical norms and requirements, the faithful may raise their voices in song.

119. In certain parts of the world, especially mission lands, people have their own musical traditions and these play a great part in their religious and social life. Thus, in keeping with art. 39 and 40, due importance is to be attached to their music and a suitable place given to it, not only in forming their attitude toward religion, but also in adapting worship to their native genius.

Therefore, when missionaries are being given training in music, every effort should be made to see that they become competent in promoting the traditional music of the people, both in schools and in sacred services, as far as may be practicable.

120. In the Latin Church the pipe organ is to be held in high esteem, for it is the traditional musical instrument that adds a wonderful splendor to the Church's ceremonies and powerfully lifts up the spirit to God and to higher things.

But other instruments also may be admitted for use in divine worship, with the knowledge and consent of the competent territorial authority and in conformity with art. 22, § 2, art. 37 and art. 40. This applies, however, only on condition that the instruments are suitable, or can be made suitable, for sacred use, are in accord with the dignity of the place of worship, and truly contribute to the uplifting of the faithful.

121. Composers, filled with the Christian spirit, should feel that their vocation is to develop sacred music and to increase its store of treasures.

Let them produce compositions having the qualities proper to genuine sacred music, not confining themselves to works that can be sung only by large choirs, but providing also for the needs of small choirs and for the active participation of the entire assembly of the faithful.

The texts intended to be sung must always be consistent with Catholic teaching; indeed they should be drawn chiefly from holy Scripture and from liturgical sources.

CHAPTER VII
SACRED ART AND SACRED FURNISHINGS

122. The fine arts are deservedly ranked among the noblest activities of human genius and this applies especially to religious art and to its highest achievement, sacred art. These arts, by their very nature, are oriented toward the infinite beauty of God, which they attempt in some way to portray by the work of human hands. They are dedicated to advancing God's praise and glory to the degree that they center on the single aim of turning the human spirit devoutly toward God.

The Church has therefore always been the friend of the fine arts, has ever sought their noble help, and has trained artists with the special aim that all things set apart for use in divine worship are truly worthy, becoming, and beautiful, signs and symbols of the supernatural world. The Church has always regarded itself as the rightful arbiter of the arts, deciding which of the works of artists are in accordance with faith, with reverence, and with honored traditional laws and are thereby suited for sacred use.

The Church has been particularly careful to see that sacred furnishings worthily and beautifully serve the dignity of worship and has admitted changes in materials, design, or ornamentation prompted by the progress of the technical arts with the passage of time.

Wherefore it has pleased the Fathers to issue the following decrees on these matters.

123. The Church has not adopted any particular style of art as its very own but has admitted styles from every period, according to the proper genius and circumstances of peoples and the requirements of the many different rites in the Church. Thus, in the course of centuries, the Church has brought into being a treasury of art that must be very carefully preserved. The art of our own days, coming from every race and region, shall also be given free scope in the Church, on condition that it serves the places of worship and sacred rites with the reverence and honor due to them. In this way contemporary art can add its own voice to that wonderful chorus of praise sung by the great masters of past ages of Catholic faith.

124. In encouraging and favoring art that is truly sacred, Ordinaries should strive after noble beauty rather than mere sumptuous display. This principle is to apply also in the matter of sacred vestments and appointments.

Let bishops carefully remove from the house of God and from other places of worship those works of artists that are repugnant to faith and morals and to Christian devotion and that offend true religious sense either by their grotesqueness or by the deficiency, mediocrity, or sham in their artistic quality.

When churches are to be built, let great care be taken that they are well suited to celebrating liturgical services and to bringing about the active participation of the faithful.

125. The practice of placing sacred images in churches so that they may be venerated by the faithful is to be maintained. Nevertheless there is to be restraint regarding their number and prominence so that they do not create confusion among the Christian people or foster religious practices of doubtful orthodoxy.

126. When deciding on works of art, local Ordinaries shall give hearing to the diocesan commission on sacred art, and if need be, to others who are especially expert, as well as to the commissions referred to in art. 44, 45, and 46. Ordinaries must be very careful to see that sacred furnishings and valuable works of art are not disposed of or damaged, for they are the adornment of the house of God.

127. Bishops should have a special concern for artists, so as to imbue them with the spirit of sacred art and liturgy. This they may do in person or through competent priests who are gifted with a knowledge and love of art.

It is also recommended that schools or academies of sacred art to train artists be founded in those parts of the world where they seem useful.

All artists who, prompted by their talents, desire to serve God's glory in holy Church, should ever bear in mind that they are engaged in a kind of sacred imitation of God the Creator and are concerned with works intended to be used in Catholic worship, to uplift the faithful, and to foster their devotion and religious formation.

128. Along with the revision of the liturgical books, as laid down in art. 25, there is to be an early revision of the canons and ecclesiastical statutes regulating the supplying of material things involved in sacred worship. This applies in particular to the worthy and well-planned construction of places of worship, the design and construction of altars, the nobility, placement, and security of the eucharistic tabernacle, the practicality and dignity of the baptistry, the appropriate arrangement of sacred images and church decorations and appointments. Laws that seem less suited to the reformed liturgy are to be brought into harmony with it or else abolished; laws that are helpful are to be retained if already in use or introduced where they are lacking.

With art. 22 of this Constitution as the norm, the territorial bodies of bishops are empowered to make adaptations to the needs and customs of their different regions; this applies especially to the material and design of sacred furnishings and vestments.

129. During their philosophical and theological studies, clerics are to be taught about the history and development of sacred art and about the sound principles on which the production of its works must be grounded. In consequence they will be able to appreciate and preserve the Church's treasured monuments and be in a position to offer good advice to artists who are engaged in producing works of art.

130. It is fitting that the use of pontifical insignia be reserved to those ecclesiastical persons who have either episcopal rank or some definite jurisdiction.

APPENDIX
DECLARATION OF THE SECOND VATICAN ECUMENICAL COUNCIL ON REVISION OF THE CALENDAR

131. The Second Vatican Ecumenical Council recognizes the importance of the wishes expressed by many on assigning the feast of Easter to a fixed Sunday and on an unchanging calendar and has considered the effects that could result from the introduction of a new calendar. Accordingly the Council issues the following declaration:

1. The Council is not opposed to the assignment of the feast of Easter to a particular Sunday of the Gregorian Calendar, provided those whom it may concern, especially other Christians who are not in communion with the Apostolic See, give their assent.

2. The Council likewise declares that it does not oppose measures designed to introduce a perpetual calendar into civil society.

Among the various systems being suggested to establish a perpetual calendar and to introduce it into civil life, only those systems are acceptable to the Church that retain and safeguard a seven-day week with Sunday and introduce no days outside the week, so that the present sequence of weeks is left intact, unless the most serious reasons arise. Concerning these the Apostolic See will make its own judgment.

The Fathers of the Council have given assent to all and to each part of the matters set forth in this Constitution. And together with the venerable Fathers, we, by the apostolic power given to us by Christ, approve, enact, and establish in the Holy Spirit each and all the decrees in this Constitution and command that what has been thus established in the Council be promulgated for the glory of God.

NOTES

1. Prayer over the gifts, Holy Thursday and 2d Sunday in Ordinary Time.
2. See Heb 13:14.
3. See Eph 2:21–22.
4. See Eph 4:13.
5. See Is 11:12.
6. See Jn 11:52.
7. See Jn 10:16.
8. See Is 61:1; Lk 4:18.
9. Ignatius of Antioch, *To the Ephesians* 7, 2.
10. See Tm 2:5.
11. *Sacramentarium Veronese* (ed Mohlberg), no. 1265.
12. Easter preface, Roman Missal.
13. Prayer after the seventh reading, Easter Vigil.
14. See Mk 16:15.
15. See Acts 26:18.
16. See Rom 6:4; Eph 2:6; Col 3:1.
17. See Jn 4:23.
18. See 1 Cor 11:26.
19. Council of Trent, sess. 13, 11 Oct 1551, Decree on the Holy Eucharist, chap. 5.
20. Council of Trent, sess. 22, 17 Sept 1562, Doctrine on the Holy Sacrifice of the Mass, chap. 2.
21. See Augustine, *In Ioannis Evangelium Tractatus 6*, chap. 1, n. 7.
22. See Rv. 21:2; Col 3:1; Heb 8:2.
23. See Phil 3:20; Col 3:4.
24. See Jn 17:3; Lk 24:47; Acts 2:38.
25. See Mt 28:20.
26. Prayer after communion, Easter Vigil.
27. Opening prayer, Mass for Monday of Easter Week.
28. See 2 Cor 6:1.
29. See Mt 6:6.
30. See 1 Thes 5:17.
31. See 2 Cor 4:10–11.
32. Prayer over the gifts, Saturday after the 2d, 4th, and 6th Sundays of Easter.
33. Cyprian, *On the Unity of the Catholic Church 7;* see *Letter 66,* n. 8, 3.
34. See Council of Trent, sess. 22, 17 Sept 1562, Doctrine on the Holy Sacrifice of the Mass, chap. 8.
35. See Ignatius of Antioch, *To the Magnesians,* 7; *To the Philadelphians,* 4; *To the Smyrians,* 8.
36. See Augustine, *In Ioannis Evangelium Tractatus 36,* chap. 6, n. 13.
37. Roman Breviary, antiphon for the Magnificat, second vespers, feast of Corpus Christi.
38. See Cyril of Alexandria, *Commentary on the Gospel of John,* book 11, chap. 11–12.
39. See 1 Tm 2:1–2.
40. Council of Trent, sess. 21, 16 July 1562, Doctrine on Communion under Both Species, chap. 1–3.
41. Council of Trent, sess. 24, 11 Nov 1563, Decree on Reform, chap. 1. See also Roman Ritual, title 8, chap. 2, n. 6.
42. See Eph 5:19; Col 3:16.

GENERAL INSTRUCTION
ON THE
ROMAN MISSAL

FOURTH EDITION

March 1975

BACKGROUND

The title of this document is misleading in that we no longer speak of or use a "missal." We have the sacramentary, which is the book of prayers that the presider needs for Mass, and we have the lectionary which contains the scripture readings and the responsorial psalms. This instruction is always included in the front matter of the sacramentary. It is our key to the use of the sacramentary and our basic text for understanding the order of the eucharistic liturgy and the ministries involved in that liturgy.

The *General Instruction* was first published in 1969 to guide the new order of the Roman Mass. It has had several minor revisions since that time. Parts of it are detailed and tedious, but for the most part it sets down briefly and clearly the rubrics which should be known thoroughly by planners and ministers. In *Elements of Rite* (Pueblo Publishing Company, 1982), Aidan Kavanagh writes:

[Rubrics] are included in liturgical books to be helpful in securing a recognizable standard of usage deemed appropriate in worshiping assemblies enjoying each other's communion. To regard them as more than this is usually both unhealthy and unproductive. To regard them as less than this is an attitude which should be watched with care and firmly resisted. . . . Grammatical rules also will not produce great speech any more than liturgical rubrics alone will result in a great act of celebration, [but] neither great speech nor great liturgy can afford to ignore the rules basic to each without risking the collapse of both.

Attend to this document in that spirit.

OUTLINE

GENERAL INSTRUCTION OF THE ROMAN MISSAL
Fourth Edition, March 1975

INTRODUCTION

1.   When Christ the Lord was about to celebrate the passover meal with his disciples and institute the sacrifice of his body and blood, he directed them to prepare a large room, arranged for the supper (Lk 22:12). The Church has always regarded this command of Christ as applying to itself when it gives directions about the preparation of the sentiments of the worshipers, the place, rites, and texts for the celebration of the eucharist. The current norms, laid down on the basis of the intent of Vatican Council II, and the new Missal that will be used henceforth in the celebration of Mass by the Church of the Roman Rite, are fresh evidence of the great care, faith, and unchanged love that the Church shows toward the eucharist. They attest as well to its coherent tradition, continuing amid the introduction of some new elements.

A WITNESS TO UNCHANGED FAITH

2.   The sacrificial nature of the Mass was solemnly proclaimed by the Council of Trent in agreement with the whole tradition of the Church.[1] Vatican Council II reaffirmed this teaching in these significant words: "At the Last Supper our Savior instituted the eucharistic sacrifice of his body and blood. He did this in order to perpetuate the sacrifice of the cross throughout the centuries until he should come again and in this way to entrust to his beloved Bride, the Church, a memorial of his death and resurrection."[2]

The Council's teaching is expressed constantly in the formularies of the Mass. This teaching, in the concise words of the Leonine Sacramentary, is that "the work of our redemption is carried out whenever we celebrate the memory of this sacrifice";[3] it is aptly and accurately brought out in the eucharistic prayers. At the anamnesis or memorial, the priest, addressing God in the name of all the people, offers in thanksgiving the holy and living sacrifice: the Church's offering and the Victim whose death has reconciled us with God.[4] The priest also prays that the body and blood of Christ may be a sacrifice acceptable to the Father, bringing salvation to the whole world.[5]

In this new Missal, then, the Church's rule of prayer (lex orandi) corresponds to its constant rule of faith (lex credendi). This rule of faith instructs us that the sacrifice of the cross and its sacramental renewal in the Mass, which Christ instituted at the Last Supper and commanded his apostles to do in his memory, are one and the same, differing only in the manner of offering, and that consequently the Mass is at once a sacrifice of praise and thanksgiving, of reconciliation and expiation.

3.   The celebration of Mass also proclaims the sublime mystery of the Lord's real presence under the eucharistic elements, which Vatican Council II[6] and other documents of the Church's magisterium[7] have reaffirmed in the same sense and as the same teaching that the Council of Trent had proposed as a matter of faith.[8] The Mass does this not only by means of the very words of consecration, by which Christ becomes present through transubstantiation, but also by that spirit and expression of reverence and adoration in which the eucharistic liturgy is carried out. For the same reason the Christian people are invited in Holy Week on Holy Thursday and on the solemnity of Corpus Christi to honor this wonderful sacrament in a special way by their adoration.

4.   Further, because of the priest's more prominent place and office in the rite, its form sheds light on the ministerial priesthood proper to the presbyter, who offers the sacrifice in the person of Christ and presides over the assembly of a holy people. The meaning of his office is declared and detailed in the preface for the chrism Mass on Thursday of Holy Week, the day celebrating the institution of the priesthood. The preface brings out the passing on of the sacerdotal power through the laying on of hands and, by listing its various offices, describes that power. It is the continuation of the power of Christ, High Priest of the New Testament.

5.   In addition, the ministerial priesthood puts into its proper light another reality of which much should be made, namely, the royal priesthood of believers. Through the ministry of presbyters the people's spiritual sacrifice to God is brought to completeness in union with the sacrifice of Christ, our one and only Mediator.[9] For the celebration of the eucharist is the action of the whole Church; in it all should do only, but all of, those parts that belong to them in virtue of their place within the people of God. In this way greater attention will be given to some aspects of the eucharistic celebration that have sometimes been neglected in the course of time. For these people are the people of God, purchased by Christ's blood, gathered together by the Lord, nourished by his word. They are a people called to offer God the prayers of the entire human family, a people giving thanks in Christ for the mystery of salvation by offering his sacrifice. Finally, they are a people growing together into unity by sharing in Christ's body and blood. These people are holy by their

origin, but becoming ever more holy by conscious, active, and fruitful participation in the mystery of the eucharist.[10]

A WITNESS TO UNBROKEN TRADITION

6.   In setting forth its decrees for the revision of the Order of Mass, Vatican Council II directed, among other things, that some rites be restored "to the vigor they had in the tradition of the Fathers";[11] this is a quotation from the Apostolic Constitution *Quo primum* of 1570, by which St. Pius V promulgated the Tridentine Missal. The fact that the same words are used in reference to both Roman Missals indicates how both of them, although separated by four centuries, embrace one and the same tradition. And when the more profound elements of this tradition are considered, it becomes clear how remarkably and harmoniously this new Roman Missal improves on the older one.

7.   The older Missal belongs to the difficult period of attacks against Catholic teaching on the sacrificial nature of the Mass, the ministerial priesthood, and the real and permanent presence of Christ under the eucharistic elements. St. Pius V was therefore especially concerned with preserving the relatively recent developments in the Church's tradition, then unjustly being assailed, and introduced only very slight changes into the sacred rites. In fact, the Roman Missal of 1570 differs very little from the first printed edition of 1474, which in turn faithfully follows the Missal used at the time of Pope Innocent III (1198–1216). Manuscripts in the Vatican Library provided some verbal emendations, but they seldom allowed research into "ancient and approved authors" to extend beyond the examination of a few liturgical commentaries of the Middle Ages.

8.   Today, on the other hand, countless studies of scholars have enriched the "tradition of the Fathers" that the revisers of the Missal under St. Pius V followed. After the Gregorian Sacramentary was first published in 1571, many critical editions of other ancient Roman and Ambrosian sacramentaries appeared. Ancient Spanish and Gallican liturgical books also became available, bringing to light many prayers of profound spirituality that had hitherto been unknown.

Traditions dating back to the first centuries before the formation of the Eastern and Western rites are also better known today because so many liturgical documents have been discovered.

The continuing progress in patristic studies has also illumined eucharistic theology through the teachings of such illustrious saints of Christian antiquity as Irenaeus, Ambrose, Cyril of Jerusalem, and John Chrysostom.

9.   The "tradition of the Fathers" does not require merely the preservation of what our immediate predecessors have passed on to us. There must also be profound study and understanding of the Church's entire past and of all the ways in which its single faith has been expressed in the quite diverse human and social forms prevailing in Semitic, Greek, and Latin cultures. This broader view shows us how the Holy Spirit endows the people of God with a marvelous fidelity in preserving the deposit of faith unchanged, even though prayers and rites differ so greatly.

ADAPTATION TO MODERN CONDITIONS

10.   As it bears witness to the Roman Church's rule of prayer *(lex orandi)* and guards the deposit of faith handed down by the later councils, the new Roman Missal in turn marks a major step forward in liturgical tradition.

The Fathers of Vatican Council II in reaffirming the dogmatic statements of the Council of Trent were speaking at a far different time in the world's history. They were able therefore to bring forward proposals and measures of a pastoral nature that could not have even been foreseen four centuries ago.

11.   The Council of Trent recognized the great catechetical value of the celebration of Mass, but was unable to bring out all its consequences for the actual life of the Church. Many were pressing for permission to use the vernacular in celebrating the eucharistic sacrifice, but the Council, judging the conditions of that age, felt bound to answer such a request with a reaffirmation of the Church's traditional teaching. This teaching is that the eucharistic sacrifice is, first and foremost, the action of Christ himself and therefore the manner in which the faithful take part in the Mass does not affect the efficacy belonging to it. The Council thus stated in firm but measured words: "Although the Mass contains much instruction for the faithful, it did not seem expedient to the Fathers that as a general rule it be celebrated in the vernacular."[12] The Council accordingly anathematized anyone maintaining that "the rite of the Roman Church, in which part of the canon and the words of consecration are spoken in a low voice, should be condemned or that the Mass must be celebrated only in the vernacular."[13] Although the Council of Trent on the one hand prohibited the use of the vernacular in the Mass, nevertheless, on the other, it did direct pastors to substitute appropriate catechesis: "Lest Christ's flock go hungry . . . the Council commands pastors and others having the care of souls that either personally or through others they frequently give instructions during Mass, especially on Sundays and holydays, on what is read at Mass and that among their instructions they include some explanations of the mystery of this sacrifice."[14]

12.   Convened in order to adapt the Church to the contemporary requirements of its apostolic task, Vatican Council II examined thoroughly, as had Trent, the pedagogic and pastoral character of the liturgy.[15] Since no Catholic would now deny the lawfulness and efficacy of a sacred rite celebrated in Latin, the Council was able to acknowledge that "use of the mother tongue frequently may be of great advantage to the people" and gave permission for its use.[16] The enthusiasm in response to this decision was so great that, under the leadership of the bishops and the Apostolic See, it has resulted in the permission for all liturgical celebrations in which the faithful participate to be in the vernacular for the sake of a better comprehension of the mystery being celebrated.

13.   The use of the vernacular in the liturgy may certainly be considered an important means for presenting more clearly the catechesis on the mystery that is part of the celebration itself. Nevertheless, Vatican Council II also ordered the observance of certain directives, prescribed by the Council of Trent but not obeyed everywhere. Among these are the obligatory homily on Sundays and holydays[17] and the permission to interpose some commentary during the sacred rites themselves.[18]

Above all, Vatican Council II strongly endorsed "that more complete form of participation in the Mass by which the faithful, after the priest's communion, receive the Lord's body from the same sacrifice."[19] Thus the Council gave impetus to the fulfillment of the further desire of the Fathers of Trent that for fuller participation in the holy eucharist "the faithful present at each Mass should communicate not only by spiritual desire but also by sacramental communion."[20]

14.   Moved by the same spirit and pastoral concern, Vatican Council II was able to reevaluate the Tridentine norm on communion under both kinds. No one today challenges the doctrinal principles on the completeness of eucharistic communion under the form of bread alone. The Council thus gave permission for the reception of communion under both kinds on some occasions, because this more explicit form of the sacramental sign offers a special means of deepening the understanding of the mystery in which the faithful are taking part.[21]

15.   Thus the Church remains faithful in its responsibility as teacher of truth to guard "things old," that is, the deposit of tradition; at the same time it fulfills another duty, that of examining and prudently bringing forth "things news" (see Mt 13:52).

Accordingly, a part of the new Roman Missal directs the prayer of the Church expressly to the needs of our times. This is above all true of the ritual Masses and the Masses for various needs and occasions, which happily combine the traditional and the contemporary. Thus many expressions, drawn from the Church's most ancient tradition and become familiar through the many editions of the Roman Missal, have remained unchanged. Other expressions, however, have been adapted to today's needs and circumstances and still others—for example, the prayers for the Church, the laity, the sanctification of human work, the community of all peoples, certain needs proper to our era—are completely new compositions, drawing on the thoughts and even the very language of the recent conciliar documents.

The same awareness of the present state of the world also influenced the use of texts from very ancient tradition. It seemed that this cherished treasure would not be harmed if some phrases were changed so that the style of language would be more in accord with the language of modern theology and would faithfully reflect the actual state of the Church's discipline. Thus there have been changes of some expressions bearing on the evaluation and use of the good things of the earth and of allusions to a particular form of outward penance belonging to another age in the history of the Church.

In short, the liturgical norms of the Council of Trent have been completed and improved in many respects by those of Vatican Council II. This Council has brought to realization the efforts of the last four hundred years to move the faithful closer to the sacred liturgy, especially the efforts of recent times and above all the zeal for the liturgy promoted by St. Pius X and his successors.

CHAPTER I
IMPORTANCE AND DIGNITY OF THE EUCHARISTIC CELEBRATION

1.　The celebration of Mass, the action of Christ and the people of God arrayed hierarchically, is for the universal and the local Church as well as for each person the center of the whole Christian life.[22] In the Mass we have the high point of the work that in Christ God accomplishes to sanctify us and the high point of the worship that in adoring God through Christ, his Son, we offer to the Father.[23] During the cycle of the year, moreover, the mysteries of redemption are recalled in the Mass in such a way that they are somehow made present.[24] All other liturgical rites and all the works of the Christian life are linked with the eucharistic celebration, flow from it, and have it as their end.[25]

2.   Therefore, it is of the greatest importance that the celebration of the Mass, the Lord's Supper, be so arranged that the ministers and the faithful who take their own proper part in it may more fully receive its good effects.[26] This is the reason why Christ the Lord instituted the eucharistic sacrifice of his body and blood and entrusted it to the Church, his beloved Bride, as the memorial of his passion and resurrection.[27]

3.   This purpose will best be accomplished if, after due regard for the nature and circumstances of each assembly, the celebration is planned in such a way that it brings about in the faithful a participation in body and spirit that is conscious, active, full, and motivated by faith, hope, and charity. The Church desires this kind of participation, the nature of the celebration demands it, and for the Christian people it is a right and duty they have by reason of their baptism.[28]

4.   The presence and active participation of the people bring out more plainly the ecclesial nature of the celebration.[29] But even when their participation is not possible, the eucharistic celebration still retains its effectiveness and worth because it is the action of Christ and the Church,[30] in which the priest always acts on behalf of the people's salvation.

5.   The celebration of the eucharist, like the entire liturgy, involves the use of outward signs that foster, strengthen, and express faith.[31] There must be the utmost care therefore to choose and to make wise use of those forms and elements provided by the Church that, in view of the circumstances of the people and the place, will best foster active and full participation and serve the spiritual well-being of the faithful.

6.   The purpose of this Instruction is to give the general guidelines for planning the eucharistic celebration properly and to set forth the rules for arranging the individual forms of celebration.[32] In accord with the *Constitution on the Liturgy*, each conference of bishops has the power to lay down norms for its own territory that are suited to the traditions and character of peoples, regions, and various communities.[33]

CHAPTER II
STRUCTURE, ELEMENTS, AND PARTS OF THE MASS

I. GENERAL STRUCTURE OF THE MASS

7.   At Mass or the Lord's Supper, the people of God are called together, with a priest presiding and acting in the person of Christ, to celebrate the memorial of the Lord or eucharistic sacrifice.[34] For this reason Christ's promise applies supremely to such a local gathering of the Church: "Where two or three come together in my name, there am I in their midst" (Mt 18:20). For at the celebration of Mass, which perpetuates the sacrifice of the cross,[35] Christ is really present to the assembly gathered in his name; he is present in the person of the minister, in his own word, and indeed substantially and permanently under the eucharistc elements.[36]

8.   The Mass is made up as it were of the liturgy of the word and the liturgy of the eucharist, two parts so closely connected that they form but one single act of worship.[37] For in the Mass the table of God's word and of Christ's body is laid for the people of God to receive from it instruction and food.[38] There are also certain rites to open and conclude the celebration.

II. DIFFERENT ELEMENTS OF THE MASS

READING AND EXPLAINING THE WORD OF GOD

9.   When the Scriptures are read in the Church, God himself is speaking to his people, and Christ, present in his own word, is proclaiming the Gospel.

The readings must therefore be listened to by all with reverence; they make up a principal element of the liturgy. In the biblical readings God's word addresses all people of every era and is understandable to them, but a living commentary on the word, that is, the homily, as an integral part of the liturgy, increases the word's effectiveness.[39]

PRAYERS AND OTHER PARTS ASSIGNED TO THE PRIEST

10.   Among the parts assigned to the priest, the eucharistic prayer is preeminent; it is the high point of the entire celebration. Next are the prayers: the opening prayer or collect, the prayer over the gifts, and the prayer after communion. The priest, presiding over the assembly in the person of Christ, addresses these prayers to God in the name of the entire holy people and all present.[40] Thus there is good reason to call them "the presidential prayers."

11.   It is also up to the priest in the exercise of his office of presiding over the assembly to pronounce the instructions and words of introduction and conclusion that are provided in the rites themselves. By their very nature these introductions do not need to be expressed verbatim in the form in which they are given in the Missal; at least in certain cases it will be advisable to adapt them somewhat to the concrete situation of the community.[41] It also belongs to the priest presiding to proclaim the word of God and to give the final blessing. He may give the faithful a very brief introduction to the Mass of the day (before the celebration begins), to the liturgy of the word (before the readings), and to the eucharistic prayer (before the preface); he may make comments concluding the entire sacred service before the dismissal. [See Appendix to the General Instruction for the Dioceses of the United States of America (GIapp), no. 11.]

12.   The nature of the presidential prayers demands that they be spoken in a loud and clear voice and that everyone present listen with attention.[42] While the priest is reciting them there should be no other prayer and the organ or other instruments should not be played.

13.   But the priest does not only pray in the name of the whole community as its president; he also prays at times in his own name that he may exercise his ministry with attention and devotion. Such prayers are said inaudibly.

OTHER TEXTS IN THE CELEBRATION

14.   Since by nature the celebration of Mass has the character of being the act of a community,[43] both the dialogues between celebrant and congregation and the acclamations take on special value;[44] they are not simply outward signs of the community's celebration, but the means of greater communion between priest and people.

15.   The acclamations and the responses to the priest's greeting and prayers create a degree of the active participation that the gathered faithful must contribute in every form of the Mass, in order to express clearly and to further the entire community's involvement.[45]

16.   There are other parts, extremely useful for expressing and encouraging the people's active participation, that are assigned to the whole congregation: the penitential rite, the profession of faith, the general intercessions, and the Lord's Prayer.

17.   Finally, of the other texts:

      a.   Some constitute an independent rite or act, such as the Gloria, the responsorial psalm, the Alleluia verse and the verse before the Gospel, the Sanctus, the memorial acclamation, and the song after communion.

b.   Others accompany another rite, such as songs at the entrance, at the preparation of the gifts, at the breaking of the bread (Agnus Dei), and at communion.

VOCAL EXPRESSION OF THE DIFFERENT TEXTS

18.   In texts that are to be delivered in a clear, loud voice, whether by the priest or by the ministers or by all, the tone of voice should correspond to the genre of the text, that is, accordingly as it is a reading, a prayer, an instruction, an acclamation, or a song; the tone should also be suited to the form of celebration and to the solemnity of the gathering. Other criteria are the idiom of different languages and the genius of peoples.

In the rubrics and in the norms that follow, the words *say (dicere)* or *proclaim (proferre)* are to be understood of both singing and speaking, and in accordance with the principles just stated.

IMPORTANCE OF SINGING

19.   The faithful who gather together to await the Lord's coming are instructed by the Apostle Paul to sing psalms, hymns, and inspired songs (see Col 3:16). Song is the sign of the heart's joy (see Acts 2:46). Thus St. Augustine says rightly: "To sing belongs to lovers."[46] There is also the ancient proverb: "One who sings well prays twice." [See GIapp, no. 19.]

With due consideration for the culture and ability of each congregation, great importance should be attached to the use of singing at Mass; but it is not always necessary to sing all the texts that are of themselves meant to be sung.

In choosing the parts actually to be sung, however, preference should be given to those that are more significant and especially to those to be sung by the priest or ministers with the congregation responding or by the priest and people together.[47]

Since the faithful from different countries come together ever more frequently, it is desirable that they know how to sing at least some parts of the Ordinary of the Mass in Latin, especially the profession of faith and the Lord's Prayer, set to simple melodies.[48]

MOVEMENTS AND POSTURES

20.   The uniformity in standing, kneeling, or sitting to be observed by all taking part is a sign of the community and the unity of the assembly; it both expresses and fosters the spiritual attitude of those taking part.[49]

21.   For the sake of uniformity in movement and posture, the people should follow the directions given during the celebration by the deacon, the priest, or another minister. Unless other provision is made, at every

Mass the people should stand from the beginning of the entrance song or when the priest enters until the end of the opening prayer or collect; for the singing of the Alleluia before the gospel; while the gospel is proclaimed; during the profession of faith and the general intercessions; from the prayer over the gifts to the end of the Mass, except at the places indicated later in this paragraph. They should sit during the readings before the gospel and during the responsorial psalm, for the homily and the presentation of the gifts, and, if this seems helpful, during the period of silence after communion. They should kneel at the consecration unless prevented by the lack of space, the number of people present, or some other good reason.

But it is up to the conference of bishops to adapt the actions and postures described in the Order of the Roman Mass to the customs of the people.[50] But the conference must make sure that such adaptations correspond to the meaning and character of each part of the celebration. [See GI app, no. 21.]

22.   Included among the external actions of the Mass are those of the priest going to the altar, of the faithful presenting the gifts, and their coming forward to receive communion. While the songs proper to these movements are being sung, they should be carried out becomingly in keeping with the norms prescribed for each.

SILENCE

23.   Silence should be observed at the designated times as part of the celebration.[51] Its function depends on the time it occurs in each part of the celebration. Thus at the penitential rite and again after the invitation to prayer, all recollect themselves; at the conclusion of a reading or the homily, all meditate briefly on what has been heard; after communion, all praise God in silent prayer.

III. INDIVIDUAL PARTS OF THE MASS

A. Introductory Rites

24.   The parts preceding the liturgy of the word, namely, the entrance song, greeting, penitential rite, Kyrie, Gloria, and opening prayer or collect, have the character of a beginning, introduction, and preparation.

The purpose of these rites is that the faithful coming together take on the form of a community and prepare themselves to listen to God's word and celebrate the eucharist properly.

ENTRANCE

25.   After the people have assembled, the entrance song begins as the

priest and the ministers come in. The purpose of this song is to open the celebration, intensify the unity of the gathered people, lead their thoughts to the mystery of the season or feast, and accompany the procession of priest and ministers.

26.   The entrance song is sung alternately either by the choir and the congregation or by the cantor and the congregation; or it is sung entirely by the congregation or by the choir alone. The antiphon and psalm of the *Graduale Romanum* or the *The Simple Gradual* may be used, or another song that is suited to this part of the Mass, the day, or the season and that has a text approved by the conference of bishops.

   If there is no singing for the entrance, the antiphon in the Missal is recited either by the faithful, by some of them, or by a reader; otherwise it is recited by the priest after the greeting. [See GI app, no. 26.]

VENERATION OF THE ALTAR AND GREETING OF THE CONGREGATION

27.   When the priest and the ministers enter the sanctuary, they reverence the altar. As a sign of veneration, the priest and deacon kiss the altar; when the occasion warrants, the priest may also incense the altar.

28.   After the entrance song, the priest and the whole assembly make the sign of the cross. Then through his greeting the priest declares to the assembled community that the Lord is present. This greeting and the congregation's response express the mystery of the gathered Church.

PENITENTIAL RITE

29.   After greeting the congregation, the priest or other qualified minister may very briefly introduce the faithful to the Mass of the day. Then the priest invites them to take part in the penitential rite, which the entire community carries out through a communal confession and which the priest's absolution brings to an end.

KYRIE ELEISON

30.   The Kyrie begins, unless it has already been included as part of the penitential rite. Since it is a song by which the faithful praise the Lord and implore his mercy, it is ordinarily prayed by all, that is, alternately by the congregation and the choir or cantor.

   As a rule each of the acclamations is said twice, but, because of the idiom of different languages, the music, or other circumstances, it may be said more than twice or a short verse (trope) may be interpolated. If the Kyrie is not sung, it is to be recited.

GLORIA

31. The Gloria is an ancient hymn in which the Church, assembled in the Holy Spirit, praises and entreats the Father and the Lamb. It is sung by the congregation, or by the congregation alternately with the choir, or by the choir alone. If not sung, it is to be recited either by all together or in alternation.

The Gloria is sung or said on Sundays outside Advent and Lent, on solemnites and feasts, and in special, more solemn celebrations.

OPENING PRAYER OR COLLECT

32. Next the priest invites the people to pray and together with him they observe a brief silence so that they may realize they are in God's presence and may call their petitions to mind. The priest then says the opening prayer, which custom has named the "collect." This expresses the theme of the celebration and the priest's words address a petition to God the Father through Christ in the Holy Spirit.

The people make the prayer their own and give their assent by the acclamation, Amen.

In the Mass only one opening prayer is said; this rule applies also to the prayer over the gifts and the prayer after communion.

The opening prayer ends with the longer conclusion, namely:

—if the prayer is directed to the Father: *We ask this (Grant this) through our Lord Jesus Christ, your Son, who lives and reigns with you and the Holy Spirit, one God, for ever and ever;*

—if it is directed to the Father, but the Son is mentioned at the end: *Who lives and reigns with you and the Holy Spirit, one God, for ever and ever;*

—if directed to the Son: *You live and reign with the Father and the Holy Spirit, one God, for ever and ever.*

The prayer over the gifts and the prayer after communion end with the shorter conclusion, namely:

—if the prayer is directed to the Father: *We ask this (Grant this) through Christ our Lord;*

—if it is directed to the Father, but the Son is mentioned at the end: *Who lives and reigns with you for ever and ever;*

—if it is directed to the Son: *You live and reign for ever and ever.*

B. Liturgy of the Word

33. Readings from Scripture and the chants between the readings form the main part of the liturgy of the word. The homily, profession of faith, and general intercessions or prayer of the faithful expand and complete this part of the Mass. In the readings, explained by the homily, God is speaking to his people,[52] opening up to them the mystery of redemption and salvation, and nourishing their spirit; Christ is present to the faithful through his own word.[53] Through the chants the people make God's word their own and through the profession of faith affirm their adherence to it. Finally, having been fed by this word, they make their petitions in the general intercessions for the needs of the church and for the salvation of the whole world.

SCRIPTURE READINGS

34.   The readings lay the table of God's word for the faithful and open up the riches of the Bible to them.[54] Since by tradition the reading of the Scripture is a ministerial, not a presidential function, it is proper that as a rule a deacon or, in his absence, a priest other than the one presiding read the gospel. A reader proclaims the other readings. In the absence of a deacon or another priest, the priest celebrant reads the gospel.[55]

35.   The liturgy itself inculcates the great reverence to be shown toward the reading of the gospel, setting it off from the other readings by special marks of honor. A special minister is appointed to proclaim it and prepares himself by a blessing or prayer. The people, who by their acclamations acknowledge and confess Christ present and speaking to them, stand as they listen to it. Marks of reverence are given to the Book of the Gospels itself.

CHANTS BETWEEN THE READINGS

36.   After the reading comes the responsorial psalm or gradual, an integral part of the liturgy of the word. The psalm as a rule is drawn from the Lectionary because the individual psalm texts are directly connected with the individual readings: the choice of psalm depends therefore on the readings. Nevertheless, in order that the people may be able to join in the responsorial psalm more readily, some texts of responses and psalms have been chosen, according to the different seasons of the years and classes of saints, for optional use, whenever the psalm is sung, in place of the text corresponding to the reading.

The psalmist or cantor of the psalm sings the verses of the psalm at the lectern or other suitable place. The people remain seated and listen, but also as a rule take part by singing the response, except when the psalm is sung straight through without the response.

The psalm when sung may be either the psalm assigned in the Lectionary or the gradual from the *Graduale ˜Romanum* or the responsorial psalm or the psalm with Alleluia as the response from *The Simple Gradual* in the form they have in those books. [See GI app, no. 36.]

37.   As the season requires, the Alleluia or another chant follows the second reading.

a.   The Alleluia is sung in every season outside Lent. It is begun either by all present or by the choir or cantor; it may then be repeated. The verses are taken from the Lectionary or the *Graduale.*

b.   The other chant consists of the verse before the gospel or another psalm or tract, as found in the Lectionary or the *Graduale.*

38.   When there is only one reading before the gospel:

a.   during a season calling for the Alleluia, there is an option to use either the psalm with Alleluia as the response, or the responsorial psalm and the Alleluia with its verse, or just the psalm, or just the Alleluia.

b.   during the season when the Alleluia is not allowed, either the responsorial psalm or the verse before the gospel may be used.

39.   If the psalm after the reading is not sung, it is to be recited. If not sung, the Alleluia or the verse before the gospel may be omitted.

40.   Sequences are optional, except on Easter Sunday and Pentecost.

HOMILY

41.   The homily is an integral part of the liturgy and is strongly recommended:[56] it is necessary for the nurturing of the Christian life. It should develop some point of the readings or of another text from the Ordinary or from the Proper of the Mass of the day, and take into account the mystery being celebrated and the needs proper to the listeners.[57]

42.   There must be a homily on Sundays and holydays of obligation at all Masses that are celebrated with a congregation; it may not be omitted without a serious reason. It is recommended on other days, especially on the weekdays of Advent, Lent, and the Easter season, as well as on other feasts and occasions when the people come to Church in large numbers.[58]

The homily should ordinarily be given by the priest celebrant.

PROFESSION OF FAITH

43.   The symbol or profession of faith in the celebration of Mass serves as a way for the people to respond and to give their assent to the word of God heard in the readings and through the homily and for them to call to mind the truths of faith before they begin to celebrate the eucharist.

44.   Recitation of the profession of faith by the priest together with the people is obligatory on Sundays and solemnities. It may be said also at special, more solemn celebrations.

If it is sung, as a rule all are to sing it together or in alternation.

45.   In the general intercessions or prayer of the faithful, the people, exercising their priestly function, intercede for all humanity. It is appropriate that this prayer be included in all Masses celebrated with a congregation, so that petitions will be offered for the Church, for civil authorities, for those oppressed by various needs, for all people, and for the salvation of the world.[59] [See GIapp, no. 45]

46.   As a rule the sequence of intentions is to be:

   a.   for the needs of the Church;

   b.   for public authorities and the salvation of the world;

   c.   for those oppressed by any need;

   d.   for the local community.

   In particular celebrations, such as confirmations, marriages, funerals, etc., the series of intercessions may refer more specifically to the occasion.

47.   It belongs to the priest celebrant to direct the general intercessions, by means of a brief introduction to invite the congregation to pray, and after the intercessions to say the concluding prayer. It is desirable that a deacon, cantor, or other person announce the intentions.[60] The whole assembly gives expression to its supplication either by a response said together after each intention or by silent prayer.

C. Liturgy of the Eucharist

48.   At the last supper Christ instituted the sacrifice and paschal meal that make the sacrifice of the cross to be continuously present in the Church when the priest, representing Christ the Lord, carries out what the Lord did and handed over to his disciples to do in his memory.[61]

   Christ took the bread and the cup and gave thanks; he broke the bread and gave it to his disciples, saying: "Take and eat, this is my body." Giving the cup, he said: "Take and drink, this is the cup of my blood. Do this in memory of me." Accordingly, the Church has planned the celebration of the eucharistic liturgy around the parts corresponding to these words and actions of Christ:

   1.   In the preparation of the gifts, the bread and wine with water are brought to the altar, that is, the same elements that Christ used.

   2.   In the eucharistic prayer thanks is given to God for the whole work of salvation and the gifts of bread and wine become the body and blood of Christ.

3. Through the breaking of the one bread the unity of the faithful is expressed and through communion they receive the Lord's body and blood in the same way the apostles received them from Christ's own hands.

PREPARATION OF THE GIFTS

49. At the beginning of the liturgy of the eucharist the gifts, which will become Christ's body and blood, are brought to the altar.

First the altar, the Lord's table, which is the center of the whole eucharistic liturgy,[62] is prepared: the corporal, purificator, missal and chalice are placed on it (unless the chalice is prepared at a side table).

The gifts are then brought forward. It is desirable for the faithful to present the bread and wine, which are accepted by the priest or deacon at a convenient place. The gifts are placed on the altar to the accompaniment of the prescribed texts. Even though the faithful no longer, as in the past, bring the bread and wine for the liturgy from their homes, the rite of carrying up the gifts retains the same spiritual value and meaning.

This is also the time to receive money or other gifts for the church or the poor brought by the faithful or collected at the Mass. These are to be put in a suitable place but not on the altar.

50. The procession bringing the gifts is accompanied by the presentation song, which continues at least until the gifts have been placed on the altar. The rules for this song are the same as those for the entrance song (no. 26). If it is not sung, the presentation antiphon is omitted. [See GIapp, no. 50.]

51. The gifts on the altar and the altar itself may be incensed. This is a symbol of the Church's offering and prayer going up to God. Afterward the deacon or other minister may incense the priest and the people.

52. The priest then washes his hands as an expression of his desire to be cleansed within.

53. Once the gifts have been placed on the altar and the accompanying rites completed, the preparation of the gifts comes to an end through the invitation to pray with the priest and the prayer over the gifts, which are a preparation for the eucharistic prayer.

EUCHARISTIC PRAYER

54. Now the center and summit of the entire celebration begins: the eucharistic prayer, a prayer of thanksgiving and sanctification. The priest invites the people to lift up their hearts to the Lord in prayer and thanks; he unites them with himself in the prayer he addresses in their name to the Father through Jesus Christ. The meaning of the prayer is that the

entire congregation joins itself to Christ in acknowledging the great things God has done and in offering the sacrifice.

55. The chief elements making up the eucharistic prayer are these:

a. Thanksgiving (expressed especially in the preface): in the name of the entire people of God, the priest praises the Father and gives thanks to him for the whole work of salvation or for some special aspect of it that corresponds to the day, feast, or season.

b. Acclamation: joining with the angels, the congregation sings or recites the Sanctus. This acclamation is an intrinsic part of the eucharistic prayer and all the people join with the priest in singing or reciting it.

c. Epiclesis: in special invocations the Church calls on God's power and asks that the gifts offered by human hands be consecrated, that is, become Christ's body and blood, and that the victim to be received in communion be the source of salvation for those who will partake.

d. Institution narrative and consecration: in the words and actions of Christ, that sacrifice is celebrated which he himself instituted at the last supper, when, under the appearances of bread and wine, he offered his body and blood, gave them to his apostles to eat and drink, then commanded that they carry on this mystery.

e. Anamnesis: in fulfillment of the command received from Christ through the apostles, the Church keeps his memorial by recalling especially his passion, resurrection, and ascension.

f. Offering: in this memorial, the Church—and in particular the Church here and now assembled— offers the spotless victim to the Father in the Holy Spirit. The Church's intention is that the faithful not only offer this victim but also learn to offer themselves and so to surrender themselves, through Christ the Mediator, to an ever more complete union with the Father and each other, so that at last God may be all in all.[63]

g. Intercessions: the intercessions make it clear that the eucharist is celebrated in communion with the entire Church of heaven and earth and that the offering is made for the Church and all its members, living and dead, who are called to share in the salvation and redemption purchased by Christ's body and blood.

h. Final doxology: the praise of God is expressed in the doxology, to which the people's acclamation is an assent and a conclusion.

The eucharistic prayer calls for all to listen in silent reverence, but also to take part through the acclamations for which the rite makes provision.

56.   Since the eucharistic celebration is the paschal meal, it is right that the faithful who are properly disposed receive the Lord's body and blood as spiritual food as he commanded.[64] This is the purpose of the breaking of the bread and the other preparatory rites that lead directly to the communion of the people:

a.   Lord's Prayer: this is a petition both for daily food, which for Christians means also the eucharistic bread, and for the forgiveness of sin, so that what is holy may be given to those who are holy. The priest offers the invitation to pray, but all the faithful say the prayer with him; he alone adds the embolism, *Deliver us*, which the people conclude with a doxology. The embolism, developing the last petition of the Lord's Prayer, begs on behalf of the entire community of the faithful deliverance from the power of evil. The invitation, the prayer itself, the embolism, and the people's doxology are sung or are recited aloud.

b.   Rite of peace: before they share in the same bread, the faithful implore peace and unity for the Church and for the whole human family and offer some sign of their love for one another.

The form the sign of peace should take is left to the conference of bishops to determine, in accord with the culture and customs of the people. [See GI app, no. 56b.]

c.   Breaking of the bread: in apostolic times this gesture of Christ at the last supper gave the entire eucharistic action its name. This rite is not simply functional, but is a sign that in sharing in the one bread of life which is Christ we who are many are made one body (see 1 Cor 10:17).

d.   Commingling: the celebrant drops a part of the host into the chalice.

e.   Agnus Dei: during the breaking of the bread and the commingling, the Agnus Dei is as a rule sung by the choir or cantor with the congregation responding; otherwise it is recited aloud. This invocation may be repeated as often as necessary to accompany the breaking of the bread. The final reprise concludes with the words, *grant us peace.*

f.   Personal preparation of the priest: the priest prepares himself by the prayer, said softly, that he may receive Christ's body and blood to good effect. The faithful do the same by silent prayer.

g.   The priest then shows the eucharistic bread for communion to the faithful and with them recites the prayer of humility in words from the Gospels.

h.   It is most desirable that the faithful receive the Lord's body from hosts consecrated at the same Mass and that, in the instances when it is permitted, they share in the chalice. Then even through the signs communion will stand out more clearly as a sharing in the sacrifice actually being offered.[65]

i.   During the priest's and the faithful's reception of the sacrament the communion song is sung. Its function is to express outwardly the communicants' union in spirit by means of the unity of their voices, to give evidence of joy of heart, and to make the procession to receive Christ's body more fully an act of community. The song begins when the priest takes communion and continues for as long as seems appropriate while the faithful receive Christ's body. But the communion song should be ended in good time whenever there is to be a hymn after communion.

An antiphon from the *Graduale Romanum* may also be used, with or without the psalm, or an antiphon with psalm from *The Simple Gradual* or another suitable song approved by the conference of bishops. It is sung by the choir alone or by the choir or cantor with the congregation.

If there is no singing, the communion antiphon in the missal is recited either by the people, by some of them, or by a reader. Otherwise the priest himself says it after he has received communion and before he gives communion to the faithful. [See GI app, no. 56i.]

j.   After communion, the priest and people may spend some time in silent prayer. If desired, a hymn, psalm, or other song of praise may be sung by the entire congregation.

k.   In the prayer after communion, the priest petitions for the effects of the mystery just celebrated and by their acclamation, Amen, the people make the prayer their own.

D. Concluding Rite

57.   The concluding rite consists of:

a.   the priest's greeting and blessing, which on certain days and occasions is expanded and expressed in the prayer over the people or another more solemn formulary.

b.   the dismissal of the assembly, which sends each member back to doing good works, while praising and blessing the Lord.

CHAPTER III
OFFICES AND MINISTRIES IN THE MASS

58.   All in the assembly gathered for Mass have an individual right and duty to contribute their participation in ways differing according to the diversity of their order and liturgical function.[66] Thus in carrying out this function, all, whether ministers or laypersons, should do all and only those parts that belong to them,[67] so that the very arrangement of the celebration itself makes the Church stand out as being formed in a structure of different orders and ministries.

I. OFFICES AND MINISTRIES OF HOLY ORDERS

59.   Every authentic celebration of the eucharist is directed by the bishop, either in person or through the presbyters, who are his helpers.[68]

Whenever he is present at a Mass with a congregation, it is fitting that the bishop himself preside over the assembly and associate the presbyters with himself in the celebration, if possible by concelebrating with them.

This is done not to add external solemnity, but to express in a clearer light the mystery of the Church, which is the sacrament of unity.[69]

Even if the bishop is not the celebrant of the eucharist but assigns someone else he should preside over the liturgy of the word and give the blessing at the end of Mass. [See GIapp, no. 59.]

60.   Within the community of believers, the presbyter is another who possesses the power of orders to offer sacrifice in the person of Christ.[70] He therefore presides over the assembly and leads its prayer, proclaims the message of salvation, joins the people to himself in offering the sacrifice to the Father through Christ in the Spirit, gives them the bread of eternal life, and shares in it with them. At the eucharist he should, then, serve God and the people with dignity and humility; by his bearing and by the way he recites the words of the liturgy he should communicate to the faithful a sense of the living presence of Christ.

61.   Among ministers, the deacon, whose order has been held in high honor since the early Church, has first place. At Mass he has his own functions: he proclaims the gospel, sometimes preaches God's word, leads the general intercessions, assists the priest, gives communion to the people (in particular, ministering the chalice), and sometimes gives directions regarding the assembly's moving, standing, kneeling, or sitting.

II. OFFICE AND FUNCTION OF THE PEOPLE OF GOD

62.   In the celebration of Mass the faithful are a holy people, a people God has made his own, a royal priesthood: they give thanks to the Father and offer the victim not only through the hands of the priest but also together with him and learn to offer themselves.[71] They should endeavor to make this clear by their deep sense of reverence for God and their charity toward all who share with them in the celebration.

They therefore are to shun any appearance of individualism or division, keeping before their mind that they have the one Father in heaven and therefore are all brothers and sisters to each other.

They should become one body, whether by hearing the word of God, or joining in prayers and song, or above all by offering the sacrifice together and sharing together in the Lord's table. There is a beautiful expression of this unity when the faithful maintain uniformity in their actions and in standing, sitting, or kneeling.

The faithful should serve the people of God willingly when asked to perform some particular ministry in the celebration.

63.   The *schola cantorum* or choir exercises its own liturgical function within the assembly. Its task is to ensure that the parts proper to it, in keeping with the different types of chants, are carried out becomingly and to encourage active participation of the people in the singing.[72] What is said about the choir applies in a similar way to other musicians, especially the organist.

64.   There should be a cantor or a choir director to lead and sustain the people in the singing. When in fact there is no choir, it is up to the cantor to lead the various songs, and the people take part in the way proper to them.[73]

III. SPECIAL MINISTRIES

65.   The acolyte is instituted to serve at the altar and to assist the priest and deacon. In particular it is for him to prepare the altar and the vessels and, as a special minister of the eucharist, to give communion to the faithful.

66.   The reader is instituted to proclaim the readings from Scripture, with the exception of the gospel. He may also announce the intentions for the general intercessions and, in the absence of the psalmist, sing or read the psalm between the readings.

The reader has his own proper function in the eucharistic celebration and should exercise this even though ministers of a higher rank may be present.

Those who exercise the ministry of reader, even if they have not received institution, must be truly qualified and carefully prepared in order that the faithful will develop a warm and lively love for Scripture[74] from listening to the reading of the sacred texts. [See GIapp, no. 66.]

67.   The cantor of the psalm is to sing the psalm or other biblical song that comes between the readings. To fulfill their function correctly, these cantors should possess singing talent and an aptitude for correct pronunciation and diction.

68.   As for other ministers, some perform different functions inside the sanctuary, others outside.

The first kind include those deputed as special ministers of communion[75] and those who carry the missal, the cross, candles, the bread, wine, water, and the thurible.

The second kind include:

a.   The commentator. This minister provides explanations and commentaries with the purpose of introducing the faithful to the celebration and preparing them to understand it better. The commentator's remarks must be meticulously prepared and marked by a simple brevity.

In performing this function the commentator stands in a convenient place visible to the faithful, but it is preferable that this not be at the lectern where the Scriptures are read.

b.   Those who, in some places, meet the people at the church entrance, seat them, and direct processions.

c.   Those who take up the collection.

69.   Expecially in larger churches and communities, a person should be assigned responsibility for planning the services properly and for their being carried out by the ministers with decorum, order, and devotion.

70.   Laymen, even if they have not received institution as ministers, may perform all the functions below those reserved to deacons. At the discretion of the rector of the church, women may be appointed to ministries that are performed outside the sanctuary.

The conference of bishops may permit qualified women to proclaim the readings before the gospel and to announce the intentions of the general intercessions. The conference may also more precisely designate a suitable place for a woman to proclaim the word of God in the liturgical assembly.[76]

71. If there are several persons present who are empowered to exercise the same ministry, there is no objection to their being assigned different parts to perform. For example, one deacon may take the sung parts, another assist at the altar; if there are several readings, it is better to distribute them among a number of readers. The same applies for the other ministries.

72. If only one minister is present at a Mass with a congregation, he may carry out several different functions.

73. All concerned should work together in the effective preparation of each liturgical celebration as to its rites, pastoral aspects and music. They should work under the direction of the rector of the church and should consult the faithful.

CHAPTER IV

THE DIFFERENT FORMS OF CELEBRATION

74. In the local Church, first place should be given, because of its meaning, to the Mass at which the bishop presides surrounded by the college of presbyters and the ministers[77] and in which the people take full and active part. For this Mass is the preeminent expression of the Church.

75. Great importance should be attached to a Mass celebrated by any community, but especially by the parish community, inasmuch as it represents the universal Church gathered at a given time and place. This is particularly true of the community's celebration of the Lord's Day.[78]

76. Of those Masses celebrated by some communities, the conventual Mass, which is a part of the daily office, or the "community" Mass have particular significance. Although such Masses do not have a special form of celebration, it is most proper that they be celebrated with singing, with the full participation of all community members, whether religious or canons. In these Masses, therefore, individuals should exercise the function proper to the order or ministry they have received. All the priests who are not bound to celebrate individually for the pastoral benefit of the faithful should thus concelebrate at the conventual or community Mass, if possible. Further, all priests belonging to the community who are obliged to celebrate individually for the pastoral benefit of the faithful may also on the same day concelebrate at the conventual or community Mass.[79]

I. MASS WITH A CONGREGATION

77.   Mass with a congregation means a Mass celebrated with the people taking part. As far as possible, and especially on Sundays and holy days of obligation, this Mass should be celebrated with song and with a suitable number of ministers.[80] But it may be celebrated without music and with only one minister.

78.   It is desirable that as a rule an acolyte, a reader, and a cantor assist the priest celebrant; this form of celebration will hereafter be referred to as the "basic" or "typical" form. But the rite to be described also allows for a greater number of ministers.

A deacon may exercise his office in any of the forms of celebration.

ARTICLES TO BE PREPARED

79.   The altar is to be covered with at least one cloth. On or near the altar there are to be candlesticks with lighted candles, at least two but even four, six, or, if the bishop of the diocese celebrates, seven. There is also to be a cross on or near the altar. The candles and cross may be carried in the entrance procession. The Book of the Gospels, if distinct from the book of other readings, may be placed on the altar, unless it is carried in the entrance procession.

80.   The following are also to be prepared:

a.   next to the priest's chair: the missal and, as may be useful, a book with the chants;

b.   at the lectern: the lectionary;

c.   on a side table: the chalice, corporal, purificator, and, if useful, a pall; a paten and ciboria, if needed, with the bread for the communion of the ministers and the people, together with cruets containing wine and water, unless all of these are brought in by the faithful at the presentation of the gifts; a communion plate for the communion of the faithful; the requisites for the washing of hands. The chalice should be covered with a veil, which may always be white.

81.   In the sacristy the vestments for the priest and ministers are to be prepared according to the various forms of celebration:

a.   for the priest: alb, stole, and chasuble;

b.   for the deacon: alb, stole and dalmatic; the last may be omitted either out of necessity or for less solemnity;

c. for the other ministers: albs or other lawfully approved vestments.

All who wear an alb should use a cincture and an amice, unless other provision is made.

A. Basic Form of Celebration

INTRODUCTORY RITES

82. Once the congregation has gathered, the priest and the ministers, clad in their vestments, go to the altar in this order:

a. a server with a lighted censer, if incense is used;

b. the servers, who, according to the occasion, carry lighted candles, and between them the crossbearer, if the cross is to be carried;

c. acolytes and other ministers;

d. a reader, who may carry the Book of the Gospels;

e. the priest who is to celebrate the Mass.

If incense is used, the priest puts some in the censer before the procession begins.

83. During the procession to the altar the entrance song is sung (see nos. 25–26).

84. On reaching the altar the priest and ministers make the proper reverence, that is, a low bow or, if there is a tabernacle containing the blessed sacrament, a genuflection.

If the cross has been carried in the procession, it is placed near the altar or at some other convenient place; the candles carried by the servers are placed near the altar or on a side table; the Book of Gospels is placed on the altar.

85. The priest goes up to the altar and kisses it. If incense is used, he incenses the altar while circling it.

86. The priest then goes to the chair. After the entrance song, and with all standing, the priest and the faithful make the sign of the cross. The priest says: *In the name of the Father, and of the Son, and of the Holy Spirit;* the people answer: *Amen.*

Then, facing the people and with hands outstretched, the priest greets all present, using one of the formularies indicated. He or some other qualified minister may give the faithful a very brief introduction to the Mass of the day.

87.   After the penitential rite, the Kyrie and Gloria are said, in keeping with the rubrics (nos. 30–31). Either the priest or the cantors or even everyone together may begin the Gloria.

88.   With his hands joined, the priest then invites the people to pray, saying: *Let us pray.* All pray silently with the priest for a while. Then the priest with hands outstretched says the opening prayer, at the end of which the people respond: *Amen.*

LITURGY OF THE WORD

89.   After the opening prayer, the reader goes to the lectern for the first reading. All sit and listen and make the acclamation at the end.

90.   After the reading, the psalmist or cantor of the psalm, or even the reader, sings or recites the psalm and the congregation sings or recites the response (see no. 36).

91.   Then, if there is a second reading before the gospel, the reader reads it at the lectern as before. All sit and listen and make the acclamation at the end.

92.   The Alleluia or other chant, according to the season, follows (see nos. 37–39).

93.   During the singing of the Alleluia or other chant, if incense is being used, the priest puts some into the censer. Then with hands joined he bows before the altar and inaudibly says the prayer. *Almighty God, cleanse my heart.*

94.   If the Book of the Gospels is on the altar, he takes it and goes to the lectern, the servers, who may carry the censer and candles, walking ahead of him.

95.   At the lectern the priest opens the book and says: *The Lord be with you.* Then he says: *A reading from . . .* , making the sign of the cross with his thumb on the book and on his forehead, mouth, and breast. If incense is used, he then incenses the book. After the acclamation of the people, he proclaims the gospel and at the end kisses the book, saying inaudibly: *May the words of the gospel wipe away our sins.* After the reading the people make the acclamation customary to the region.

96.   If no reader is present, the priest himself proclaims all the readings at the lectern and there also, if necessary, the chants between the readings. If incense is used, he puts some into the censer at the lectern and then, bowing, says the prayer, *Almighty God, cleanse my heart.*

97.   The homily is given at the chair or at the lectern.

98.   The profession of faith is said by the priest together with the people (see no. 44). At the words, *by the power of the Holy Spirit,* etc., all bow; on the solemnities of the Annunciation and Christmas all kneel.

99.   Next, with the people taking their proper part, follow the general intercessions (prayer of the faithful), which the priest directs from his chair or at the lectern (see nos. 45–47).

LITURGY OF THE EUCHARIST

100.   After the general intercessions, the presentation song begins (see no. 50). The servers place the corporal, purificator, chalice, and missal on the altar.

101.   It is fitting for the faithful's participation to be expressed by their presenting both the bread and wine for the celebration of the eucharist and other gifts to meet the needs of the church and of the poor.

The faithful's offerings are received by the priest, assisted by the ministers, and put in a suitable place; the bread and wine for the eucharist are taken to the altar.

102.   At the altar the priest receives the paten with the bread from a minister. With both hands he holds it slightly raised above the altar and says the accompanying prayer. Then he places the paten with the bread on the corporal.

103.   Next, as a minister presents the cruets, the priest stands at the side of the altar and pours wine and a little water into the chalice, saying the accompanying prayer softly. He returns to the middle of the altar, takes the chalice, raises it a little with both hands, and says the appointed prayer. Then he places the chalice on the corporal and may cover it with a pall.

104.   The priest bows and inaudibly says the prayer, *Lord God, we ask you to receive.*

105.   If incense is used, he incenses the gifts and the altar. A minister incenses the priest and the congregation.

106.   After the prayer, *Lord God, we ask you to receive,* or after the incensation, the priest washes his hands at the side of the altar and inaudibly says the prescribed prayer as a minister pours the water.

107. The priest returns to the center and, facing the people and extending then joining his hands, pronounces the invitation: *Pray, brothers and sisters.* After the people's response, he says the prayer over the gifts with hands outstretched. At the end the people make the acclamation: *Amen.*

108. The priest then begins the eucharistic prayer. With hands outstretched, he says: *The Lord be with you.* As he says: *Lift up your hearts,* he raises his hands; with hands outstretched, he adds: *Let us give thanks to the Lord our God.* When the people have answered: *It is right to give him thanks and praise,* the priest continues the preface. At its conclusion, he joins his hands and sings or says aloud with the ministers and people the Sanctus-Benedictus (see no. 55 b).

109. The priest continues the eucharistic prayer according to the rubrics that are given for each of them. If the priest celebrant is a bishop, after the words *N. our Pope* or the equivalent, he adds: *and for me your unworthy servant.* The local Ordinary must be mentioned in this way: *N. our Bishop* (or *Vicar, Prelate, Prefect, Abbot).* Coadjutor and auxiliary bishops may be mentioned in the eucharistic prayer. When several are named, this is done with the collective formula, *N. our Bishop and his assistant bishops.*[81] All these phrases should be modified grammatically to fit with each one of the eucharistic prayers.

A little before the consecration, the server may ring a bell as a signal to the faithful. Depending on local custom, he also rings the bell at the showing of both the host and the chalice.

110. After the doxology at the end of the eucharistic prayer, the priest, with hands joined, says the introduction to the Lord's Prayer. With hands outstretched he then sings or says this prayer with the people.

111. After the Lord's Prayer, the priest alone, with hands outstretched, says the embolism, *Deliver us.* At the end the congregation makes the acclamation, *For the kingdom.*

112. Then the priest says aloud the prayer, *Lord Jesus Christ.* After this prayer, extending then joining his hands, he gives the greeting of peace: *The peace of the Lord be with you always.* The people answer: *And also with you.* Then the priest may add: *Let us offer each other the sign of peace.* All exchange some sign of peace and love, according to the local custom. The priest may give the sign of peace to the ministers.

113. The priest then takes the eucharistic bread and breaks it over the paten. He places a small piece in the chalice, saying inaudibly: *May this mingling.* Meanwhile the Agnus Dei is sung or recited by the choir and congregation (see no. 56 e).

114. Then the priest inaudibly says the prayer, *Lord Jesus Christ, Son of the living God,* or *Lord Jesus Christ, with faith in your love and mercy.*

115. After the prayer the priest genuflects, takes the eucharistic bread, and, holding it slightly above the paten while facing the people says: *This is the Lamb of God.* With the people he adds, once only: *Lord, I am not worthy to receive you.*

116. Next, facing the altar, the priest says inaudibly: *May the body of Christ bring me to everlasting life* and reverently consumes the body of Christ. Then he takes the chalice, saying: *May the blood of Christ bring me to everlasting life,* and reverently drinks the blood of Christ.

117. He then takes the paten or a ciborium and goes to the communicants. If communion is given only under the form of bread, he raises the eucharistic bread slightly and shows it to each one, saying: *The body of Christ.* The communicants reply: *Amen* and, holding the communion plate under their chin, receive the sacrament.

118. For communion under both kinds, the rite described in nos. 240–252 is followed.

119. The communion song is begun while the priest is receiving the sacrament (see no. 56 i).

120. After communion the priest returns to the altar and collects any remaining particles. Then, standing at the side of the altar or at a side table, he purifies the paten or ciborium over the chalice, then purifies the chalice, saying inaudibly: *Lord, may I receive these gifts,* etc., and dries it with a purificator. If this is done at the altar, the vessels are taken to a side table by a minister. It is also permitted, especially if there are several vessels to be purified, to leave them, properly covered and on a corporal, either at the altar or at a side table and to purify them after Mass when the people have left.

121. Afterward the priest may return to the chair. A period of silence may now be observed, or a hymn of praise or a psalm may be sung (see no. 56 j).

122. Then, standing at the altar or at the chair and facing the people, the priest says, with hands outstretched: *Let us pray.* There may be a brief period of silence, unless this has been already observed immediately after communion. He recites the prayer after communion, at the end of which the people make the response: *Amen.*

123. If there are any brief announcements, they may be made at this time.

124. Then the priest, with hands outstretched, greets the people: *The Lord be with you.* They answer: *And also with you.* The priest immediately adds: *May almighty God bless you* and, as he blesses with the sign of the cross, continues: *the Father, and the Son, and the Holy Spirit.* All answer: *Amen.* On certain days and occasions another, more solemn form of blessing or the prayer over the people precedes this form of blessing as the rubrics direct.

Immediately after the blessing, with hands joined, the priest adds: *Go in the peace of Christ,* or: *Go in peace to love and serve the Lord,* or: *The Mass is ended, go in peace,* and the people answer: *Thanks be to God.*

125. As a rule, the priest then kisses the altar, makes the proper reverence with the ministers, and leaves.

126. If another liturgical service follows the Mass, the concluding rites (greeting, blessing, and dismissal) are omitted.

B. Functions of the Deacon

127. When there is a deacon present to exercise his ministry, the norms in the preceding section apply, with the following exceptions.

In general the deacon: a. assists the priest and walks at his side; b. at the altar, assists with the chalice or the book; c. if there is no other minister present, carries out other ministerial functions as required. [See GI app, no. 127.]

INTRODUCTORY RITES

128. Vested and carrying the Book of the Gospels, the deacon precedes the priest on the way to the altar or else walks at the priest's side.

129. With the priest he makes the proper reverence and goes up to the altar. After placing the Book of the Gospels on it, along with the priest he kisses the altar. If incense is used, he assists the priest in putting some in the censer and in incensing the altar.

130. After the incensing, he goes to the chair with the priest, sits next to him, and assists him as required.

LITURGY OF THE WORD

131. If incense is used, the deacon assists the priest when he puts incense in the censer during the singing of the Alleluia or other chant. Then he bows before the priest and asks for the blessing, saying in a low voice: *Father, give me your blessing.* The priest blesses him: *The Lord be in your heart.* The deacon answers: *Amen.* If the Book of the Gospels is on the altar, he takes it and goes to the lectern; the servers, if there are any, precede, carrying candles and the censer when used. At the lectern the deacon greets the people, incenses the book, and proclaims the gospel. After the reading, he kisses the book, saying inaudibly: *May the words of the gospel wipe away our sins,* and returns to the priest. If there is no homily or profession of faith, he may remain at the lectern for the general intercessions, but the servers leave.

132. After the priest introduces the general intercessions, the deacon announces the intentions at the lectern or other suitable place.

LITURGY OF THE EUCHARIST

133. At the presentation of the gifts, while the priest remains at the chair, the deacon prepares the altar, assisted by other ministers, but the care of the sacred vessels belongs to the deacon. He assists the priest in receiving the people's gifts. Next, he hands the priest the paten with the bread to be consecrated, pours wine and a little water into the chalice, saying inaudibly the prayer, *Through the mystery of this water and wine,* then passes the chalice to the priest (He may also prepare the chalice and pour the wine and water at a side table.) If incense is used, the deacon assists the priest with the incensing of the gifts and the altar; afterward he, or another minister, incenses the priest and the people.

134. During the eucharistic prayer, the deacon stands near but slightly behind the priest, so that when necesary he may assist the priest with the chalice or the missal.

135. At the final doxology of the eucharistic prayer, the deacon stands next to the priest, holding up the chalice as the priest raises the paten with the eucharistic bread, until the people have said the acclamation: *Amen.*

136. After the priest has said the prayer for peace and the greeting: *The peace of the Lord be with you always,* and the people have made the response: *And also with you,* the deacon may invite all to exchange the sign of peace, saying: *Let us offer each other the sign of peace.* He himself receives the sign of peace from the priest and may offer it to other ministers near him.

137. After the priest's communion, the deacon receives under both kinds and then assists the priest in giving communion to the people. But if communion is given under both kinds, the deacon ministers the chalice to the communicants and is the last to drink from it.

138. After communion, the deacon returns to the altar with the priest and collects any remaining fragments. He then takes the chalice and other vessels to the side table, where he purifies them and arranges them in the usual way; the priest returns to the chair. But it is permissible to leave the vessels to be purified, properly covered and on a corporal, at a side table and to purify them after Mass, when the people have left.

CONCLUDING RITES

139. Following the prayer after communion, if there are any brief announcements, the deacon may make them, unless the priest prefers to do so himself.

140. After the priest's blessing, the deacon dismisses the people, saying: *Go in the peace of Christ*, or: *Go in peace to love and serve the Lord*, or: *The Mass is ended, go in peace.*

141. Along with the priest, the deacon kisses the altar, makes the proper reverence, and leaves in the manner followed for the entrance procession.

C. Functions of the Acolyte

142. The acolyte may have functions of various kinds and several may occur at the same time. It is therefore desirable that these functions be suitably distributed among several acolytes. But if there is only a single acolyte present, he should perform the more important functions and the rest are distributed among other ministers.

INTRODUCTORY RITES

143. In the procession to the altar the acolyte may carry the cross, walking between two servers with lighted candles. When he reaches the altar, he places the cross near it and takes his own place in the santuary.

144. Throughout the celebration it belongs to the acolyte to go to the priest or the deacon, whenever necessary, in order to present the book to them and to assist them in any other way required. Thus it is appropriate that, if possible, he have a place from which he can conveniently carry out his ministry both at the chair and at the altar.

LITURGY OF THE EUCHARIST

145. After the general intercessions, when no deacon is present, the acolyte places the corporal, purificator, chalice and missal on the altar, while the priest remains at the chair. Then, if necessary, the acolyte assists the priest in receiving the gifts of the people and he may bring the bread and wine to the altar and present them to the priest. If incense, is used, the acolyte gives the censer to the priest and assists him in incensing the gifts and altar.

146. The acolyte may assist the priest as a special minister in giving communion to the people.[82] If communion is given under both kinds, the acolyte ministers the chalice to the communicants or he holds the chalice when communion is given by intinction.

147. After communion, the acolyte helps the priest or deacon to purify and arrange the vessels. If no deacon is present, the acolyte takes the vessels to the side table, where he purifies and arranges them.

D. Functions of the Reader

INTRODUCTORY RITES

148. In the procession to the altar, when no deacon is present, the reader may carry the Book of the Gospels. In that case he walks in front of the priest; otherwise he walks with the other ministers.

149. Upon reaching the altar, the reader makes the proper reverence along with the priest, goes up to the altar, and places the Book of the Gospels on it. Then he takes his place in the sanctuary with the other ministers.

LITURGY OF THE WORD

150. At the lectern the reader proclaims the readings that precede the gospel. If there is no cantor of the psalm, he may also sing or recite the responsorial psalm after the first reading.

151. After the priest gives the introduction to the general intercessions, the reader may announce the intentions when no deacon is present.

152. If there is no entrance song or communion song and the antiphons in the Missal are not said by the faithful, the reader recites them at the proper time.

II. CONCELEBRATED MASSES

153. Concelebration effectively brings out the unity of the priesthood, of the sacrifice, and of the whole people of God. The rite itself prescribes concelebration at the ordination of bishops and of priests and at the chrism Mass.

Unless the good of the faithful requires or suggests otherwise, concelebration is also recommended at:

    a. the evening Mass on Holy Thursday;

    b. the Mass for councils, meetings of bishops and synods;

    c. the Mass for the blessing of an abbot;

    d. the conventual Mass and the principal Mass in churches and oratories;

    e. the Mass for any kind of meeting of priests, either secular or religious.[83] (See GIapp, no. 153.]

154. Where there is a large number of priests, the authorized superior may permit concelebration several times on the same day, but either at different times or in different places.[84]

155. The right to regulate, in accord with the law, the discipline for concelebration in his diocese, even in churches and oratories of exempt religious, belongs to the bishop.

156. No one is ever to be admitted into a concelebration once Mass has already begun.[85]

157. A concelebration in which the priests of any diocese concelebrate with their own bishop, especially at the chrism Mass on Holy Thursday and on the occasion of a synod or pastoral visitation, is to be held in high regard. Concelebration is likewise recommended whenever priests gather together with their bishop during a retreat or at any other meeting. That sign of the unity of the priesthood and of the Church itself which marks every concelebration stands out even more clearly in the instances mentioned.[86]

158. For a particular reason, having to do either with the meaning of the rite or of the liturgical feast, to celebrate or concelebrate more than once on the same day is permitted as follows:

    a. One who has celebrated or concelebrated the chrism Mass on Holy Thursday may also celebrate or concelebrate the evening Mass.

b. One who has celebrated or concelebrated the Mass of the Easter Vigil may celebrate or concelebrate the second Mass of Easter.

c. All priests may celebrate or concelebrate the three Masses of Christmas provided the Masses are at their proper times of day.

d. One who concelebrates with the bishop or his delegate at a synod or pastoral visitation, or concelebrates on the occasion of a meeting of priests, may celebrate another Mass for the benefit of the people.[87] This holds also, in analogous circumstances, for gatherings of religious.

159. The structure of a concelebrated Mass, whatever its form, follows the norms for an individual celebration, except for the points prescribed or changed in the next section.

160. If neither a deacon nor other ministers assist in a concelebrated Mass, their functions are carried out by the concelebrants.

INTRODUCTORY RITES

161. In the sacristy or other suitable place, the concelebrants put on the vestments usual for individual celebrants. For a good reason, however, as when there are more concelebrants than vestments, the concelebrants may omit the chasuble and simply wear the stole over the alb; but the principal celebrant always wears the chasuble.

162. When everything is ready, there is the usual procession through the church to the altar. The concelebrating priests go ahead of the principal celebrant.

163. On reaching the altar, the concelebrants and the celebrant make the prescribed reverence, kiss the altar, then go to their chairs. When incense is used, the principal celebrant incenses the altar, then goes to the chair.

LITURGY OF THE WORD

164. During the liturgy of the word, the concelebrants remain at their places, sitting or standing as the principal celebrant does.

165. As a rule the principal celebrant or one of the concelebrants gives the homily.

LITURGY OF THE EUCHARIST

166. The rites for the preparation of the gifts are carried out by the principal celebrant; the other concelebrants remain at their places.

167. At the end of the preparation of the gifts, the concelebrants come near the altar and stand around it in such a way that they do not interfere with the actions of the rite and that the people have a clear view. They should not be in the deacon's way when he has to go to the altar in the performance of his ministry.

Manner of Reciting the Eucharistic Prayer

168. The preface is said by the principal celebrant alone; the Sanctus is sung or recited by all the concelebrants with the congregation and the choir.

169. After the Sanctus, the concelebrants continue the eucharistic prayer in the way to be described. Unless otherwise indicated, only the principal celebrant makes the gestures.

170. The parts said by all the concelebrants together are to be recited in such a way that the concelebrants say them in a softer voice and the principal celebrant's voice stands out clearly. In this way the congregation should be able to hear the text without difficulty.

A. Eucharistic Prayer I, the Roman Canon

171. The prayer, *We come to you, Father,* is said by the principal celebrant alone, with hands outstretched.

172. The intercessions, *Remember, Lord, your people* and *In union with the whole Church,* may be assigned to one of the concelebrants; he alone says these prayers, with hands outstretched and aloud.

173. The prayer, *Father, accept this offering,* is said by the principal celebrant alone, with hands outstretched.

174. From *Bless and approve our offering* to *Almighty God, we pray* inclusive, all the concelebrants recite everything together in this manner:

a.   They say *Bless and approve our offering* with hands outstretched toward the offerings.

b.   They say *The day before he suffered* and *When supper was ended* with hands joined.

c.   While saying the words of the Lord, each extends his right hand toward the bread and toward the chalice, if this seems appropriate; they look at the eucharistic bread and chalice as these are shown and afterward bow low.

d.   They say *Father, we celebrate the memory of Christ* and *Look with favor* with hands outstretched.

e.   *From Almighty God, we pray* to *the sacred body and blood of your Son* inclusive, they bow with hands joined; then they stand upright and cross themselves at the words, *let us be filled.*

175. The intercessions, *Remember, Lord, those who have died* and *For ourselves, too,* may be assigned to one of the concelebrants; he alone says these prayers, with hands outstretched and aloud.

176. At the words, *Though we are sinners,* all the concelebrants strike their breast.

177. The prayer, *Through Christ our Lord you give us all these gifts,* is said by the principal celebrant alone.

178. In this eucharistic prayer the parts from *Bless and approve our offering* to *Almighty God, we pray* inclusive and the concluding doxology may be sung.

B. Eucharistic Prayer II

179. The prayer, *Lord, you are holy indeed,* is said by the principal celebrant alone, with hands outstretched.

180. From *Let your Spirit come* to *May all of us who share* inclusive, all the concelebrants together say the prayer in this manner:

a.   They say *Let your Spirit come* with hands outstretched toward the offerings.

b.   They say *Before he was given up to death* and *When supper was ended* with hands joined.

c.   While saying the words of the Lord, each extends his right hand toward the bread and toward the chalice, if this seems appropriate; they look at the eucharistic bread and the chalice as they are shown and afterward bow low.

d.   They say *In memory of his death* and *May all of us who share* with hands outstretched.

181. The intercessions for the living, *Lord, remember your Church,* and for the dead, *Remember our brothers and sisters,* may be assigned to one of the concelebrants; he alone says the intercessions, with hands outstretched.

182. In this eucharistic prayer the parts from *Before he was given up to death* to *In memory of his death* inclusive and the concluding doxology may be sung.

C. Eucharistic Prayer III

183. The prayer, *Father, you are holy indeed,* is said by the principal celebrant alone, with hands outstretched.

184. From *And so, Father, we bring you these gifts* to *Look with favor* inclusive, all the concelebrants together say the prayer in this manner:

a. They say *And so, Father, we bring you these gifts* with hands outstretched toward the offerings.

b. They say *On the night he was betrayed* and *When supper was ended* with hands joined.

c. While saying the words of the Lord, each extends his right hand toward the bread and toward the chalice, if this seems appropriate; they look at the eucharistic bread and chalice as these are shown and afterward bow low.

d. They say *Father, calling to mind* and *Look with favor* with hands outstretched.

185. The intercessions, *May he make us an everlasting gift* and *Lord, may this sacrifice,* may be assigned to one of the concelebrants; he alone says these prayers, with hands outstretched.

186. In this eucharistic prayer the parts from *On the night he was betrayed* to *Father calling to mind* inclusive and the concluding doxology may be sung.

D. Eucharistic Prayer IV

187. The prayer, *Father, we acknowledge,* is said by the principal celebrant alone, with hands outstretched.

188. From *Father, may this Holy Spirit* to *Lord, look upon this sacrifice* inclusive, all the concelebrants together say the prayer in this manner:

a. They say *Father, may this Holy Spirit* with hands outstretched toward the offerings.

b. They say *He always loved those* and *In the same way* with hands joined.

c. While saying the words of the Lord, each extends his right hand toward the bread and toward the chalice, if this seems appropriate; they look at the eucharistic bread and chalice as these are shown and afterward bow low.

d. They say *Father, we now celebrate* and *Lord, look upon this sacrifice* with hands outstretched.

189. The intercessions, *Lord, remember those,* may be assigned to one of the concelebrants; he alone says them, with hands outstretched.

190. In this eucharistic prayer the parts from *He always loved those* to *Father, we now celebrate* inclusive and the concluding doxology may be sung.

191. The concluding doxology of the eucharistic prayer may be sung or said either by the principal celebrant alone or together with all the concelebrants.

COMMUNION RITE

192. Next, with hands joined, the celebrant introduces the Lord's Prayer; with hands outstretched, he then says this prayer itself with the other concelebrants and the congregation.

193. The embolism, *Deliver us,* is said by the principal celebrant alone, with hands outstretched. All the concelebrants together with the congregation say the final acclamation, *For the kingdom.*

194. After the deacon (or one of the concelebrants) says: *Let us offer each other the sign of peace,* all exchange the sign of peace. The concelebrants who are nearer the principal celebrant receive the sign of peace from him ahead of the deacon.

195. During the Agnus Dei, some of the concelebrants may help the principal celebrant break the eucharistic bread for communion, both for the concelebrants and for the congregation.

196. After the commingling, the principal celebrant alone says inaudibly the prayer, *Lord Jesus Christ, Son of the living God,* or *Lord Jesus Christ, with faith in your love and mercy.*

197. After this prayer, the principal celebrant genuflects and steps back a little. One by one the concelebrants come to the middle of the altar, genuflect, and reverently take the body of Christ from the altar. Then holding the eucharistic bread in the right hand, with the left hand under it, they return to their places. The concelebrants, may, however, remain in their places and take the body of Christ from the paten presented to them by the principal celebrant or by one or more of the concelebrants, or from the paten as it is passed from one to the other.

198. Then the principal celebrant takes the eucharistic bread, holds it slightly raised above the paten, and, facing the congregation, says: *This is the Lamb of God.* With the concelebrants and the congregation he continues: *Lord, I am not worthy.*

199. Then the principal celebrant, facing the altar, says inaudibly: *May the body of Christ bring me to everlasting life* and reverently consumes the body of Christ. The concelebrants do the same. After them the deacon receives the body of Christ from the principal celebrant.

200. The blood of the Lord may be taken by drinking from the chalice directly, through a tube, with a spoon, or even by intinction.

201. If communion is received directly from the chalice, either of two procedures may be followed.

a. The principal celebrant takes the chalice and says inaudibly: *May the blood of Christ bring me to everlasting life.* He drinks a little and hands the chalice to the deacon or a concelebrant. Then he gives communion to the faithful or returns to the chair. The concelebrants approach the altar one by one or, if two chalices are used, two by two. They drink the blood of Christ and return to their seats. The deacon or a concelebrant wipes the chalice with a purificator after each concelebrant communicates.

b. The principal celebrant stands at the middle of the altar and drinks the blood of Christ in the usual manner.

But the concelebrants may receive the blood of the Lord while remaining in their places. They drink from the chalice presented by the deacon or by one of their number, or else passed from one to the other. Either the one who drinks from the chalice or the one who presents it always wipes it off. After communicating, each one returns to his seat.

202. If communion is received through a tube, this is the procedure. The principal celebrant takes the tube and says inaudibly: *May the blood of Christ bring me to everlasting life.* He drinks a little and immediately cleans the tube by sipping some water from a container at hand on the altar, then places the tube on the paten. The deacon or one of the concelebrants puts the chalice at a convenient place in the middle of the altar or at the right side on another corporal. A container of water for purifying the tubes is placed near the chalice, with a paten to hold them afterward.

The concelebrants come forward one by one, take a tube, and drink a little from the chalice. They then purify the tube, by sipping a little water, and place it on the paten.

203. If communion is received by using a spoon, the same procedure is followed as for communion with a tube. But care is to be taken that after each communion the spoon is placed in a container of water. After communion has been completed, the acolyte carries this container to a side table to wash and dry the spoons.

204. The deacon receives communion last. He then drinks what remains in the chalice and takes it to the side table. There he or the acolyte washes and dries the chalice and arranges it in the usual way.

205. The concelebrants may also receive from the chalice at the altar immediately after receiving the body of the Lord.

In this case the principal celebrant receives under both kinds as he would when celebrating Mass alone, but for the communion from the chalice he follows the rite that in each instance has been decided on for the concelebrants.

After the principal celebrant's communion, the chalice is placed on another corporal at the right side of the altar. The concelebrants come forward one by one, genuflect, and receive the body of the Lord; then they go to the side of the altar and drink the blood of the Lord, following the rite decided upon, as has just been said.

The communion of the deacon and the purification of the chalice take place as already described.

206. If the concelebrants receive communion by intinction, the principal celebrant receives the body and blood of the Lord in the usual way, making sure that enough remains in the chalice for their communion. Then the deacon or one of the concelebrants arranges the paten with the eucharistic bread and the chalice conveniently in the center of the altar or at the right side on another corporal. The concelebrants approach the altar one by one, genuflect, and take a particle, dip part of it into the chalice, and, holding a paten under their chins, communicate. Afterward they return to their places as at the beginning of Mass.

The deacon receives communion also by intinction and to the concelebrant's words: *The body and blood of Christ*, makes the response: *Amen.* At the altar the deacon drinks all that remains in the chalice, takes it to the side table and there he or the acolyte purifies and dries it, then arranges it in the usual way.

CONCLUDING RITES

207. The principal celebrant does everything else until the end of Mass in the usual way; the other concelebrants remain at their seats.

208. Before leaving, the concelebrants make the proper reverence to the altar; as a rule, the principal celebrant kisses the altar.

III. MASS WITHOUT A CONGREGATION

INTRODUCTION

209. This section gives the norms for Mass celebrated by a priest with only one server to assist him and to make the responses.

210. In general this form of Mass follows the rite of Mass with a congregation. The server takes the people's part to the extent possible.

211. Mass should not be celebrated without a server or the participation of at least one of the of the faithful, except for some legitimate and reasonable cause. In this case the greetings and the blessing at the end of Mass are omitted.

212. The chalice is prepared before Mass, either on a side table near the altar or on the altar itself; the missal is placed on the left side of the altar.

INTRODUCTORY RITES

213. After he reverences the altar, the priest crosses himself, saying: *In the name of the Father,* etc. He turns to the server and gives one of the forms of greeting. For the penitential rite the priest stands at the foot of the altar.

214. The priest then goes up to the altar and kisses it, goes to the missal at the left side of the altar, and remains there until the end of the general intercessions.

215. He reads the entrance antiphon and says the Kyrie and the Gloria, in keeping with the rubrics.

216. Then, with hands joined, the priest says: *Let us pray.* After a suitable pause, he says the opening prayer, with hands outstretched. At the end the server responds: *Amen.*

LITURGY OF THE WORD

217. After the opening prayer, the server or the priest himself reads the first reading and psalm, the second reading, when it is to be said, and the Alleluia verse or other chant.

218. The priest, remains in the same place, bows and says: *Almighty God, cleanse my heart.* He then reads the gospel and at the conclusion kisses the book, saying inaudibly: *May the words of the gospel wipe away our sins.* The server says the acclamation.

219. The priest then says the profession of faith with the server, if the rubrics call for it.

220. The general intercessions may be said even in this form of Mass; the priest gives the intentions and the server makes the response.

221. The antiphon for the preparation of the gifts is omitted. The minister places the corporal, purificator, and chalice on the altar, unless they have already been put there at the beginning of Mass.

222. Preparation of the bread and wine, including the pouring of the water, are carried out as at a Mass with a congregation, with the formularies given in the Order of Mass. After placing the bread and wine on the altar, the priest washes his hands at the side of the altar as the server pours the water.

223. The priest says the prayer over the gifts and the eucharistic prayer, following the rite described for Mass with a congregation.

224. The Lord's Prayer and the embolism, *Deliver us*, are said as at Mass with a congregation.

225. After the acclamation concluding the embolism, the priest says the prayer, *Lord Jesus Christ, you said.* He then adds: *The peace of the Lord be with you always,* and the server answers: *And also with you.* The priest may give the sign of peace to the server.

226. Then, while he says the Agnus Dei with the server, the priest breaks the eucharistic bread over the paten. After the Agnus Dei, he places a particle in the chalice, saying inaudibly: *May this mingling.*

227. After the commingling, the priest inaudibly says the prayer, *Lord Jesus Christ, Son of the living God,* or *Lord Jesus Christ, with faith in your love and mercy.* Then he genuflects and takes the eucharistic bread. If the server is to receive communion, the priest turns to him and, holding the eucharistic bread a little above the paten, says: *This the Lamb of God,* adding once with the server: *Lord I am not worthy.* Facing the altar, the priest then receives the body of Christ. If the server is not receiving communion, the priest, after making a genuflection, takes the host and, facing the altar, says once inaudibly: *Lord, I am not worthy,* and eats the body of Christ. The blood of Christ is received in the way described in the Order of Mass with a congregation.

228. Before giving communion to the server, the priest says the communion antiphon.

229. The chalice is washed at the side of the altar and then may be carried by the server to a side table or left on the altar, as at the beginning.

230. After the purification of the chalice, the priest may observe a period of silence. Then he says the prayer after communion.

CONCLUDING RITES

231. The concluding rites are carried out as at Mass with a congregation, but the dismissal formulary is omitted.

IV. SOME GENERAL RULES FOR ALL FORMS OF MASS

VENERATION OF THE ALTAR AND THE BOOK OF THE GOSPELS

232. According to traditional liturgical practice, the altar and the Book of the Gospels are kissed as a sign of veneration. But if this sign of reverence is not in harmony with the traditions or the culture of the region, the conference of bishops may substitute some other sign, after informing the Apostolic See.

GENUFLECTIONS AND BOWS

233. Three genuflections are made during Mass: after the showing of the eucharistic bread, after the showing of the chalice, and before communion.

If there is a tabernacle with the blessed sacrament in the sanctuary, a genuflection is made before and after Mass and whenever anyone passes in front of the blessed sacrament.

234. There are two kinds of bow, a bow of the head and bow of the body:

a. A bow of the head is made when the three divine Persons are named together and at the name of Jesus, Mary, and the saint in whose honor Mass is celebrated.

b. A bow of the body, or profound bow, is made: toward the altar if there is no tabernacle with the blessed sacrament; during the prayers, *Almightly God, cleanse* and *Lord God, we ask you to receive;* within the profession of faith at the words, *by the power of the Holy Spirit;* in Eucharistic Prayer I (Roman Canon) at the words, *Almighty God, we pray.* The same kind of bow is made by the deacon when he asks the blessing before the gospel. In addition, the priest bends over slightly as he says the words of the Lord at the consecration.

INCENSATION

235. The use of incense is optional in any form of Mass:

a. during the entrance procession;

b. at the beginning of Mass, to incense the altar;

c. at the procession and proclamation of the gospel;

d. at the preparation of the gifts, to incense them, as well as the altar, priest, and people;

e. at the showing of the eucharistic bread and chalice after the consecration.

236. The priest puts the incense in the censer and blesses it with the sign of the cross, saying nothing.

This is the way to incense the altar:

a. If the altar is freestanding, the priest incenses it as he walks around it.

b. If the altar is not freestanding, he incenses it while walking first to the right side, then to the left.

If there is a cross on or beside the altar, he incenses it before he incenses the altar. If the cross is behind the altar, the priest incenses it when he passes in front of it.

PURIFICATIONS

237. Whenever a particle of the eucharistic bread adheres to his fingers, especially after the breaking of the bread or the communion of the people, the priest cleanses his fingers over the paten or, if necessary, washes them. He also gathers any particles that may fall outside the paten.

238. The vessels are purified by the priest or else by the deacon or acolyte after the communion or after Mass, if possible at a side table. Wine and water alone are used for the purification of the chalice, then drunk by the one who purifies it. The paten is usually to be wiped with the purificator.

239. If the eucharistic bread or any particle of it should fall, it is to be picked up reverently. If any of the precious blood spills, the area should be washed and the water poured into the sacrarium.

COMMUNION UNDER BOTH KINDS

240. Holy communion has a more complete form as a sign when it is received under both kinds. For in this manner of reception a fuller light shines on the sign of the eucharistic banquet. Moreover there is a clearer expression of that will by which the new and everlasting covenant is ratified in the blood of the Lord and of the relationship of the eucharistic banquet to the eschatological banquet in the Father's kingdom.[88] [See GI app, no. 240.]

241. For the faithful who take part in the rite or are present at it, pastors should take care to call to mind as clearly as possible Catholic teaching according to the Council of Trent on the manner of communion. Above all

they should instruct the people that according to Catholic faith Christ, whole and entire, as well as the true sacrament are received even under one kind only; that, therefore, as far as the effects are concerned, those who receive in this manner are not deprived of any grace necessary for salvation.[89]

Pastors are also to teach that the Church has power in its stewardship of the sacraments, provided their substance remains intact. The Church may make those rules and changes that, in view of the different conditions, times, and places, it decides to be in the interest of reverence of the sacraments or the well-being of the recipients.[90] At the same time the faithful should be guided toward a desire to take part more intensely in a sacred rite in which the sign of the eucharistic meal stands out more explicitly.

242. At the discretion of the Ordinary and after the prerequisite catechesis, communion from the chalice is permitted in the case of:[91]

1. newly baptized adults at the Mass following their baptism; adults at the Mass at which they receive confirmation; baptized persons who are being received into the full communion of the Church;

2. the bride and bridegroom at their wedding Mass;

3. deacons at the Mass of their ordination;

4. an abbess at the Mass in which she is blessed; those consecrated to a life of virginity at the Mass of their consecration; professed religious, their relatives, friends, and the other members of their community at the Mass of first or perpetual vows or renewal of vows;

5. those who receive institution for a certain ministry at the Mass of their institution; lay missionary helpers at the Mass in which they publicly receive their mission; others at the Mass in which they receive an ecclesiastical mission;

6. the sick person and all present at the time viaticum is to be administered when Mass is celebrated in the sick person's home;

7. the deacon and ministers who exercise their office at Mass;

8. when there is a concelebration, in the case of:

a. all who exercise a liturgical function at this concelebration and also all seminarians present;

b. in their churches or oratories, all members of institutes professing the evangelical counsels and other societies whose members dedicate themselves to God by religious vows or by an offering or promise; also all those who reside in the houses of members of such institutes and societies;

9. priests who are present at major celebrations and are not able to celebrate or concelebrate;

10. all who make a retreat at a Mass in which they actively participate and which is specially celebrated for the group; also all who take part in the meeting of any pastoral body at a Mass they celebrate as a group;

11. those listed in nos. 2 and 4, at Masses celebrating their jubilees;

12. godparents, relatives, wife or husband, and lay catechists of newly baptized adults at the Mass of their initiation;

13. relatives, friends and special benefactors who take part in the Mass of a newly ordained priest;

14. members of communities at the conventual or community Mass, in accord with the provisions of this Instruction, no. 76.

Further, the conferences of bishops have the power to decide to what extent and under what considerations and conditions Ordinaries may allow communion under both kinds in other instances that are of special significance in the spiritual life of any community or group of the faithful.

Within such limits, Ordinaries may designate the particular instances, but on condition that they grant permission not indiscriminately but for clearly defined celebrations and that they point out matters for caution. They are also to exclude occasions when there will be a larger number of communicants. The groups receiving this permission must also be specific, well-ordered, and homogeneous. [See GI app, no. 242.]

243. Preparation for giving communion under both kinds:

a. If communion is received from the chalice with a tube, silver tubes are needed for the celebrant and each communicant. There should also be a container of water for purifying the tubes and a paten on which to put them afterward.

b. If communion is given with a spoon, only one spoon is necessary.

c. If communion is given by intinction, care is to be taken that the eucharistic bread is not too thin or too small, but a little thicker than usual so that after being partly dipped into the precious blood it can still easily be given to the communicant.

1. Rite of Communion under Both Kinds Directly from the Chalice

244. If there is a deacon or another assisting priest or an acolyte:

a.   The celebrant receives the Lord's body and blood as usual, making sure enough remains in the chalice for the other communicants. He wipes the outside of the chalice with a purificator.

b.   The priest gives the chalice with purificator to the minister and himself takes the paten or ciborium with the hosts; then both station themselves conveniently for the communion of the people.

c.   The communicants approach, make the proper reverence, and stand in front of the priest. Showing the host he says: *The body of Christ.* The communicant answers: *Amen* and receives the body of Christ from the priest.

d.   The communicant then moves to the minister of the chalice and stands before him. The minister says: *The blood of Christ,* the communicant answers: *Amen,* and the minister holds out the chalice with purificator. For the sake of convenience, communicants may raise the chalice to their mouths themselves. Holding the purificator under the mouth with one hand, they drink a little from the chalice, taking care not to spill it, and then return to their places. The minister wipes the outside of the chalice with the purificator.

e.   The minister places the chalice on the altar after all who are receiving under both kinds have drunk from it. If there are others who are not receiving communion under both kinds, the priest gives these communion, then returns to the altar. The priest or minister drinks whatever remains in the chalice and carries out the usual purifications.

245.   If there is no deacon, other priest or acolyte:

a.   The priest receives the Lord's body and blood as usual, making sure enough remains in the chalice for the other communicants. He wipes the outside of the chalice with the purificator.

b.   The priest then stations himself conveniently for communion and distributes the body of Christ in the usual way to all who are receiving under both kinds. The communicants approach, make the proper reverence, and stand in front of the priest. After receiving the body of Christ, they step back a little.

c.   After all have received, the celebrant places the ciborium on the altar and takes the chalice with the purificator. All those receiving from the chalice come forward again and stand in front of the priest. He says: *The blood of Christ,* the communicant answers: *Amen,* and the priest presents the chalice with purificator. The communicants hold the purificator under their mouths with one hand, taking care that none of the precious blood is spilled, drink a little from the chalice, and then return to their places. The priest wipes the outside of the chalice with the purificator.

d.   After the communion from the chalice, the priest places it on the altar and if there are others receiving under one kind only, he gives them communion in the usual way, then returns to the altar. He drinks whatever remains in the chalice and carries out the usual purifications.

2. Rite of Communion under Both Kinds by Intinction

246. If there is a deacon, another priest assisting, or an acolyte present:

a.   The priest hands this minister the chalice with purificator and he himself takes the paten or ciborium with the hosts. The priest and the minister of the chalice station themselves conveniently for distributing communion.

b.   The communicants approach, make the proper reverence, stand in front of the priest, and hold the communion plate below their chins. The celebrant dips a particle into the chalice and, showing it, says: *The body and blood of Christ.* The communicants respond: *Amen,* receive communion from the priest, and return to their places.

c.   The communion of those who do not receive under both kinds and the rest of the rite take place as already described.

247. If there is no deacon, assisting priest, or acolyte present:

a.   After drinking the blood of the Lord, the priest takes the ciborium or paten with the hosts, between the index and middle fingers of one hand and holds the chalice between the thumb and index finger of the same hand. Then he stations himself conveniently for communion.

b.   The communicants approach, make the proper reverence, stand in front of the priest, and hold a plate beneath their chins. The priest takes a particle, dips it into the chalice, and, showing it, says: *The body and blood of Christ.* The communicants respond: *Amen,* receive communion from the priest, and return to their places.

c.   It is also permitted to place a small table covered with a cloth and corporal at a suitable place. The priest places the chalice or ciborium on the table in order to make the distribution of communion easier.

d.   The communion of those who do not receive under both kinds, the consumption of the blood remaining in the chalice, and the purifications take place as already described.

3. Rite of Communion under Both Kinds Using a Tube

248. In this case the priest celebrant also uses a tube when receiving the blood of the Lord.

249. If there is a deacon, another assisting priest, or an acolyte present:

a. For the communion of the body of the Lord, everything is done as described in nos. 224 b and c.

b. The communicant goes to the minister of the chalice and stands in front of him. The minister says: *The blood of Christ* and the communicant responds: *Amen.* The communicant receives the tube from the minister, places it in the chalice, and drinks a little. The communicant then removes the tube, careful not to spill any drops, and places it in a container of water held by the minister. The communicant sips a little water to purify the tube, then puts it into another container presented by the minister.

250. If there is no deacon, other assisting priest, or acolyte present, the priest celebrant offers the chalice to each communicant in a way described already for communion from the chalice (no. 245). The minister standing next to him holds the container of water for purifying the tube.

4. Rite of Communion under Both Kinds Using a Spoon

251. If a deacon, another assisting priest, or an acolyte is present, he holds the chalice and, saying: *The blood of Christ*, ministers the blood of the Lord with a spoon to the individual communicants, who hold the plate beneath their chins. He is to take care that the spoon does not touch the lips or tongues of the communicants.

252. If there is no deacon, other assisting priest, or acolyte present, the priest celebrant himself gives them the Lord's blood, after all receiving communion under both kinds have received the Lord's body.

CHAPTER V
ARRANGEMENT AND FURNISHING OF CHURCHES FOR THE EUCHARISTIC CELEBRATION

I. GENERAL PRINCIPLES

253. For the celebration of the eucharist, the people of God normally assemble in a church or, if there is none, in some other fitting place worthy of so great a mystery. Churches and other places of worship should therefore be suited to celebrating the liturgy and to ensuring the active participation of the faithful. Further, the places and requisities for worship should be truly worthy and beautiful, signs and symbols of heavenly realities.[92]

254. At all times, therefore, the Church seeks out the service of the arts and welcomes the artistic expressions of all peoples and regions.[93] The Church is intent on keeping the works of art and the treasures handed

down from the past[94] and, when necessary, on adapting them to new needs. It strives as well to promote new works of art that appeal to the contemporary mentality.[95]

In commissioning artists and choosing works of art that are to become part of a church, the highest standard is therefore to be set, in order that art may aid faith and devotion and be true to the reality it is to symbolize and the purpose it is to serve.[96]

255. All churches are to be solemnly dedicated or at least blessed. But cathedral and parish churches are always to be dedicated. The faithful should give due honor to the cathedral of their diocese and to their own church as symbols of the spiritual Church that their Christian vocation commits them to build up and extend.

256. All who are involved in the construction, restoration, and remodeling of churches are to consult the diocesan commission on liturgy and art. The local Ordinary is to use the counsel and help of this commission whenever it comes to laying down norms on this matter, approving plans for new buildings, and making decisions on the more important issues.[97]

II. ARRANGEMENT OF A CHURCH FOR THE LITURGICAL ASSEMBLY

257. The people of God assembled at Mass possess an organic and hierarchical structure, expressed by the various ministries and actions for each part of the celebration. The general plan of the sacred edifice should be such that in some way it conveys the image of the gathered assembly. It should also allow the participants to take the place most appropriate to them and assist all to carry out their individual functions properly.

The congregation and the choir should have a place that facilitates their active participation.[98]

The priest and his ministers have their place in the sanctuary, that is, in the part of the church that brings out their distinctive role, namely, to preside over the prayers, to proclaim the word of God, or to minister at the altar.

Even though these elements must express a hierarchical arrangement and the diversity of offices, they should at the same time form a complete and organic unity, clearly expressive of the unity of the entire holy people. The character and beauty of the place and all its appointments should foster devotion and show the holiness of the mysteries celebrated there.

III. SANCTUARY

258. The sanctuary should be clearly marked off from the body of the church either by being somewhat elevated or by its distinctive design and appointments. It should be large enough to accommodate all the rites.[99]

IV. ALTAR

259. At the altar the sacrifice of the cross is made present under sacramental signs. It is also the table of the Lord and the people of God are called together to share in it. The altar is, as well, the center of the thanksgiving that the eucharist accomplishes.[100]

260. In a place of worship, the celebration of the eucharist must be on an altar, either fixed or movable. Outside a place of worship, especially if the celebration is only for a single occasion, a suitable table may be used, but always with a cloth and corporal.

261. A fixed altar is one attached to the floor so that it cannot be moved; a movable altar is one that can be transferred from place to place.

262. In every church there should ordinarily be a fixed, dedicated altar, which should be freestanding to allow the ministers to walk around it easily and Mass to be celebrated facing the people. It should be so placed as to be a focal point on which the attention of the whole congregation centers naturally.[101]

263. According to the Church's traditional practice and the altar's symbolism, the table of a fixed altar should be of stone and indeed of natural stone. But at the discretion of the conference of bishops some other solid, becoming, and well-crafted material may be used. [See GIapp, no. 263.]

    The pedestal or base of the table may be of any sort of material, as long as it is becoming and solid.

264. A movable altar may be constructed of any becoming, solid material suited to liturgical use, according to the traditions and customs of different regions.

265. Altars both fixed and movable are dedicated according to the rite described in the liturgical books, but movable altars may simply be blessed.

266. The practice of placing under the altar to be dedicated relics of saints, even of nonmartyrs, is to be maintained. Care must be taken to have solid evidence of the authenticity of such relics.

267. Other altars should be fewer in number. In new churches they should be placed in chapels separated in some way from the body of the church.[102]

V. ALTAR FURNISHINGS

268. At least one cloth should be placed on the altar out of reverence for the celebration of the memorial of the Lord and the banquet that gives us his body and blood. The shape, size, and decoration of the altar cloth should be in keeping with the design of the altar.

269. Candles are to be used at every liturgical service as a sign of reverence and festiveness. The candlesticks are to be placed either on or around the altar in a way suited to the design of the altar and the sanctuary. Everything is to be well balanced and must not interfere with the faithful's clear view of what goes on at the altar or is placed on it.

270. There is also to be a cross, clearly visible to the congregation, either on the altar or near it. [See GI app, no. 270.]

VI. CHAIR FOR THE PRIEST CELEBRANT AND THE MINISTERS, THAT IS, THE PLACE WHERE THE PRIEST PRESIDES

271. The priest celebrant's chair ought to stand as a symbol of his office of presiding over the assembly and of directing prayer. Thus the best place for the chair is at the back of the sanctuary and turned toward the congregation, unless the structure or other circumstances are an obstacle (for example, if too great a distance would interfere with communication between the priest and people). Anything resembling a throne is to be avoided. The seats for the ministers should be so placed in the sanctuary that they can readily carry out their appointed functions.[103]

VII. LECTERN (AMBO) OR PLACE FROM WHICH THE WORD OF GOD IS PROCLAIMED

272. The dignity of the word of God requires the church to have a place that is suitable for proclamation of the word and is a natural focal point for the people during the liturgy of the word.[104]

As a rule the lectern or ambo should be stationary, not simply a movable stand. In keeping with the structure of each church, it must be so placed that the ministers may be easily seen and heard by the faithful.

The readings, responsorial psalm, and the Easter Proclamation (Exsultet) are proclaimed from the lectern; it may be used also for the homily and general intercessions (prayer of the faithful).

It is better for the commentator, cantor, or choir director not to use the lectern.

VIII. PLACES FOR THE FAITHFUL

273. The places for the faithful should be arranged with care so that the people are able to take their rightful part in the celebration visually and mentally. As a rule, there should be benches or chairs for their use. But the custom of reserving seats for private persons must be abolished.[105] Chairs or benches should be set up in such a way that the people can easily take the positions required during various celebrations and have unimpeded access to receive communion.

The congregation must be enabled not only to see the priest and the other ministers but also, with the aid of modern sound equipment, to hear them without difficulty.

IX. CHOIR, ORGAN AND OTHER MUSICAL INSTRUMENTS

274. In relation to the design of each church, the *schola cantorum* should be so placed that its character as a part of the assembly of the faithful that has a special function stands out clearly. The location should also assist the choir's liturgical ministry and readily allow each member complete, that is, sacramental participation in the Mass.[106]

275. The organ and other lawfully approved musical instruments are to be placed suitably in such a way that they can sustain the singing of the choir and congregation and be heard with ease when they are played alone. [See GI app, no. 275.]

X. RESERVATION OF THE EUCHARIST

276. Every encouragement should be given to the practice of eucharistic reservation in a chapel suited to the faithful's private adoration and prayer.[107] If this is impossible because of the structure of the church, the sacrament should be reserved at an altar or elsewhere, in keeping with local custom, and in a part of the church that is worthy and properly adorned.[108]

277. The eucharist is to be reserved in a single, solid, immovable tabernacle that is opaque and is locked in such a way as to provide every possible security against the danger of desecration. Thus as a rule there should be only one tabernacle in each church. [109]

XI. IMAGES FOR VENERATION BY THE FAITHFUL

278. In keeping with the Church's very ancient tradition, it is lawful to set up in places of worship images of Christ, Mary, and the saints for veneration by the faithful. But there is need both to limit their number and to situate them in such a way that they do not distract the people's attention from the celebration.[110] There is to be only one image of any one saint. In general, the devotion of the entire community is to be the criterion regarding images in the adornment and arrangement of a church.

XII. GENERAL PLAN OF THE CHURCH

279. The style in which a church is decorated should be a means to achieve noble simplicity, not ostentation. The choice of materials for church appointments must be marked by concern for genuineness and by the intent to foster instruction of the faithful and the dignity of the place of worship.

280. Proper planning of a church and its surroundings that meets contemporary needs require attention not only to the elements belonging directly to liturgical services but also to those facilities for the comfort of the people that are usual in places of public gatherings.

CHAPTER VI
REQUISITIES FOR CELEBRATING MASS

I. BREAD AND WINE

281. Following the example of Christ, the Church has always used bread and wine with water to celebrate the Lord's Supper.

282. The bread must be made only from wheat and must have been baked recently; according to the long-standing tradition of the Latin Church, it must be unleavened.

283. The nature of the sign demands that the material for the eucharistic celebration truly have the appearance of food. Accordingly, even though unleavened and baked in the traditional shape, the eucharistic bread, should be made in such a way that in a Mass with a congregation the priest is able actually to break the host into parts and distribute them to at least some of the faithful. (When, however, the number of communicants is large or other pastoral needs require it, small hosts are in no way ruled out.) The action of the breaking of the bread, the simple term for the eucharist in apostolic times, will more clearly bring out the force and

meaning of the sign of the unity of all in the one bread and of their charity, since the one bread is being distributed among the members of one family.

284. The wine for the eucharist must be from the fruit of the vine (see Lk 22:18), natural, and pure, that is not mixed with any foreign substance.

285. Care must be taken to ensure that the elements are kept in good condition: that the wine does not turn to vinegar or the bread spoil or become too hard to be broken easily.

286. If the priest notices after the consecration or as he receives communion that water instead of wine was poured into the chalice, he pours the water into another container, then pours wine with water into the chalice and consecrates it. He says only the part of the institution narrative related to the consecration of the chalice, without being obligated to consecrate the bread again.

II. SACRED FURNISHINGS IN GENERAL

287. As in the case of architecture, the Church welcomes the artistic style of every region for all sacred furnishings and accepts adaptations in keeping with the genius and traditions of each people, provided they fit the purpose for which the sacred furnishings are intended.[111]

In this matter as well the concern is to be for the noble simplicity that is the perfect companion of genuine art.

288. In the choice of materials for sacred furnishings, others besides the traditional are acceptable that by contemporary standards are considered to be of high quality, are durable, and well suited to sacred uses. The conference of bishops is to make the decisions for each region. [See GI app, no. 288.]

III. SACRED VESSELS

289. Among the requisites for the celebration of Mass, the sacred vessels hold a place of honor, especially the chalice and paten, which are used in presenting, consecrating, and receiving the bread and wine.

290. Vessels should be made from materials that are solid and that in the particular region are regarded as noble. The conference of bishops will be the judge in this matter. But preference is to be given to materials that do not break easily or become unusable.

291. Chalices and other vessels that serve as receptacles for the blood of the Lord are to have a cup of nonabsorbent material. The base may be of any other solid and worthy material.

292. Vessels that serve as receptacles for the eucharistic bread, such as a paten, ciborium, pyx, monstrance, etc., may be made of other materials that are prized in the region, for example, ebony or other hard woods, as long as they are suited to sacred use.

293. For the consecration of hosts one rather large paten may properly be used; on it is placed the bread for the priest as well as for the ministers and the faithful.

294. Vessels made from metal should ordinarily be gilded on the inside if the metal is one that rusts; gilding is not necessary if the metal is more precious than gold and does not rust.

295. The artist may fashion the sacred vessels in a shape that is in keeping with the culture of each region, provided each type of vessel is suited to the intended liturgical use.

296. For the blessing or consecration of vessels the rites prescribed in the liturgical books are to be followed.

IV. VESTMENTS

297. In the Church, the Body of Christ, not all members have the same function. This diversity of ministries is shown outwardly in worship by the diversity of vestments. These should therefore symbolize the function proper to each ministry. But at the same time the vestments should also contribute to the beauty of the rite.

298. The vestment common to ministers of every rank is the alb, tied at the waist with a cincture, unless it is made to fit without a cincture. An amice should be put on first if the alb does not completely cover the street clothing at the neck. A surplice may not be substituted for the alb when the chasuble or dalmatic is to be worn or when a stole is used instead of the chasuble or dalmatic.

299. Unless otherwise indicated, the chasuble, worn over the alb and stole, is the vestment proper to the priest celebrant at Mass and other rites immediately connected with Mass.

300. The dalmatic, worn over the alb and stole, is the vestment proper to the deacon.

301. Ministers below the order of deacon may wear the alb or other vestment that is lawfully approved in each region.

302. The priest wears the stole around his neck and hanging down in front. The deacon wears it over his left shoulder and drawn across the chest to the right side, where it is fastened.

303. The cope is worn by the priest in processions and other services, in keeping with the rubrics proper to each rite.

304. Regarding the design of vestments, the conferences of bishops may determine and propose to the Apostolic See adaptations that correspond to the needs and usages of their regions.[112]

305. In addition to the traditional materials, natural fabrics proper to the region may be used for making vestments; artificial fabrics that are in keeping with the dignity of the liturgy and the person wearing them may also be used. The conference of bishops will be the judge in this matter.[113] [See GI app, no. 305.]

306. The beauty of a vestment should derive from its material and design rather than from lavish ornamentaion. Representations on vestments should consist only of symbols, images, or pictures portraying the sacred. Anything out of keeping with the sacred is to be avoided.

307. Variety in the color of the vestments is meant to give effective, outward expression to the specific character of the mysteries of the faith being celebrated and, in the course of the year, to a sense of progress in the Christian life.

308. Traditional usage should be retained for the vestment colors.

    a. White is used in the offices and Masses of the Easter and Christmas seasons; on feasts and memorials of the Lord, other than of his passion; on feasts and memorials of Mary, the angels, saints who were not martyrs, All Saints (1 November), John the Baptist (24 June), John the Evangelist (27 December), the Chair of St. Peter (22 February), and the Conversion of St. Paul (25 January).

    b. Red is used on Passion Sunday (Palm Sunday) and Good Friday, Pentecost, celebrations of the Lord's passion, birthday feasts of the apostles and evangelists, and celebrations of martyrs.

    c. Green is used in the offices and Masses of Ordinary Time.

    d. Violet is used in Lent and Advent. It may also be worn in offices and Masses for the dead.

    e. Black may be used in Masses for the dead.

    f. Rose may be used on *Gaudete* Sunday (Third Sunday of Advent) and *Laetare* Sunday (Fourth Sunday of Lent).

The conference of bishops may choose and propose to the Apostolic See adaptations suited to the needs and culture of peoples. [See GI app, no. 308.]

309. On solemn occasions more precious vestments may be used, even if not the color of the day.

310. Ritual Masses are celebrated in their proper color, in white, or in a festive color; Masses for various needs and occasions are celebrated in the color proper to the day or the season or in violet if they bear a penitential character, for example, ritual Masses nos. 23, 28 and 40; votive Masses are celebrated in the color suited to the Mass itself or in the color proper to the day or season.

V. OTHER REQUISITES FOR CHURCH USE

311. Besides vessels and vestments for which some special material is prescribed, any other furnishings that either have a liturgical use or are in any other way introduced into a church should be worthy and suited to their particular purpose.

312. Even in minor matters, every effort should be made to respect the canons of art and to combine cleanliness and a noble simplicity.

CHAPTER VII
CHOICE OF THE MASS AND ITS PARTS

313. The pastoral effectiveness of a celebration will be heightened if the texts of readings, prayers, and songs correspond as closely as possible to the needs, religious dispositions, and aptitude of the participants. This will be achieved by an intelligent use of the broad options described in this chapter.

In planning the celebration, then, the priest should consider the general spiritual good of the assembly rather than his personal outlook. He should be mindful that the choice of texts is to be made in consultation with the ministers and others who have a function in the celebration, including the faithful in regard to the parts that more directly belong to them.

Since a variety of options is provided for the different parts of the Mass, it is necessary for the deacon, readers, psalmists, cantors, commentator, and choir to be completely sure beforehand of those texts for which they are responsible so that nothing is improvised. A harmonious planning and execution will help dispose the people spiritually to take part in the eucharist.

I. CHOICE OF MASS

314. On solemnities the priest is bound to follow the calendar of the church where he is celebrating.

315. On Sundays, on weekdays of Advent, the Christmas season, Lent, and the Easter season, on feasts, and on obligatory memorials:

a. if Mass is celebrated with a congregation, the priest should follow the calendar of the church where he is celebrating;

b. if Mass is celebrated without a congregation, the priest may choose either the calendar of the church or his own calendar.

316. On optional memorials:

a. On the weekdays of Advent from 17 December to 24 December, during the octave of Christmas, and on the weekdays of Lent, apart from Ash Wednesday and in Holy Week, the priest celebrates the Mass of the day; but he may take the opening prayer from a memorial listed in the General Roman Calendar for that day, except on Ash Wednesday and during Holy Week.

b. On the weekdays of Advent before 17 December, the weekdays of the Christmas season from 2 January on, and the weekdays of the Easter season, the priest may choose the weekday Mass, the Mass of the saint or of one of the saints whose memorial is observed, or the Mass of a saint inscribed in the martyrology for that day.

c. On the weekdays in Ordinary Time, the priest may choose the weekday Mass, the Mass of an optional memorial, the Mass of a saint inscribed in the martyrology for that day, a Mass for various needs and occasions, or a votive Mass.

If he celebrates with a congregation, the priest should first consider the spiritual good of the faithful and avoid imposing his own personal preferences. In particular, he should not omit the readings assigned for each day in the weekday lectionary too frequently or without sufficient reason, since the Church desires that a richer portion of God's word be provided for the people.[114]

For similar reasons he should use Masses for the dead sparingly. Every Mass is offered for both the living and the dead and there is a remembrance of the dead in each eucharistic prayer.

Where the faithful are attached to the optional memorials of Mary or the saints, at least one Mass of the memorial should be celebrated to satisfy their devotion.

When an option is given between a memorial in the General Roman Calendar and one in a diocesan or religious calendar, the preference should be given, all things being equal and depending on tradition, to the memorial in the particular calendar.

II. CHOICE OF INDIVIDUAL TEXTS

317. In the choice of texts for the several parts of the Mass, the following rules are to be observed. They apply to Masses of the season and of the saints.

READINGS

318. Sundays and holydays have three readings, that is, from the Old Testament, from the writings of an apostle, and from a Gospel. Thus God's own teaching brings the Christian people to a knowledge of the continuity of the work of salvation.

Accordingly, it is expected that there will be three readings, but for pastoral reasons and by decree of the conference of bishops the use of only two readings is allowed in some places. In such a case, the choice between the first two readings should be based on the norms in the Lectionary and on the intention to lead the people to a deeper knowledge of Scripture; there should never be any thought of choosing a text because it is shorter or easier. [See GIapp, no. 318.]

319. In the weekday lectionary, readings are provided for each day of every week throughout the year; therefore, unless a solemnity or feast occurs, these readings are for the most part to be used on the days to which they are assigned.

The continuous reading during the week, however, is sometimes interrupted by the occurrence of a feast or particular celebration. In this case the priest, taking into consideration the entire week's plan of readings is allowed either to combine omitted parts with other readings or to give preference to certain readings.

In Masses with special groups, the priest may choose texts more suited to the particular celebration, provided they are taken from the texts of an approved lectionary.

320. The Lectionary has a special selection of texts from Scripture for Masses that incorporate certain sacraments or sacramentals or that are celebrated by reason of special circumstances.

These selections of readings have been assigned so that by hearing a more pertinent passage from God's word the faithful may be led to a better understanding of the mystery they are taking part in and may be led to a more ardent love for God's word.

Therefore the texts for proclamation in the liturgical assembly are to be chosen on the basis of their pastoral relevance and the options allowed in this matter.

321. The many prefaces enriching the Roman Missal are intended to develop in different ways the theme of thanksgiving in the eucharistic prayer and bring out more clearly the different facets of the mystery of salvation.

322. The choice of the eucharistic prayer may be guided by the following norms.

a. Eucharistic Prayer I, the Roman Canon, which may be used on any day, is particularly apt on days when there is a special text for the prayer, *In union with the whole Church,* or in Masses that have a special form of the prayer, *Father, accept this offering;* also on the feasts of the apostles and saints mentioned in it and on Sundays, unless for pastoral considerations another eucharistic prayer is preferred.

b. Eucharistic Prayer II has features that make it particularly suitable for weekdays and special circumstances.

Although it has its own preface, it may also be used with other prefaces, especially those that summarize the mystery of salvation, such as the Sunday prefaces or the common prefaces.

When Mass is celebrated for a dead person, the special formulary may be inserted in the place indicated, namely, before the intercession, *Remember our brothers and sisters.*

c. Eucharistic Prayer III may be said with any preface. Its use is particularly suited to Sundays and holydays.

The special formulary for a dead person may be used with this prayer in the place indicated, namely, at the prayer, *In mercy and love unite all your children.*

d. Eucharistic Prayer IV has a fixed preface and provides a fuller summary of the history of salvation. It may be used when a Mass has no preface of its own.

Because of the structure of this prayer no special formulary for the dead may be inserted.

e. A eucharistic prayer that has its own preface may be used with that preface, even when the Mass calls for the preface of the season.

323. In any Mass the prayers belonging to that Mass are used, unless otherwise noted.

In Masses on a memorial, however, the opening prayer or collect may be from the Mass itself or from the common; the prayer over the gifts and prayer after communion, unless they are proper, may be taken either from the common or from the weekdays of the current season.

On the weekdays in Ordinary Time, the prayers may be taken from the preceding Sunday, from another Sunday in Ordinary Time, or from the prayers for various needs and occasions listed in the Missal. It is always permissible even to use the opening prayer from these Masses.

This provides a rich collection of texts that create an opportunity continually to rephrase the themes of prayer for the liturgical assembly and also to adapt the prayer to the needs of the people, the Church, and the world. During the more important seasons of the year, however, the proper seasonal prayers appointed for each day in the Missal already make this adaptation.

SONG

324. The norms laid down in their proper places are to be observed for the choice of chants between the readings and the songs for the processions at the entrance, presentation of the gifts, and communion.

SPECIAL PERMISSIONS

325. In addition to the permissions just given to choose more suitable texts, the conferences of bishops have the right in some circumstances to make further adaptions of readings, but on condition that the texts are taken from an approved lectionary.

CHAPTER VIII
MASSES AND PRAYERS FOR VARIOUS NEEDS AND
OCCASIONS AND MASSES FOR THE DEAD

I. MASSES AND PRAYERS FOR VARIOUS NEEDS AND OCCASIONS

326. For well-disposed Christians the liturgy of the sacraments and sacramentals causes almost every event in human life to be made holy by divine grace that flows from the paschal mystery.[115] The eucharist, in turn, is the sacrament of sacraments. Accordingly, the Missal provides formularies for Masses and prayers that may be used in the various circumstances of Christian life, for the needs of the whole world, and for the needs of the Church, both local and universal.

327. In view of the broad options for choosing the readings and prayers, the Masses for various needs and occasions should be used sparingly, that is, when the occasion requires.

328. In all the Masses for various needs and occasions, unless otherwise indicated, the weekday readings and the chants between them may be used, if they are suited to the celebration.

329. The Masses for various needs and occasions are of three types:

a. the ritual Masses, which are related to the celebration of certain sacraments or sacramentals;

b. the Masses for various needs and occasions, which are used either as circumstances arise or at fixed times;

c. the votive Masses of the mysteries of the Lord or in honor of Mary or a particular saint or of all the saints, which are options provided in favor of the faithful's devotion.

330. Ritual Masses are prohibited on the Sundays of Advent, Lent, and the Easter season, on solemnities, on days within the octave of Easter, on All Souls, on Ash Wednesday, and during Holy Week. In addition, the norms in the ritual books or in the Masses themselves also apply.

331. From the selection of Masses for various needs and occasions, the competent authority may choose Masses for those special days of prayer that the conferences of bishops may decree during the course of the year. [See GIapp, no. 331.]

332. In cases of serious need or pastoral advantage, at the direction of the local Ordinary or with his permission, an appropriate Mass may be celebrated on any day except solemnities, the Sundays of Advent, Lent, and the Easter season, days within the octave of Easter, on All Souls, Ash Wednesday, and during Holy Week.

333. On obligatory memorials, on the weekdays of Advent until 16 December, of the Christmas season after 2 January, and of the Easter season after the octave of Easter, Masses for various needs and occasions are per se forbidden. But if some real need or pastoral advantage requires, at the discretion of the rector of the church or the priest celebrant, the Masses corresponding to such need or advantage may be used in a celebration with a congregation.

334. On weekdays in Ordinary Time when there is an optional memorial or the office is of that weekday, any Mass or prayer for various needs and occasions is permitted, but ritual Masses are excluded.

II. MASSES FOR THE DEAD

335. The Church offers Christ's paschal sacrifice for the dead so that on the basis of the communion existing between all Christ's members, the petition for spiritual help on behalf of some members may bring others comforting hope.

336. The funeral Mass has first place among the Masses for the dead and may be celebrated on any day except solemnities that are days of obligation, Holy Thursday, the Easter triduum, and the Sundays of Advent, Lent, and the Easter season.

337. On the occasions of news of a death, final burial, or the first anniversary, Mass for the dead may be celebrated even on days within the Christmas octave, on obligatory memorials, and on weekdays, except Ash Wednesday and during Holy Week.

Other Masses for the dead, that is, daily Masses, may be celebrated on weekdays in Ordinary Time when there is an optional memorial or the office is of the weekday, provided such Masses are actually offered for the dead.

338. At the funeral Mass there should as a rule be a short homily, but never a eulogy of any kind. The homily is also recommended at other Masses for the dead celebrated with a congregation.

339. All the faithful, and especially the family, should be urged to share in the eucharistic sacrifice offered for the deceased person by receiving communion.

340. If the funeral Mass is directly joined to the burial rite, once the prayer after communion has been said and omitting the rite of dismissal, the rite of final commendation or of farewell takes place, but only when the body is present. [See GIapp, no. 340.]

341. In the planning and choosing of the variable parts of the Mass for the dead, especially the funeral Mass (for example, prayers, readings, general intercessions) pastoral considerations bearing upon the deceased, the family, and those attending should rightly be foremost.

Pastors should, moreover, take into special account those who are present at a liturgical celebration or hear the Gospel only because of the funeral. These may be non-Catholics or Catholics who never or rarely share in the eucharist or who have apparently lost the faith. Priests are, after all, ministers of Christ's Gospel for all people.

NOTES

1. See Council of Trent, sess. 22, 17 Sept 1562.
2. CSL 47; see LG 3, 28; PO, 2, 4, 5.
3. *Sacramentarium Veronese,* (ed. Mohlberg), no. 93.
4. See eucharistic prayer III.
5. See eucharistic prayer IV.
6. See CSL 7, 47; PO 5, 18.
7. See Pius XII, encyclical *Humani Generis:* AAS 42 (1950) 570-571; Paul VI, encyclical *Mysterium fidei:* AAS 57 (1965) 762-769; Solemn Profession of Faith, 30 June 1968: AAS 60 (1968) 442-443; CR, instruction EM, 25 May 1967, nos. 3, 9.
8. See Council of Trent, sess. 13, 11 Oct 1551.
9. See PO 2.
10. See CSL 11.
11. SCL 50.
12. Council of Trent, sess. 22, 17 Sept 1562, Doctrine on the Holy Sacrifice of the Mass, chap. 8.
13. *Ibid.,* chap. 9.
14. *Ibid.,* chap. 8.
15. See CSL 33.
16. See CSL 36.
17. See CSL 52.
18. See CSL 35, 3.
19. CSL 55.
20. Council of Trent, sess. 22, 17 Sept 1562, Doctrine of on the Holy Sacrifice of the Mass, chap. 6.
21. See CSL 55.
22. See CSL 41; LG 11; PO 2, 5, 6; Decree on the Pastoral Office of Bishops in the Church, *Christus Dominus,* no. 30; Decree on Ecumenism, *Unitatis redintegratio,* no. 15; EM 3e, 6.
23. See CSL 10.
24. See CSL 102.
25. See PO 5; CSL 10.
26. See CSL 14, 19, 26, 28, 30.
27. See CSL 47.
28. See CSL 14.
29. See CSL 41.
30. See PO 13.
31. See CSL 59.
32. For Masses with special groups see instruction *Actio pastoralis,* 15 May 1969; CDW, Directory for Masses with Children; for the manner of joining the liturgy of the hours with the Mass, General Instruction of the Liturgy of the Hours, nos. 93-98.
33. See CSL 37-40.
34. See PO 5; CSL 33.
35. See Council of Trent, sess. 22, 17 Sept 1562, chap. 1; Paul VI, Solemn Profession of Faith, 30 June 1968, no. 24: AAS 60 (1968) 442.
36. See CSL 7; Paul VI encyclical Mysterium fidei; AAS 57 (1965) 764; EM 9.
37. See CSL 56; EM 10.
38. See CSL 48, 51; DV 21; PO 4.
39. See CSL 7, 33, 52.
40. See CSL 33.
41. See CDW, circular letter on the eucharistic prayers. 27 April 1973, no. 14.
42. See CR, instruction MS, 5 March 1967, no. 14.
43. See CSL 26, 27.
44. See CSL 30.
45. See MS 16a.
46. Augustine, Sermon 336, 1: *Patrologiae cursus completus: Series latina,* (ed. Migne), 38, 1472.
47. See MS 7, 16.
48. See CSL 54; CR, IOe, 26 Sept 1964, no. 59; MS 47.
49. See CSL 30.
50. See CSL 39.
51. See CSL 30; MS 17.
52. See CSL 33.
53. See CSL 7.
54. See CSL 51.
55. See IOe 50.
56. See CSL 52.
57. See IOe 54.
58. See IOe 53.
59. See CSL 53.

60. See IOe 56.

61. See CSL 47; EM 3a, b.

62. See IOe 91.

63. See CSL 48; PO 5, EM 12.

64. See EM 12, 33a.

65. *Ibid.*, 31, 32, on communion twice in one day. See also CCL, can. 917.

66. See CSL 14, 26.

67. See CSL 28.

68. See LG 26, 28; CSL 42.

69. See CSL 26.

70. See PO 2; LG 28.

71. See CSL 48; EM 12.

72. See MS 19.

73. *Ibid.*, 21.

74. See CSL 24.

75. See CDW, instruction *Immensae caritatis*, 29 Jan 1973, no. 1

76. See CDW, instruction *Liturgicae instaurationes*, 5 Sept 1970, no. 7.

77. See CSL 41.

78. See CSL 42; EM 26; LG 28; PO 5.

79. See EM 47.

80. *Ibid.*, 26; MS 16, 27.

81. See CDW, Decree, 9 Oct 1972.

82. See Paul VI, *motu proprio Ministeria quaedam*, 15 Aug 1972, no. 6.

83. See CSL 57; CCL 902.

84. See EM 47.

85. See Rite of Concelebration, introduction, no. 6.

86. See CR, general decree *Ecclesiae semper*, 7 Mar 1965; EM 47.

87. See Rite of Concelebration, introduction no. 9; CDW, Declaration on Concelebration, 7 Aug 1972.

88. See EM 32.

89. See Council of Trent, sess. 21, 16 July 1562, Decree on Eucharistic Communion, chap. 1-3.

90. *Ibid.*, chap. 2.

91. See CDW, instruction *Sacramentali Communione*, 29 June 1970.

92. See CSL 122-124; PO 5; IOe 90; EM 24.

93. See CSL 123.

94. See EM 24.

95. See CSL 123, 129; IOe 13c.

96. See CSL 123.

97. See CSL 126.

98. See IOe 97-98.

99. *Ibid.*, 91.

100. See EM 24.

101. See IOe 91.

102. *Ibid.*, 93.

103. *Ibid.*, 92.

104. *Ibid.*, 96.

105. See CSL 32; IOe 98.

106. See MS 23.

107. See EM 53.

108. *Ibid.*, 54, IOe 95.

109. See EM 52; IOe 96; CDW, instruction *Nullo umquam tempore*, 28 May 1938, no. 4: AAS 30 (1938) 199-200; Roman Ritual, Holy Communion and Worship of the Eucharist outside Mass, no. 10-11; CCL 938.

110. See CSL 125.

111. See CSL 128; EM 24.

112. See CSL 128.

113. *Ibid.*

114. See CSL 51.

115. See CSL 61.

APPENDIX

TO THE

GENERAL INSTRUCTION

FOR THE DIOCESES
OF THE UNITED STATES

OUTLINE

Adaptations for the dioceses of the United States
are given on the following:

The numbers assigned to each entry refer to
articles of the *General Instruction.*

APPENDIX TO THE *GENERAL INSTRUCTION*
FOR THE DIOCESES OF THE UNITED STATES

The following notes, related to the individual sections of the *General Instruction of the Roman Missal*, include adaptations made by the National Conference of Catholic Bishops for the dioceses of the United States, as well as supplementary references.

For further documentation concerning the Eucharistic celebration, see Congregation of Rites, *Instruction on Eucharistic Worship* (25 May 1967), especially "Some General Principles of Particular Importance in the Catechesis of the People on the Mystery of the Eucharist" (nos. 5–15) and "The Celebration of the Memorial of the Lord" (nos. 16–48); and Sacred Congregation for the Sacraments and Divine Worship, *On Certain Norms concerning Worship of the Eucharistic Mystery* (17 April 1980).

The number at the beginning of each section below refers to the respective section of the *General Instruction*. Unless otherwise indicated, decisions of the National Conference of Catholic Bishops were taken at the plenary session of November 1969.

11. INTRODUCTIONS AND INVITATIONS

With regard to the adaptation of words of introduction, see the circular letter of the Congregation for Divine Worship, 27 April 1973. No. 14 reads:

Among the possibilities for further accommodating any individual celebration, it is important to consider the admonitions, the homily and the general intercessions. First of all are the admonitions. These enable the people to be drawn into a fuller understanding of the sacred action, or any of its parts, and lead them into a true spirit of participation. The *General Instruction of the Roman Missal* entrusts the more important admonitions to the priest for preparation and use. He may introduce the Mass to the people before the celebration begins, during the liturgy of the word prior to the actual readings, and in the Eucharistic prayer before the preface; he may also conclude the entire sacred action before the dismissal. The *Order of Mass* provides others as well, which are important to certain portions of the rite, such as during the penitential rite, or before the Lord's Prayer. By their very nature these brief admonitions do not require that everyone use them in the form in which they appear in the *Missal.* Provision can be made in certain cases that they be adapted to some degree to the varying circumstances of the community. In all cases it is well to remember the nature of an admonition, and not make them into a sermon or homily; care should be taken to keep them brief and not too wordy, for otherwise they become tedious.

19. SINGING

See the statement of the Bishops' Committee on the Liturgy, *The Place of Music in Eucharistic Celebrations* (Washington, 1968); revised ed., *Music in Catholic Worship* (Washington, 1972).

The settings for liturgical texts to be sung by the priest and ministers that are given in the *Sacramentary* are chant adaptations prepared by the International Commission on English in the Liturgy, rather than new melodies. Other settings for the ministerial chants are those approved by the National Conference of Catholic Bishops (November 1965).

No official approbation is needed for new melodies for the Lord's Prayer at Mass or for the chants, acclamations and other song of the congregation.

In accord with no. 55 of the instruction of the Congregation of Rites on music in the liturgy (5 March 1967), the Conference of Bishops has determined that vernacular texts set to music composed in earlier periods may be used in liturgical services even though they may not conform in all details with the legitimately approved versions of liturgical texts (November 1967). This decision authorizes the use of choral and other music in English when the older text is not precisely the same as the official version.

21. ACTIONS AND POSTURES

At its meeting in November 1969, the National Conference of Catholic bishops voted that in general, the directives of the *Roman Missal* concerning the posture of the congregation at Mass should be left unchanged, but that no. 21 of the *General Instruction* should be adapted so that the people kneel beginning after the singing or recitation of the Sanctus until after the Amen of the eucharistic prayer, that is, before the Lord's Prayer.

26. ENTRANCE SONG

As a further alternative to the singing of the entrance antiphon and psalm of the *Roman Gradual (Missal)* or the *Simple Gradual*, the Conference of Bishops has approved the use of other collections of psalms and antiphons in English, as supplements to the *Simple Gradual*, including psalms arranged in responsorial form, metrical and similar versions of psalms, provided they are used in accordance with the principles of the *Simple Gradual* and are selected in harmony with the liturgical season, feast or occasion (decree confirmed by the Consilium for the Implementation of the Constitution on the Liturgy, 17 December 1968).

With regard to texts of other sacred songs from the psalter that may be used as the entrance song, the following criterion was adopted by the Conference of Bishops in November 1969:

The entrance rite should create an atmosphere of celebration. It serves the function of putting the assembly in the proper frame of mind for listening to the word of God. It helps people to become conscious of themselves as a worshiping community. The choice of texts for the entrance song should not conflict with these purposes.

In general, during the most important seasons of the Church year, Eastertime, Lent, Christmas and Advent, it is preferable that most songs used at the entrance be seasonal in nature.

There are thus four options for the entrance song:
1. the entrance antiphon and psalm of the *Roman Gradual;*
2. the entrance antiphon and psalm of the *Simple Gradual;*
3. song from other collections of psalms and antiphons;
4. other sacred song chosen in accord with the above criteria.

The same options exist for the sacred song at the offertory and communion, but not for the chants between the readings (below).

Only if none of the above alternatives is employed and there is no entrance song, is the antiphon in the Missal recited.

36. CHANTS BETWEEN THE READINGS

As a further alternative to (1) the singing of the psalm with its response in the *Lectionary,* (2) the gradual in the *Roman Gradual,* or (3) the responsorial or alleluia psalm in the *Simple Gradual,* the Conference of Bishops has approved the use of other collections of psalms and antiphons in English, as supplements to the *Simple Gradual,* including psalms arranged in responsorial form, metrical and similar versions of psalms, provided they are used in accordance with the principles of the *Simple Gradual* and are selected in harmony with the liturgical season, feast or occasion (decree confirmed by the Consilium for the Implementation of the Constitution on the Liturgy, 17 December 1968).

The choice of texts that are *not* from the psalter (permitted at the entrance, offertory and communion) is not extended to the chants between the readings.

For further information concerning the use of the chants between the readings, see the Foreword and the Introduction (VIII) to the *Lectionary for Mass* (New York, Collegeville, Minn., 1970). In particular, see the common texts for sung responsorial psalms (nos. 174–175), which may be used in place of the text corresponding to the reading whenever the psalm is sung.

During Lent the alleluia is not sung with the verse before the Gospel. Instead one of the following (or similar) acclamations may be sung before and after the verse before the Gospel:

Praise and honor to you, Lord Jesus Christ, King of endless glory!

Praise and honor to you, Lord Jesus Christ!

Glory and praise to you, Lord Jesus Christ!

Glory to you, Word of God, Lord Jesus Christ!

If the psalm after the reading is not sung, it is recited. The alleluia or the verse before the Gospel may be omitted if not sung (see no. 39 of the *General Instruction*). The people stand for the singing of the alleluia before the Gospel (see no. 21 of the *General Instruction*).

45. GENERAL INTERCESSIONS

See the statement of the Bishops' Committee on the Liturgy, *General Prayer or Prayer of the Faithful*, July 1969.

50. OFFERTORY SONG

The choice of texts for the offertory song is governed by the same rule as the entrance song, with the several options described above (no. 26). If there is no offertory song, the offertory antiphon is omitted.

With regard to texts not from the psalter that may be used as the offertory song, the following criterion was adopted by the National Conference of Bishops in November 1969:

The offertory song need not speak of bread and wine or of offering. The proper function of the offertory song is rather to accompany and celebrate the communal aspects of the procession. The text, therefore, may be an appropriate song of praise or of rejoicing in keeping with the season. Those texts are not acceptable that speak of the offering completely apart from the action of Christ.

In general, during the most important seasons of the Church year, Easter time, Lent, Christmas and Advent, it is preferable that most songs used during the offertory be seasonal in character. During the remainder of the Church year, however, topical songs may be used during the offertory procession provided that these texts do not conflict with the paschal character of every Sunday *(Constitution on the Liturgy, 102, 106)*.

With regard to the offertory song, the statement of the Bishops' Committee on the Liturgy of 1968 *(The Place of Music in Eucharistic Celebrations)* gives additional comments:

The procession can be accompanied by song. Song is not always necessary or desirable. Organ or instrumental music is also fitting at this time. The song need not speak of bread or wine or offering. The proper function of this song is to accompany and celebrate the communal aspects of the procession. The text, therefore, can be any appropriate song of praise or of rejoicing in keeping with the season. (See approved criteria above.) The song need not accompany the entire preparation rite. (The song, if any, continues at least until the priest has placed the bread and wine on the altar, while saying the accompanying prayers quietly; see no. 50 of the *General Instruction*, nos. 19–21 of the *Order of Mass.)*

If there is no singing or organ or instrumental music, this may be a period of silence (see no. 23 of the *General Instruction*). In fact, it is good to give the assembly a period of quiet (that is, while the gifts are prepared and placed on the altar, until the introduction to the prayer over the gifts: "Pray, brethren . . .") before demanding, at the preface, their full attention to the eucharistic prayer.

56b. SIGN OF PEACE

The Conference of Bishops has left the development of specific modes of exchanging the sign of peace to local usage. Neither a specific form nor specific words are determined (November 1969).

56i. COMMUNION SONG

The choice of texts for the communion song is governed by the same rule as the entrance song, with the several options described above (no. 26).

With regard to the texts not from the psalter that may be used as the communion song, the following criterion was adopted by the National Conference of Catholic Bishops in November 1969:

The communion song should foster a sense of unity. It should be simple and not demand great effort. It gives expression to the joy of unity in the body of Christ and the fulfillment of the mystery being celebrated. Most benediction hymns, by reason of their concentration on adoration rather than on communion, are not acceptable, as indicated in the instruction on music in the liturgy, no. 36.

In general, during the most important seasons of the church year, Eastertime, Lent, Christmas and Advent, it is preferable that most songs used at the communion be seasonal in nature. During the remainder of the church year, however, topical songs may be used during the communion procession provided these texts do not conflict with the paschal character of every Sunday *(Constitution on the Liturgy, 102, 106)*.

Only if none of the above alternatives is employed and there is no communion song, is the antiphon in the *Missal* recited. Until the publication of the complete new Missal, the antiphon from the present *Missal* is said in such cases (Congregation for Divine Worship, instruction, 20 October 1969, no. 13).

59. CELEBRATION BY THE BISHOP

See Congregation of Rites, instruction on the simplification of pontifical rites and insignia, 21 June 1968.

For occasions when the bishop is present at a celebration of the eucharist but, for a just reason, does not elect to be the principal celebrant, he may assign another to celebrate the liturgy of the eucharist while he presides over the introductory rites, the liturgy of the word and the concluding rite of the Mass. For directives on the manner in which this is done, see *Newsletter* of the Bishops' Committee on the Liturgy, May–June, 1981.

66. WOMEN AS READERS

The Conference of Bishops has given permission for women to serve as readers in accord with no. 66 of the *General Instruction* (November 1969).

In February 1971, the Bishops' Committee on the Liturgy prepared a commentary on the liturgical ministry of women:

a. With the exception of service at the altar itself, women may be admitted to the exercise of other liturgical ministries. In particular the designation of women to serve in such ministries as reader, cantor, leader of singing, commentator, director of liturgical participation, etc., is left to the judgment of the pastor or the priest who presides over the celebration, in the light of the culture and mentality of the congregation.

b. Worthiness of life and character and other qualifications are required in women who exercise liturgical ministries in the same way as for men who exercise the same ministries.

c. Women who read one or other biblical reading during the liturgy of the word (other than the Gospel, which is reserved to a deacon or priest) should do so from the lectern or ambo where the other readings are proclaimed: the reservation of a single place for all the biblical readings is more significant than the person of the reader, whether ordained or lay, whether woman or man (cf. *General Instruction*, no. 272).

d. Other ministries performed by women, such as leading the singing or otherwise directing the congregation, should be done either within or outside the sanctuary area, depending on circumstances or convenience.

127. OFFICE OF DEACON

The various ministries of the deacon at Mass may be distributed among several deacons, present and wearing their vestments. (See Congregation of Rites, instruction, 21 June 1968, nos. 4, 5). Other deacons who are present but not called upon to function in the celebration normally should not vest or occupy a specific place in the liturgy, unless they are participating as the *order of deacons*, e.g., at the liturgy of ordination of another deacon. (See Bishops' Committee on the Liturgy, *Newsletter*, October 1981.)

153. CONCELEBRATED MASS

See the statement of the Bishops' Committee on the Liturgy, "Concelebration," *Newsletter*, June 1966.

240. COMMUNION UNDER BOTH KINDS

On 17 June 1977, the Congregation of Sacraments and Divine Worship approved the request of the National Conference of Catholic Bishops to permit the optional practice of communion in the hand. The Bishops' Committee on the Liturgy, in its catechesis about this optional practice, drew attention to these considerations:

a. Proper catechesis must be provided to assure the proper and reverent reception of communion without any suggestion of wavering on the part of the Church in its faith in the eucharistic presence.

b. The practice must remain the option of the communicant. The priest or minister of communion does not make the decision as to the manner of reception of communion. It is the communicant's personal choice.

c. When communion is distributed under both kinds by intinction, the host is not placed in the hands of the communicants, nor may the communicants receive the host and dip it into the chalice. Intinction should not be introduced as a means of circumventing the practice of communion in the hand.

d. Children have the option to receive communion in the hand or on the tongue. No limitations because of age have been established. Careful preparation for first reception of the eucharist will provide the necessary instruction. (See also the Roman Ritual, *Holy Communion and Worship of the Eucharist outside Mass*, no. 21.)

242. COMMUNION UNDER BOTH KINDS

See the statement of the Bishops' Committee on the Liturgy, "Communion under Both Kinds," *Newsletter,* July 1966.

In accord with the instruction of the Congregation for Divine Worship on communion under both kinds (29 June 1970), the National Conference of Catholic Bishops in November 1970, added the following cases:

15. other members of the faithful present on the special occasions enumerated in no. 242 of the *General Instruction;*

16. at funeral Masses and at Masses for a special family observance;

17. at Masses on days of special religious or civil significance for the people of the United States;

18. at Masses on Holy Thursday and at the Mass of the Easter Vigil, the norms of the instruction of 29 June 1970, being observed;

19. at weekday Masses.

At its meeting in November 1978, the National Conference of Catholic Bishops further extended the occasions on which holy communion under both kinds might be given when it approved the motion that holy communion may be given under both kinds to the faithful at Masses on Sundays and holydays of obligation if, in the judgment of the ordinary, communion may be given in an orderly and reverent manner.

263. MATERIALS FOR FIXED ALTARS

Materials other than natural stone may be used for fixed altars provided these are worthy, solid and properly constructed, subject to the further judgment of the local ordinary in doubtful cases.

270. ALTAR CROSS

Only a single cross should be carried in a procession in order to give greater dignity and reverence to the cross. It is desirable to place the cross that has been carried in the procession near the altar so that it may serve as the cross of the altar. Otherwise it should be put away during the service. (See Congregation of Rites, instruction, 21 June 1968, no. 20).

275. MUSICAL INSTRUMENTS

The Conference of Bishops has decreed that musical instruments other than the organ may be used in liturgical services provided they are played in a manner that is suitable to public worship. (November 1967; see *Constitution on the Liturgy*, 120). This decision deliberately refrains from singling out specific instruments. Their use depends on circumstances, the nature of the congregation, etc. In particular cases, if there should be doubt as to the suitability of the instruments, it is the responsibility of the diocesan bishop, in consultation with the diocesan liturgical and music commissions, to render a decision.

288. MATERIALS FOR SACRED FURNISHINGS

Materials other than the traditional ones may be used for sacred furnishings provided they are suitable for liturgical use, subject to the further judgment of the local ordinary in doubtful cases.

305. MATERIALS FOR VESTMENTS

Fabrics, both natural and artificial, other than the traditional ones may be used for sacred vesture provided they are suitable for liturgical use, subject to the further judgment of the local ordinary in doubtful cases.

308. COLOR OF VESTMENTS

White, violet or black vestments may be worn at funeral services and at other offices and Masses for the dead (November 1970).

318. READINGS ON SUNDAYS AND FEASTS

According to the decision of the National Conference of Catholic Bishops, the complete pattern of three readings for Sundays and feast days should be completely implemented.

331. DAYS OF PRAYER

The Conference of Bishops has decreed that there be observed in the dioceses of the United States, at times to be designated by the local ordinary in consultation with the diocesan liturgical commission, days or periods of prayer for the fruits of the earth, prayer for human rights and equality, prayer for world justice and peace, and penitential observance outside Lent (November 1971). This is in addition to observances customary on certain civic occasions such as Independence Day, Labor Day and Thanksgiving Day, for which either proper text or texts of the *Sacramentary* and *Lectionary for Mass* are provided.

The Bishops' Committee on the Liturgy presented the above decision in these terms: The expression of such days or periods of prayer should be left as general as possible, so that the time, length, occasion, and more specific intentions of prayer should be determined locally rather than nationally. In this way no arbitrary rule is imposed until it becomes evident that a pattern of such supplications is emerging from practice. See also General Norms for the Liturgical Year and the Calendar, nos. 45–47.

340. FUNERAL MASS

Although the rite of final commendation at the catafalque or pall is excluded, it is permitted to celebrate the funeral service, including the commendations, in those cases where it is physically or morally impossible for the body of the deceased person to be present (November 1970).

For other adaptations in the funeral Mass and service, see the *Rite of Funerals* (1971); *Newsletter* of the Bishops' Committee on the Liturgy, April–May 1971. The following refer directly to the eucharistic celebration:

It is appropriate that the paschal candle be carried in the entrance procession.

If the introductory rites have taken place at the church door, the priest venerates the altar and goes to his chair. The penitential rite is omitted, and the priest says or sings the opening prayer.

It is desirable that the first and second readings be read by relatives or friends of the deceased person.

The homily may properly include an expression of praise and gratitude to God for his gifts, particularly the gift of a Christian life to the deceased person. The homily should relate Christian death to the paschal mystery of the Lord's victorious death and resurrection and to the hope of eternal life.

It is desirable that members of the family or friends of the deceased person participate in the usual offering of the bread and wine for the celebration of the eucharist, together with other gifts for the needs of the Church and the poor.

If incense is used, the priest, after incensing the gifts and the altar, may incense the body. The deacon or another minister then incenses the priest and people.

LECTIONARY FOR MASS: INTRODUCTION

SECOND EDITION

BACKGROUND

The lectionary is the book which holds the church's arrangement of the scriptures for the Sundays and weekdays of the seasons and of Ordinary Time. Following the directives of the *Constitution on the Sacred Liturgy,* a basic revision of the lectionary was published in 1969. This introduced the three-year cycle of Sunday readings and a two-year cycle of weekday readings. In 1981, some minor revisions in the readings were published together with a magnificent introduction to the whole lectionary. That introduction is the document included here. There are likely to be further revisions in the lectionary itself, but this document will remain a marvelous statement of when, why, and how the church opens and reads from her sacred book, the Bible.

Lectors and preachers should have a familiarity with all that is in this introduction, but it also has much to say to those who plan the seasons and feasts and the order of the Sunday Mass. Of particular value are: the careful study of the structure of the liturgy of the word (chapter 2); the attention to the ministers (chapter 3); the overview of the seasons and cycles (chapter 5).

OUTLINE

B. Books for proclamation of the word of
God   35-37

LECTIONARY FOR MASS: INTRODUCTION

PROLOGUE
CHAPTER 1
GENERAL PRINCIPLES FOR THE LITURGICAL
CELEBRATION OF THE WORD OF GOD

1. Preliminaries

A. IMPORTANCE OF THE WORD OF GOD IN A LITURGICAL CELEBRATION

1.   Vatican Council II,[1] the teaching of the popes,[2] and various postconciliar documents of the Roman congregations[3] have already made many excellent statements about the importance of the word of God and about reestablishing the use of Scripture in every celebration of the liturgy. The Introduction of the 1969 edition of the Order of Readings for Mass has clearly stated and briefly explained some of the more important principles.[4]

On the occasion of this new edition of the Order of Readings for Mass, requests have come from many quarters for a more detailed expositon of the same principles. In response, this expanded and more helpful arrangement of the Introduction first gives a general statement on the close relationship between the word of God and the liturgical celebration,[5] then deals in greater detail with the word of God in the celebration of Mass, and, finally, explains the precise structure of the Order of Readings for Mass.

B. TERMS USED TO REFER TO THE WORD OF GOD

2.   For the sake of clear and precise language on this topic, a definition of terms might well be expected as a prerequisite. Nevertheless this Introduction will simply use the same terms employed in conciliar and postconciliar documents. Furthermore it will use "sacred Scripture" and "word of God" interchangeably throughout when referring to the books written under the inspiration of the Holy Spirit, thus avoiding any confusion of language or meaning.[6]

C. SIGNIFICANCE OF THE WORD OF GOD IN THE LITURGY

3.   The many riches contained in the one word of God are admirably

brought out in the different kinds of liturgical celebrations and liturgical assemblies. This takes place as the unfolding mystery of Christ is recalled during the course of the liturgical year, as the Church's sacraments and sacramentals are celebrated, or as the faithful respond individually to the Holy Spirit working within them.[7] For then the liturgical celebration, based primarily on the word of God and sustained by it, becomes a new event and enriches the word itself with new meaning and power. Thus in the liturgy the Church faithfully adheres to the way Christ himself read and explained the Scriptures, beginning with the "today" of his coming forward in the synagogue and urging all to search the Scriptures.[8]

2. Liturgical celebration of the word of God

A. PROPER CHARACTER OF THE WORD OF GOD IN THE LITURGICAL CELEBRATION

4.   In the celebration of the liturgy the word of God is not voiced in only one way[9] nor does it always stir the hearts of the hearers with the same power. Always, however, Christ is present in his word;[10] as he carries out the mystery of salvation, he sanctifies us and offers the Father perfect worship.[11]

Moreover, the word of God unceasingly calls to mind and extends the plan of salvation, which achieves its fullest expression in the liturgy. The liturgical celebration becomes therefore the continuing, complete, and effective presentation of God's word.

That word constantly proclaimed in the liturgy is always, then, a living, active word[12] through the power of the Holy Spirit. It expresses the Father's love that never fails in its effectiveness toward us.

B. THE WORD OF GOD IN THE PLAN OF SALVATION

5.   When in celebrating the liturgy the Church proclaims both the Old and New Testament, it is proclaiming one and the same mystery of Christ.

The New Testament lies hidden in the Old; the Old Testament comes fully to light in the New.[13] Christ himself is the center and fullness of all of Scripture, as he is of the entire liturgy.[14] Thus the Scriptures are the living waters from which all who seek life and salvation must drink.

The more profound our understanding of the liturgical celebration, the higher our appreciation of the importance of God's word. Whatever we say of the one, we can in turn say of the other, because each recalls the mystery of Christ and each in its own way causes that mystery to be ever present.

C. THE WORD OF GOD IN THE LITURGICAL PARTICIPATION OF THE FAITHFUL

6.   In celebrating the liturgy, the Church faithfully echoes the Amen that Christ, the meditator between God and humanity, uttered once for all

as he shed his blood to seal God's new covenant in the Holy Spirit.[15]

When God shares his word with us, he awaits our response, that is, our listening and our adoring "in Spirit and in truth" (Jn 4:23). The Holy Spirit makes our response effective, so that what we hear in the celebration of the liturgy we carry out in the way we live: "Be doers of the word and not hearers only" (Jas 1:22).

The liturgical celebration and the faithful's participation receive outward expression in actions, gestures, and words. These derive their full meaning not simply from their origin in human experience but from the word of God and the economy of salvation, their point of reference. Accordingly, the faithful's participation in the liturgy increases to the degree that as they listen to the word of God spoken in the liturgy they strive harder to commit themselves to the Word of God made flesh in Christ. They endeavor to conform their way of life to what they celebrate in the liturgy, and then in turn to bring to the celebration of the liturgy all that they do in life.[16]

3. The word of God in the life of the "People of the Covenant"

A. THE WORD OF GOD IN THE CHURCH'S LIFE

7.   In the hearing of God's word the Church is built up and grows, and in the signs of the liturgical celebration God's many wonderful, past works in the history of salvation are symbolically presented anew. God in turn makes use of the assembly of the faithful who celebrate the liturgy in order that his word may speed on in triumph and his name be exalted among all peoples.[17]

Whenever, therefore, the Church, gathered by the Holy Spirit for liturgical celebration,[18] announces and proclaims the word of God, it has the experience of being a new people in whom the covenant made in the past is fulfilled. Baptism and confirmation in the Spirit have made all the faithful messengers of God's word because of the grace of hearing they have received. They must therefore be the bearers of the same word in the Church and in the world, at least by the witness of their way of life.

The word of God proclaimed in the celebration of his mysteries does not address present conditions alone but looks back to past events and forward to what is yet to come. Thus God's word shows us what we should hope for with such a longing that in this changing world our hearts will be set on the place of our true joy.[19]

B. HOW THE WORD OF GOD IS PROPOSED IN THE CHURCH

8.   By Christ's own will there is an ordered diversity of members in the new people of God and each has different duties and responsibilities toward the word of God. Accordingly, the faithful listen to God's word and

dwell on its meaning, but only those expound the word of God who have the office of teaching by virtue of ordination or who have been entrusted with exercising that ministry.

This is how in teaching, life, and worship the Church keeps alive and passes on to every generation all that it is, all that it believes. Thus with the passage of the centuries, the Church is ever to advance toward the fullness of divine truth until God's word is wholly accomplished in it.[20]

C. CONNECTION BETWEEN THE WORD OF GOD PROCLAIMED AND THE WORKING OF THE HOLY SPIRIT.

9.   The working of the Holy Spirit is needed if the word of God is to make what we hear outwardly have its effect inwardly. Because of the Holy Spirit's inspiration and support, the word of God becomes the foundation of the liturgical celebration and the rule and support of all our life.

The working of the Holy Spirit precedes, accompanies, and brings to completion the whole celebration of the liturgy. But the Spirit also brings home[21] to each person individually everything that in the proclamation of the word of God is spoken for the good of the whole assembly of the faithful. In strengthening the unity of all, the Holy Spirit at the same time fosters a diversity of gifts and furthers their multiform operation.

D. CLOSE RELATIONSHIP BETWEEN THE WORD OF GOD AND THE MYSTERY OF THE EUCHARIST

10.   The Church has honored the word of God and the eucharistic mystery with the same reverence, although not with the same worship, and has always and everywhere intended and endorsed such honor. Moved by the example of its Founder, the Church has never ceased to celebrate his paschal mystery of coming together to read "in all the Scriptures the things written about him" (Lk 24:27) and to carry out the work of salvation through the celebration of the memorial of the Lord and through the sacraments. "The preaching of the word is necessary for the sacramental ministry. For the sacraments are sacraments of faith and faith has its origin and sustenance in the word."[22]

The Church is nourished spiritually at the table of God's word and at the table of the eucharist:[23] from the one it grows in wisdom and from the other in holiness. In the word of God the divine covenant is announced; in the eucharist the new and everlasting covenant is renewed. The spoken word of God brings to mind the history of salvation; the eucharist embodies it in the sacramental signs of the liturgy.

It can never be forgotten, therefore, that the divine word read and proclaimed by the Church in the liturgy has as its one goal the sacrifice of the New Covenant and the banquet of grace, that is, the eucharist. The celebration of Mass in which the word is heard and the eucharist is offered and received forms but one single act of divine worship.[24] That act offers the sacrifice of praise to God and makes available to God's creatures the fullness of redemption.

PART ONE

THE WORD OF GOD IN THE CELEBRATION
OF THE MASS

CHAPTER II

CELEBRATION OF THE LITURGY OF THE WORD AT MASS

1. Elements of the liturgy of the word and their rites

11.   "Readings from Scripture and the chants between the readings form the main part of the liturgy of the word. The homily, profession of faith and general intercessions or prayer of the faithful expand and complete this part of the Mass."[25]

A. BIBLICAL READINGS

12.   In the celebration of Mass the biblical readings with their accompanying scriptural chants may not be omitted, shortened, or, worse still, replaced by nonbiblical readings.[26] For it is from the word of God handed down in writing that even now "God is speaking to his people"[27] and it is from the continued use of Scripture that the people of God, docile to the Holy Spirit under the light of faith, receive the power to be Christ's living witnesses before the world.

13.   The reading of the gospel is the high point of the liturgy of the word. For this the other readings, in their established sequence from the Old to the New Testament, prepare the assembly.

14.   A speaking style on the part of the readers that is audible, clear and intelligent is the first means of transmitting the word of God properly to the assembly. The readings, taken from the approved editions,[28] may be sung in a way suited to different languages. This singing, however, must serve to stress the words, not obscure them. On occasions when the readings are in Latin, they are to be sung to the melody given in the *Ordo cantus Missae.*[29]

15.   There may be concise introductions before the readings, especially the first. The style proper to such comments must be respected, that is, they must be simple, faithful to the text, brief, well prepared, and properly varied to suit the text they introduce.[30]

16.   In a Mass with a congregation the readings are always to be proclaimed at the lectern.[31]

17.   Of all the rites connected with the liturgy of the word, the reverence due to the gospel reading must receive special attention.[32] Where there is a Book of the Gospels that has been carried in by the deacon or reader during the entrance procession,[33] it is most fitting that the deacon or a priest, when there is no deacon, take the book from the altar[34] and carry it to the lectern. He is preceded by servers with candles and incense or other symbols of reverence that may be customary. As the faithful stand and acclaim the Lord, they show honor to the Book of the Gospels. The deacon who is to read the gospel, bowing in front of the one presiding, asks and receives the blessing. When no deacon is present, the priest, bowing before the altar, prays quietly: *Almighty God, cleanse my heart* . . .[35]

At the lectern the one who proclaims the gospel greets the people, who are standing, and announces the reading as he makes the sign of the cross on forehead, mouth, and breast. If incense is used, he next incenses the book, then reads the gospel. When finished, he kisses the book, saying the appointed words quietly.

Even if the gospel itself is not sung, it is appropriate for *The Lord be with you, A reading from the holy gospel* . . . , and at the end *This is the Gospel of the Lord* to be sung, in order that the assembly may also sing its acclamations. This is a way both of bringing out the importance of the gospel reading and of stirring up the faith of those who hear it.

18.   At the conclusion of the other readings, *This is the word of the Lord* may be sung, even by someone other than the reader; all respond with the acclamation. In this way the gathered assembly pays reverence to the word of God it has listened to in faith and gratitude.

B. RESPONSORIAL PSALM

19.   The responsorial psalm, also called the gradual, has great liturgical and pastoral significance because it is "an integral part of the liturgy of the word."[36] Accordingly, the people must be continually instructed on the way to perceive the word of God speaking in the psalms and to turn these psalms into the prayer of the Church. This, of course, "will be achieved more readily if a deeper understanding of the psalms, in the meaning in which they are used in the liturgy, is more diligently promoted among the clergy and communicated to all the faithful by means of appropriate catechesis."[37]

A brief remark may be helpful about the choice of the psalm and response as well as their correspondence to the readings.

20.   As a rule the responsorial psalm should be sung. There are two

established ways of singing the psalm after the first reading: responsorially and directly. In responsorial singing, which, as as far as possible, is to be given preference, the psalmist or cantor of the psalm sings the psalm verse and the whole congregation joins in by singing the response. In direct singing of the psalm there is no intervening response by the community; either the psalmist or cantor of the psalm sings the psalm alone as the community listens or else all sing it together.

21.   The singing of the psalm, or even of the response alone, is a great help toward understanding and meditating on the psalm's spiritual meaning.

To foster the congregation's singing, every means available in the various cultures is to be employed. In particular use is to be made of all the relevant options provided in the Order of Readings for Mass[38] regarding responses corresponding to the different liturgical seasons.

22.   When not sung, the psalm after the reading is to be recited in a manner conducive to meditation on the word of God.[39]

The responsorial psalm is sung or recited by the psalmist or cantor at the lectern.[40]

C. ACCLAMATION BEFORE THE READING OF THE GOSPEL

23.   The Alleluia, or, as the liturgical season requires, the verse before the gospel, is also a "rite or act standing by itself."[41] It serves as the assembled faithful's greeting of welcome to the Lord who is about to speak to them and as an expression of their faith through song.

The Alleluia or the verse before the gospel must be sung and during it all stand. It is not to be sung only by the cantor who intones it or by the choir, but by the whole congregation together.[42]

D. HOMILY

24.   Through the course of the liturgical year the homily sets forth the mysteries of faith and the standards of the Christian life on the basis of the sacred text. Beginning with the *Constitution on the Liturgy*, the homily as part of the liturgy of the word[43] has been repeatedly and strongly recommended and in some cases it is obligatory. As a rule it is to be given by the one presiding.[44] The purpose of the homily at Mass is that the spoken word of God and the liturgy of the eucharist may together become "a proclamation of God's wonderful works in the history of salvation, the mystery of Christ."[45] Through the readings and homily Christ's paschal mystery is proclaimed; through the sacrifice of the Mass it becomes present.[46] Moreover Christ himself is also always present and active in the preaching of his Church.[47]

Whether the homily explains the biblical word of God proclaimed in the readings or some other texts of the liturgy,[48] it must always lead the community of the faithful to celebrate the eucharist wholeheartedly, "so that they may hold fast in their lives to what they have grasped by their faith."[49] From this living explanation, the word of God proclaimed in the readings and the Church's celebration of the day's liturgy will have greater impact. But this demands that the homily be truly the fruit of meditation, carefully prepared, neither too long nor too short, and suited to all those present, even children and the uneducated.[50]

At a concelebration, the celebrant or one of the concelebrants as a rule gives the homily.[51]

25.   On the prescribed days, that is, Sundays and holy days of obligation, there must be a homily in all Masses celebrated with a congregation, even Masses on the preceding evening; the homily may not be omitted without a serious reason.[52] There is also to be a homily in Masses with children and with special groups.[53]

A homily is strongly recommended on the weekdays of Advent, Lent, and the Easter season for the sake of the faithful who regularly take part in the celebration of Mass; also on other feasts and occasions when a large congregation is present.[54]

26.   The priest celebrant gives the homily either at the chair, standing or sitting, or at the lectern.[55]

27.   Any necessary announcements are to be kept completely separate from the homily; they must take place following the prayer after communion.[56]

E. SILENCE

28.   The liturgy of the word must be celebrated in a way that fosters meditation; clearly, any sort of haste that hinders reflectiveness must be avoided. The dialogue between God and his people taking place through the Holy Spirit demands short intervals of silence, suited to the assembly, as an opportunity to take the word of God to heart and to prepare a response to it in prayer.

Proper times for silence during the liturgy of the word are, for example, before this liturgy begins, after the first and the second reading, after the homily.[57]

F. PROFESSION OF FAITH

29.   The symbol or profession of faith, said when the rubrics require, has as its purpose in the celebration of Mass that the gathered faithful may respond and give assent to the word of God heard in the readings and

through the homily, and that before they begin to celebrate in the eucharist the mystery of faith, they may call to mind the rule of faith in a formulary approved by the Church.[58]

G. GENERAL INTERCESSIONS OR PRAYER OF THE FAITHFUL

30. Enlightened by God's word and in a sense responding to it, the assembly of the faithful prays in the general intercessions as a rule for the needs of the universal Church and the local community, for the salvation of the world and those oppressed by any burden, and for special categories of people.

The celebrant introduces the prayer; the deacon, another minister, or some of the faithful may propose intentions that are short and phrased with a measure of flexibility. In these petitions "the people, exercising their priestly function, make intercession for all,"[59] with the result that, as the liturgy of the word has its full effects in them, they are better prepared to proceed to the liturgy of the eucharist.

31. For the general intercessions the celebrant presides at the chair and the intentions are announced at the lectern.[60]

The congregation takes part in the general intercessions while standing and by saying or singing a common response after each intention or by silent prayer.[61]

2. Aids to the proper celebration of the liturgy of the word

A. PLACE FOR PROCLAIMING THE WORD OF GOD

32. There must be a place in the church that is somewhat elevated, fixed, and of a suitable design and nobility. It should reflect the dignity of God's word and be a clear reminder to the people that in the Mass the table of God's word and of Christ's body is placed before them.[62] The place for the readings must also truly help the people's listening and attention during the liturgy of the word. Great pains must therefore be taken, in keeping with the design of each church, over the harmonious and close relationship of the lectern with the altar.

33. Either permanently or at least on occasions of greater solemnity, the lectern should be decorated simply and in keeping with its design.

Since the lectern is the place from which the ministers proclaim the word of God, it must of its nature be reserved for the readings, the responsorial psalm, and the Easter proclamation *(Exsultet)*. The lectern may rightly be used for the homily and the general intercessions, however, because of their close connection with the entire liturgy of the word. It is better for the commentator, cantor, or director of singing, for example, not to use the lectern.[63]

34.   In order that the lectern may properly serve its liturgical purpose, it is to be rather large, since on occasion several ministers must use it at the same time. Provisions must also be made for the readers to have enough light to read the text and, as required, to have sound equipment enabling the congregation to hear them without difficulty.

B. BOOKS FOR PROCLAMATION OF THE WORD OF GOD

35.   Along with the ministers, the actions, the lectern, and other elements, the books containing the readings of the word of God remind the hearers of the presence of God speaking to his people. Since, in liturgical celebrations the books too serve as signs and symbols of the sacred, care must be taken to ensure that they truly are worthy and beautiful.[64]

36.   The proclamation of the gospel always stands as the high point of the liturgy of the word. Thus the liturgical traditions of both the East and the West have consistently continued to preserve some distinction between the books for the readings. The Book of the Gospels was always designed with the utmost care and was more ornate and shown greater respect than any of the other books of readings. In our times also, then, it is very desirable that cathedrals and at least the larger, more populous parishes and the churches with a larger attendance possess a beautifully designed Book of the Gospels, separate from the other book of readings. For good reason it is the Book of the Gospels that is presented to the deacon at his ordination and that is laid upon the head of the bishop-elect and held there at his ordination.[65]

37.   Because of the dignity of the word of God, the books of readings used in the celebration are not to be replaced by other pastoral aids, for example, by leaflets printed for the faithful's preparation of the readings or for their personal meditation.

CHAPTER III
OFFICES AND MINISTRIES IN THE CELEBRATION OF THE LITURGY OF THE WORD WITHIN MASS

1. Function of the one presiding at the liturgy of the word

38.   The one presiding at the liturgy of the word brings the spiritual nourishment it contains to those present, especially in the homily. Even if he too is a listener to the word of God proclaimed by others, the duty of proclaiming it has been entrusted above all to him. Personally or through others he sees to it that the word of God is properly proclaimed. He then as a rule reserves to himself the task of composing comments to help the people to listen more attentively and to preach a homily that fosters in them a richer understanding of the word of God.

39.   The first requirement for one who is to preside over the celebration is a thorough knowledge of the structure of the Order of Readings so that he will know how to inspire good effects in the hearts of the faithful. Through study and prayer he must also develop a full understanding of the coordination and connection of the various texts in the liturgy of the word, so that the Order of Readings will become the source of a sound understanding of the mystery of Christ and his saving work.

40.   The one presiding is to make ready use of the various options provided in the Lectionary regarding readings, responses, responsorial psalms, and gospel acclamations;[66] but he is to do so with the agreement[67] of all concerned and after listening to the faithful in regard to what belongs to them.[68]

41.   The one presiding exercises his proper office and the ministry of the word of God also as he preaches the homily.[69] In this way he leads his brothers and sisters to an affective knowledge of holy Scripture. He opens their souls to gratitude for the wonderful works of God. He strengthens their faith in the word that in the celebration becomes a sacrament through the Holy Spirit. Finally, he prepares them for a fruitful reception of communion and invites them to embrace the demands of the Christian life.

42.   The one presiding is responsible for preparing the faithful for the liturgy of the word on occasion by means of introductions before the readings.[70] These comments can help the gathered assembly toward a better hearing of the word of God, because they enliven the people's faith and their desire for good. He may also carry out this responsibility through other persons, the deacon, for example, or a commentator.[71]

43. As he directs the general intercessions and through their introduction and conclusion connects them, if possible, with the day's readings and the homily, the one presiding leads the faithful toward the liturgy of the eucharist.[72]

2. Role of the faithful in the liturgy of the word

44. Christ's word gathers the people of God as one and increases and sustains them. "This applies above all to the liturgy of the word in the celebration of Mass: there is an inseparable union between the proclamation of the death of the Lord, the response of the people listening, and the offering through which Christ has confirmed the New Covenant in his blood. The people share in this offering by their inner intentions and the reception of the sacrament."[73] For "not only when things are read 'that were written for our instruction' (Rom 15:4), but also when the Church prays or sings or acts, the faith of those taking part is nourished and their minds are raised to God, so that they may offer him their worship as intelligent beings and receive his grace more abundantly."[74]

45. In the liturgy of the word, the congregation of the faithful still today receives from God the word of his covenant through the faith that comes by hearing. The faithful must respond to that word in the same faith so that more and more they may become the people of the New Covenant.

The people of God have a spiritual right to receive abundantly from the treasury of God's word. Its riches are presented to them through use of the Order of Readings, the homily, and pastoral efforts.

For their part, the faithful at the celebration of Mass are to listen to the word of God with an inward and outward reverence that will bring them continuous growth in the spiritual life and draw them more deeply into the mystery they celebrate.[75]

46. As a help toward celebrating the memorial of the Lord with devotion, the faithful should be keenly aware of the one presence of Christ in both the word of God—"it is he who speaks when the holy Scriptures are read in the Church"—and "especially under the eucharistic elements."[76]

47. To be received and integrated into the life of Christ's faithful, the word of God demands a living faith.[77] Hearing the word of God unceasingly proclaimed arouses that faith.

The Scriptures, and above all in their liturgical proclamation, are the source of life and power. As Paul attests, the Gospel is the saving power of God for everyone who believes.[78] Love of the Scriptures is therefore the force that renews the entire people of God.[79] All the faithful without exception must therefore always be ready to listen gladly to God's word.[80] When this word is proclaimed in the Church and put into living practice, it enlightens the faithful through the working of the Holy Spirit and draws them into the entire mystery of the Lord as a reality to be lived.[81] The word of God reverently received moves the heart and its desires toward conversion and toward a life filled with both individual and community faith,[82] since God's word is the sustenance of the Christian life and the source of the prayer of the entire Church.[83]

48.   The close connection between the liturgy of the word and the liturgy of the eucharist in the Mass should prompt the faithful to be present right from the beginning of the celebration,[84] to take part attentively, and to dispose themselves to hear the word, especially by learning beforehand more about Scripture. That same connection should also awaken in them a desire for a liturgical understanding of the texts read and for the willingness to respond through singing.[85]

    When they hear the word of God and reflect deeply on it, the faithful receive the power to respond to it actively with full faith, hope, and charity through prayer and self-giving, and not only during Mass but in their entire Christian life.

3. Ministries in the liturgy of the word

49.   Liturgical tradition assigns responsibility for the biblical readings in the celebration of Mass to ministers: to readers and the deacon. But when there is no deacon or another priest present, the priest celebrant is to read the gospel[86] and when there is no reader present, all the readings.[87]

50.   The deacon's part in the liturgy of the word at Mass is to proclaim the gospel, sometimes to give the homily, as occasion suggests, and to propose the intentions of the general intercessions to the people.[88]

51.   "The reader has his own proper function in the eucharistic celebration and should exercise this even though ministers of a higher rank may be present."[89] The reader's ministry, which is conferred through a liturgical rite, must be held in respect. When there are instituted readers available, they are to carry out their office at least on Sundays and major feasts, especially at the principal Mass of the day. These readers may also be given responsibility for assisting in the planning of the liturgy of the word, and, to the extent necessary, of seeing to the preparation of others of the faithful who may be appointed on a given occasion to serve as readers at Mass.[90]

52.   The liturgical assembly truly requires readers, even those not instituted. Proper measures must therefore be taken to ensure that there are qualified laypersons who have been trained to carry out this

ministry.[91] Whenever there is more than one reading, it is better to assign the readings to different readers, if available.

53. In Masses without a deacon, the function of announcing the intentions for the general intercessions is to be assigned to the cantor, particularly when they are to be sung, to a reader, or to another person.[92]

54. During the celebration of Mass with a congregation, a second priest, a deacon, and an instituted reader must wear the distinctive vestment of their office when they go to the lectern to read the word of God. Those who carry out the ministry of reader just for the occasion or even regularly but without institution may go to the lectern in ordinary attire that is in keeping with local custom.

55. "It is necessary that those who exercise the ministry of reader, even if they have not received institution, be truly qualified and carefully prepared so that the faithful may develop a warm and living love for Scripture from listening to the sacred texts read."[93]

Their preparation must above all be spiritual, but what may be called a technical preparation is also needed. The spiritual preparation presupposes at least a biblical and liturgical formation. The purpose of their biblical formation is to give readers the ability to understand the readings in context and to perceive by the light of faith the central point of the revealed message. The liturgical formation ought to equip the readers to have some grasp of the meaning and structure of the liturgy of the word and of the significance of its connection with the liturgy of the eucharist. The technical preparation should make the readers more skilled in the art of reading publicly, either with power of their own voice or with the help of sound equipment.

56. The psalmist, that is the cantor of the psalm, is responsible for singing, responsorially or directly, the chants between the readings—the psalm or other biblical canticle, the gradual and Alleluia, or other chant. The psalmist may, as occasion requires, intone the Alleluia and verse.[94]

For carrying out the function of psalmist it is advantageous to have in each ecclesial community laypersons with a talent for singing and correct diction. The points made about the formation of readers apply to cantors as well.

57. The commentator also fulfills a genuine liturgical ministry, which consists in presenting to the assembly of the faithful, from a suitable place, relevant explanations and comments that are clear, of marked simplicity, meticulously prepared, as a rule written out, and approved beforehand by the celebrant.[95]

PART TWO
STRUCTURE OF THE ORDER OF READINGS
FOR MASS

CHAPTER IV
GENERAL PLAN OF THE READINGS FOR MASS

1. Pastoral Aim of the Order of Readings for Mass

58.   On the basis of the intention of Vatican Council II, the Order of Readings provided by the Lectionary of the Roman Missal has been composed above all for a pastoral purpose. To achieve this aim, not only the principles underlying this new Order of Readings but also the lists of texts that it provides have been discussed and revised over and over again, with the cooperation of a great many experts in exegesis, pastoral studies, catechetics, and liturgy from all parts of the world. The Order of Readings is the fruit of this combined effort.

The prolonged use of this Order of Readings to proclaim and explain sacred Scripture in the eucharistic celebration will, it is hoped, prove to be an effective step toward achieving the objective stated repeatedly by Vatican Council II.[96]

59.   The decision on revising the Lectionary for Mass was to draw up and edit a single, rich, and full Order of Readings that would be in complete accord with the intent and prescriptions of the Council.[97] At the same time, however, the Order was meant to be of a kind that would meet the requirements and usages of particular Churches and liturgical assemblies. For this reason, those responsible for the revision took pains to safeguard the liturgical tradition of the Roman Rite, but valued highly the merits of all the systems of selecting, arranging, and using the biblical readings in other liturgical families and in certain particular Churches. The revisers made use of those elements that experience has confirmed, but with an effort to avoid certain shortcomings found in the preceding form of the tradition.

60.   The present Order of Readings for Mass, then, is an arrangement of biblical readings that provides the faithful with a knowledge of the whole of God's word, in a pattern suited to the purpose. Throughout the liturgical year, but above all during the seasons of Easter, Lent, and Advent, the choice and sequence of readings are aimed at giving the faithful an ever-deepening perception of the faith they profess and of the history of salvation.[98] Accordingly, the Order of Readings corresponds to the requirements and interests of the Christian people.

61.   The celebration of the liturgy is not in itself simply a form of catechesis, but it does contain an element of teaching. The Lectionary of the Roman Missal brings this out[99] and therefore deserves to be regarded as a pedagogical resource aiding catechesis.

This is so because the Order of Readings for Mass aptly presents from Scripture the principal deeds and words belonging to the history of salvation. As its many phases and events are recalled in the liturgy of the word, the faithful will come to see that the history of salvation is contained here and now in the representation of Christ's paschal mystery celebrated through the eucharist.

62.   The pastoral advantage of having in the Roman Rite a single Order of Readings for the Lectionary is obvious on other grounds. All the faithful, particularly those who for various reasons do not always take part in Mass with the same assembly, will everywhere be able to hear the same readings on any given day or in any liturgical season and to reflect on the application of these readings to their own circumstances. This is the case even in places that have no priest and where a deacon or someone else deputed by the bishop conducts a celebration of the word of God.[100]

63.   Pastors may wish to respond specifically from the word of God to the concerns of their own congregations. Although they must be mindful that they are above all to be the heralds of the entire mystery of Christ and the Gospel, they may rightfully use the options provided in the Order of Readings for Mass. This applies particularly to the celebration of a ritual or votive Mass, a Mass in honor of the saints, or one of the Masses for various needs and occasions. In the light of the general norms, special faculties are granted for the readings in Masses with particular groups.[101]

2. Principles Used in Drawing up the Order of Readings for Mass

64.   To achieve the purpose of the Order of Readings for Mass, the parts have been selected and arranged in such a way as to take into account the sequence of the liturgical seasons and the hermeneutical principles discovered and formulated through contemporary biblical research.

It was judged helpful to state here the principles guiding the composition of the Order of Readings for Mass.

A. SELECTION OF TEXTS

65.   The course of readings in the Proper of Seasons is arranged as follows. Sundays and the solemnities of the Lord present the more important biblical passages. In this way the more significant parts of God's revealed word can be read to the assembly of the faithful within a reasonable period of time. Weekdays present a second series of texts from Scripture and in a sense these complement the message of salvation

explained on Sundays and the solemnities of the Lord. But neither series in these main parts of the Order of Readings—the series for Sundays and the solemnities of the Lord and for weekdays—depends on the other. The Order of Readings for Sundays and the solemnities of the Lord extends over three years; for weekdays, over two. Thus each runs its course independently of the other.

The course of readings in other parts of the Order of Readings is governed by its own rules. This applies to the series of readings for celebrations of the saints, ritual Masses, Masses for various needs and occasions, votive Masses, or Masses for the dead.

B. ARRANGEMENT OF THE READINGS FOR SUNDAYS AND SOLEMNITIES OF THE LORD

66.   The following are features proper to the readings for Sundays and the solemnities of the Lord:

1. Each Mass has three readings: the first from the Old Testament, the second from an apostle (that is, either from a letter or from Revelation, depending on the season), and the third from the gospels. This arrangement brings out the unity of the Old and New Testaments and of the history of salvation, in which Christ is the central figure, commemorated in his paschal mystery.

2. A more varied and richer reading of Scripture on Sundays and the solemnities of the Lord results from the three-year cycle provided for these days, in that the same texts are read only every fourth year.[102]

3. The principles governing the Order of Readings for Sundays and the solemnities of the Lord are called the principles of "harmony" and of "semicontinuous reading." One or the other applies according to the different seasons of the year and the distinctive character of the particular liturgical season.

67.   The best instance of harmony between the Old and New Testament readings occurs when it is one that Scripture itself suggests. This is the case when the teaching and events recounted in texts of the New Testament bear a more or less explicit relationship to the teaching and events of the Old Testament. The present order of Readings selects Old Testament texts mainly because of their correlation with New Testament texts read in the same Mass, and particularly with the gospel text.

Harmony of another kind exists between texts of the readings for each Mass during Advent, Lent, and Easter, the seasons that have a distinctive importance or character.

In contrast, the Sundays in Ordinary Time do not have a distinctive character. Thus the texts of both the apostolic and gospel readings are arranged in an order of semicontinuous reading, whereas the Old

Testament reading is harmonized with the gospel.

68.   The decision was made not to extend to Sundays the arrangements suited to the liturgical seasons mentioned, that is, not to have an organic harmony of themes designed to aid homiletic instruction. Such an arrangement would be in conflict with the genuine conception of liturgical celebration. The liturgy is always the celebration of the mystery of Christ and makes use of the word of God on the basis of its own tradition, guided not by merely logical or extrinsic concerns but by the desire to proclaim the Gospel and to lead those who believe to the fullness of the truth.

C. ARRANGEMENT OF THE READINGS FOR WEEKDAYS

69.   The weekday readings have been arranged in the following way:

1. Each Mass has two readings: the first is from the Old Testament or from an apostle (from a letter or Revelation), and during the Easter season from Acts; the second, from the gospels.

2. The yearly cycle for Lent has its proper principles of arrangement, which take into account the baptismal and penitential themes of this season.

3. The cycle for the weekdays of Advent, the Christmas season, and the Easter season is also yearly and the readings thus remain the same each year.

4. For the thirty-four weeks of Ordinary Time, the gospel readings are arranged in a single cycle, repeated each year. But the first reading is arranged in a two-year cycle and is thus read every other year. Year I is used during odd-numbered years; Year II, during even-numbered years.

Like the Order for Sundays and the solemnities of the Lord, then, the weekday Order of Readings is governed by similar application of the principles of harmony and of semicontinuous reading, especially in the case of seasons with their own distinctive character.

D. READINGS FOR CELEBRATIONS OF THE SAINTS

70.   Two groups of readings are provided for celebrations of the saints:

1. The proper of Saints provides the first group, for solemnities, feasts, or memorials and particularly when there are proper texts for such celebrations. Sometimes in the Proper, however, there is a reference to the most appropriate among the texts in the Commons as the one to be given preference.

2. The Commons of Saints provide the second, more extensive group

of readings. There are, first, appropriate texts for the different classes of saints (martyrs, pastors, virgins, etc.), then a great many texts that deal with holiness in general. These are for alternative use whenever the Commons are indicated as the source for the choice of readings.

71.   As to their sequence, all the texts in this part of the Order of Readings appear in the order in which they are to be read at Mass. Thus the Old Testament texts are first, then the texts of an apostle, followed by the psalms and verses between the readings, and finally the texts from the gospels. The rationale of this arrangement is that, unless otherwise noted, the celebrant may choose at will from such texts, in view of the pastoral needs of the assembly taking part in the celebration.

E. READINGS FOR RITUAL MASSES, MASSES FOR VARIOUS NEEDS AND OCCASIONS, VOTIVE MASSES, AND MASSES FOR THE DEAD

72.   For ritual Masses, Masses for various needs and occasions, votive masses, and Masses for the dead, the texts for the readings are arranged as just described, that is, many texts are grouped together in the order of their use, as in the Commons of Saints.

F. MAIN CRITERIA APPLIED IN CHOOSING AND ARRANGING THE READINGS

73.   In addition to the guiding principles already given for the arrangement of readings in the individual parts of the Order of Readings, others of a more general nature are:

1. Reservation of some books on the basis of the liturgical seasons

74.   In this Order of Readings, some biblical books are set aside for particular liturgical seasons on the basis of both the intrinsic importance of subject matter and liturgical tradition. For example, the Western (Ambrosian and Hispanic) and Eastern tradition of reading Acts during the Easter season is respected. This usage results in a clear presentation of how the Church derives the beginning of its entire life from the paschal mystery. Another tradition of both the West and the East that is retained is the reading of the Gospel of John in the latter weeks of Lent and in the Easter season.

Tradition assigns the reading of Isaiah, especially the first part, to Advent. Some texts of this book, however, are read during the Christmas season, to which 1 John is also assigned.

2. Length of texts

75.   A *via media* is followed in regard to the length of texts. A distinction has been made between narratives, which require reading a fairly long

passage but which usually hold the people's attention, and texts that should not be lengthy because of the profundity of their teaching.

In the case of certain rather long texts, longer and shorter versions are provided to suit different situations. The editing of the shorter version has been carried out with great caution.

3. Difficult texts

76.   In readings for Sundays and solemnities, texts that present real difficulties are avoided for pastoral reasons. The difficulties may be objective, in that the texts themselves raise complex literary, critical, or exegetical problems; or, at least to a certain extent, the difficulties may lie in the faithful's ability to understand the texts. But there could be no justification for depriving the faithful of the spiritual riches of certain texts on the grounds of difficulty if its source is the inadequacy either of the religious education that every Christian should have or of the biblical formation that every pastor should have. Often a difficult reading is clarified by its correlation with another in the same Mass.

4. Omission of texts

77.   The omission of verses in readings from Scripture has at times been the practice in many liturgical traditions, including the Roman. Admittedly such omissions may not be made lightly, for fear of distorting the meaning of the text or the intent and style of Scripture. Yet on pastoral grounds it was decided to continue the tradition in the present Order of Readings, but at the same time to ensure that the essential meaning of the text remained intact. One reason for the decision is that otherwise some texts would have been unduly long. It would also have been necessary to omit completely certain readings of high spiritual value for the faithful because those readings include some verse that is unsuitable pastorally or that involves truly difficult problems.

3. Principles to Be Followed in the Use of the Order of Readings

A. OPTIONS IN THE CHOICE OF SOME TEXTS

78.   The Order of Readings sometimes leaves it to the celebrant to choose between alternative texts or to choose one from the several listed together for the same readings. The option seldom exists on Sundays, solemnities, or the greater feasts in order not to obscure the proper character of the particular liturgical season or needlessly interrupt the semicontinuous reading of some biblical book. On the other hand, the option is given readily in celebrations of the saints, in ritual Masses, Masses for various needs and occasions, votive Masses, and Masses for the dead.

These options, together with those indicated in the General Instruction of the Roman Missal and the *Ordo cantus Missae*,[103] have a pastoral aim. In planning the liturgy of the word, then, the priest should consider "the general spiritual good of the assembly rather than his personal outlook. He should be mindful that the choice of texts is to be made in consultation with the ministers and others who have a function in the celebration and should listen to the faithful in regard to the parts that more directly belong to them."[104]

1. The two readings before the gospel

79.   In Masses assigned three readings, the three are to be used. If, however, for pastoral reasons the conference of bishops has permitted use of only two readings,[105] the choice between the two first readings is to be made in such a way as to safeguard the Church's intent to instruct the faithful more completely in the mystery of salvation. Thus, unless the contrary is indicated in the text of the Lectionary, the reading to be chosen as the first reading is the one that is closer to the theme of the gospel, or, in accord with the intent just mentioned, that is more helpful toward a coherent catechesis over an extended period, or that preserves the semicontinuous reading of some biblical book.[106]

2. Long and short forms of texts

80.   A pastoral criterion must also guide the choice between the longer and shorter forms of a text. The main consideration must be the capacity of the hearers to listen profitably either to the longer or to the shorter reading; or to listen to a more complete text that will be explained through the homily.

3. When two texts are provided

81.   When a choice is allowed between alternative texts, whether they are fixed or optional, the first consideration must be the best interests of those taking part. It may be a matter of using the easier text or the one more relevant to the gathered assembly or, as pastoral advantage may suggest, of repeating or replacing a text that is assigned as proper to one celebration and optional to another.

The issue may arise when it is feared that some text will create difficulties for a particular congregation or when the same text would have to be repeated within a few days, as on a Sunday and on a following weekday.

4. Weekday readings

82.   The arrangement of weekday readings provides texts for every day of the week throughout the year. In most cases, therefore, these readings are to be used on their assigned days, unless a solemnity, feast, or memorial with proper readings occurs.[107]

The one using the Order of Readings for weekdays must check to see whether one reading or another from the same biblical book will have to be omitted because of some celebration occurring during the week. With the plan of readings for the entire week in mind, the priest in that case arranges to omit the less significant selections or suitably combines them with other readings, if they contribute to an integral view of a particular theme.

5. Celebrations of the saints

83.   When they exist, proper readings are given for celebrations of the saints, that is, biblical passages about the saint or the event in the saint's life that the Mass is celebrating. Even in the case of a memorial these readings must take the place of the weekday readings for the same day. This Order of Readings makes explicit note of every case of proper readings on a memorial.

In some cases there are accommodated readings, those, namely, that bring out some particular aspect of a saint's spiritual life or apostolate. Use of such readings does not seem binding, except for compelling pastoral reasons. For the most part references are given to readings in the Commons in order to facilitate choice. But these are merely suggestions: in place of an accommodated reading or the particular reading proposed from a Common, any other reading from the Commons referred to may be selected.

The first concern of a priest celebrating with a congregation is the spiritual benefit of the faithful and he will be careful not to impose his personal preference on them. Above all he will make sure not to omit too often or needlessly the readings assigned for each day in the weekday Lectionary: the Church's desire is to provide the faithful with a richer share at the table of God's word.[108]

There are also general readings, that is, those placed in the Commons either for some determined class of saints (martyrs, virgins, pastors, etc.) or for the saints in general. Because in these cases several texts are listed for the same reading, it will be up to the priest to choose the one best suited to the congregation.

In all celebrations of saints the readings may be taken not only from the Commons to which the references are given in each case, but also from the Common of Holy Men and Women, whenever there is special reason for doing so.

84.   For celebrations of the saints:

a. On solemnities and feasts the readings must be those that are given in the Proper or the Commons. For solemnities and feasts of the General Roman Calendar proper readings are always assigned.

b. On solemnities belonging to particular calendars, three readings are to be assigned, unless the conference of bishops has decreed that there are to be only two readings.[109] The first reading is from the Old Testament (but during the Easter season, from Acts or Revelation); the second from an apostle; the third, from the gospels.

c. On feasts and memorials, which have only two readings, the first can be chosen from either the Old Testament or from an apostle; the second is from the gospels. Following the Church's traditional practice, however, the first reading during the Easter season is to be taken from an apostle, the second, as far as possible, from the Gospel of John.

6. Other parts of the Order of Readings

85. In the Order of Readings for ritual Masses the references given are to the texts already published for the individual rites. This obviously does not include the texts belonging to celebrations that must not be integrated with Mass.[110]

86. The Order of Readings for Masses for various needs and occasions, votive Masses, and Masses for the dead provides many texts that can be of assistance in adapting such celebrations to the situation, circumstances, and concerns of the particular groups taking part.[111]

87. In ritual Masses, Masses for various needs and occasions, votive Masses, and Masses for the dead, since many texts are given for the same reading, the choice of readings follows the criteria already indicated for the choice of readings from the Common of Saints.

88. On a day when some ritual Mass is not permitted and the norms in the individual rite allow the choice of one reading from those provided for ritual Masses, the general spiritual welfare of the participants must be the primary consideration.[112]

B. REPSONSORIAL PSALM AND ACCLAMATION BEFORE THE GOSPEL

89. Among the chants between the readings, the psalm after the first reading is very important. As a rule the psalm to be used is the one assigned to the reading. But in the case of readings for the Common of Saints, ritual Masses, Masses for various needs and occasions, votive Masses, and Masses for the dead the choice is left up to the priest celebrating. He will base his choice on the principle of the pastoral benefit of those participating.

But to make it easier for the people to join in the response to the psalm, the Order of Readings lists certain other texts of psalms and responses that have been chosen according to the various seasons or classes of saints. Whenever the psalm is sung, these texts may replace the text corresponding to the reading.[113]

90.   The chant between the second reading and the gospel is either specified in each Mass and correlated with the gospel or else it is left as a choice to be made from those in the series belonging to a liturgical season or to one of the Commons.

91.   During Lent one of the acclamations from those given in the text of the Order of Readings[114] may be used, depending on the occasion. This acclamation is made before and after the verse before the gospel.

> [The forms customary for this acclamation are:
> Praise to you, Lord Jesus Christ, king of endless glory!
> Praise and honor to you, Lord Jesus Christ!
> Glory and praise to you, Lord Jesus Christ!
> Glory to you, Word of God, Lord Jesus Christ!]

CHAPTER V

DESCRIPTION OF THE ORDER OF READINGS

92.   It seems useful to provide here a brief description of the Order of Readings, at least for the principal celebrations and the different seasons of the liturgical year. With these in mind, readings were selected on the basis of the rules already stated. This description is meant to assist priests to understand the structure of the Order of Readings so that their use of it will become more perceptive and the Order of Readings a source of good for Christ's faithful.

1. Advent

A. SUNDAYS

93.   Each gospel reading has a distinctive theme: the Lord's coming at the end of time (First Sunday of Advent), John the Baptist (Second and Third Sunday), and the events that prepared immediately for the Lord's birth (Fourth Sunday).

The Old Testament readings are prophecies about the Messiah and the Messianic age especially from Isaiah.

The readings from an apostle serve as exhortations and as proclamations, in keeping with the different themes of Advent.

B. WEEKDAYS

94.   There are two series of readings: one to be used from the beginning of Advent until 16 December; the other from 17 to 24 December.

In the first part of Advent there are readings from Isaiah, distributed in accord with the sequence of the book itself and including salient texts that are also read on the Sundays. For the choice of the weekday gospel the first reading has been taken into consideration.

On Thursday of the second week the readings of the gospel about John the Baptist begin. The first reading is either a continuation of Isaiah or a text chosen in view of the gospel.

In the last week before Christmas the events that immediately prepared for the Lord's birth are presented from Matthew (Chapter 1) and Luke (Chapter 1). The texts in the first reading, chosen in view of the gospel reading, are from different Old Testament books and include important Messianic prophecies.

2. Christmas season

A. SOLEMNITIES, FEASTS, AND SUNDAYS

95.   For the vigil and the three Masses of Christmas both the prophetic readings and the others have been chosen from the Roman tradition.

The gospel on the Sunday within the octave of Christmas, feast of the Holy Family, is about Jesus' childhood and the other readings are about the virtues of family life.

On the octave of Christmas, solemnity of Mary, Mother of God, the readings are about the Virgin Mother of God and the giving of the holy Name of Jesus.

On the second Sunday after Christmas, the readings are about the mystery of the incarnation.

On Epiphany, the Old Testament reading and the gospel continue the Roman tradition; the text for the reading from the apostolic letters is about the calling of all peoples to salvation.

On the feast of the Baptism of the Lord, the texts chosen are about this mystery.

B. WEEKDAYS

96.   From 29 December on, there is a continuous reading of the whole of 1 John, which actually begins earlier, on 27 December, feast of St. John the Evangelist, and on 28 December, feast of the Holy Innocents. The gospels relate manifestations of the Lord: events of Jesus' childhood from Luke (29–30 December); passages from John 1 (31 December–5 January); other manifestations from the four gospels (7–18 January).

3. Lent

97.   The gospel readings are arranged as follows:

The first and second Sundays retain the accounts of the Lord's temptations and transfiguration, with readings, however, from all three Synoptics.

On the next three Sundays, the gospels about the Samaritan woman, the man born blind, and the raising of Lazarus have been restored in Year A. Because these gospels are of major importance in regard to Christian initiation, they may also be read in Year B and Year C, especially in places where there are catechumens.

Other texts, however, are provided for Year B and Year C: for Year B, a text from John about Christ's coming glorification through his cross and resurrection and for Year C, a text from Luke about conversion.

On Passion Sunday (Palm Sunday) the texts for the procession are selections from the Synoptic Gospels concerning the Lord's triumphal entrance into Jerusalem. For the Mass the reading is the account of the Lord's passion.

The Old Testament readings are about the history of salvation, which is one of the themes proper to the catechesis of Lent. The series of texts for each Year presents the main elements of salvation history from its beginning until the promise of the New Covenant.

The readings from the letters of the apostles have been selected to fit the gospel and the Old Testament readings and, to the extent possible, to provide a connection between them.

B. WEEKDAYS

98.   The readings from the gospels and the Old Testament were selected because they are related to each other. They treat various themes of the Lenten catechesis that are suited to the spiritual significance of this season. Beginning with Monday of the fourth week of Lent, there is a semicontinuous reading of the Gospel of John, made up of texts that correspond more closely to the themes proper to Lent.

Because the readings about the Samaritan woman, the man born blind, and the raising of Lazarus are now assigned to Sundays, but only for Year A (in Year B and Year C they are optional), provision has been made for their use on weekdays. Thus at the beginning of the Third, Fourth, and Fifth Weeks of Lent optional Masses with these texts for the gospel have been inserted and may be used in place of the readings of the day on any weekday of the respective week.

In the first half of Holy Week the readings are about the mystery of Christ's passion. For the chrism Mass the readings bring out both Christ's messianic mission and its continuation in the Church by means of the sacraments.

4. The Easter triduum and the Easter season

A. THE EASTER TRIDUUM

99.   On Holy Thursday at the evening Mass the remembrance of the supper preceding Christ's departure casts its own special light because of the Lord's example in washing the feet of his disciples and Paul's account of the institution of the Christian Passover in the eucharist.

On Good Friday the liturgical service has as its center John's narrative of the passion of him who was portrayed in Isaiah as the Servant of Yahweh and who became the one High Priest by offering himself to the Father.

On the holy night of the Easter Vigil there are seven Old Testament readings, recalling the wonderful works of God in the history of salvation. There are two New Testament readings, the announcement of the resurrection according to one of the Synoptic Gospels and a reading from St. Paul on Christian baptism as the sacrament of Christ's resurrection.

The gospel reading for the Mass on Easter day is from John on the finding of the empty tomb. There is also, however, the option to use the gospel texts from the Easter Vigil or, when there is an evening Mass on Easter Sunday, to use the account in Luke of the Lord's appearance to the disciples on the road to Emmaus. The first reading is from Acts, which throughout the Easter season replaces the Old Testament reading. The reading from St. Paul concerns the living out of the paschal mystery in the Church.

B. SUNDAYS

100. The gospel readings for the first three Sundays recount the appearances of the risen Christ. The readings about the Good Shepherd are assigned to the Fourth Sunday. On the Fifth, Sixth, and Seventh Sundays, there are excerpts from the Lord's discourse and prayer at the last supper.

The first reading is from Acts, in a three-year cycle of parallel and progressive selections: material is presented on the life of the primitive Church, its witness, and its growth.

For the reading from the apostles, 1 Peter is in Year A, 1 John in Year B, Revelation in Year C. These are the texts that seem to fit in especially well with the spirit of joyous faith and sure hope proper to this season.

101. As on the Sundays, the first reading is a semicontinuous reading from Acts. The gospel readings during the Easter octave are accounts of the Lord's appearances. After that there is a semicontinuous reading of the Gospel of John, but with texts that have a paschal character in order to complete the reading from John during Lent. This paschal reading is made up in large part of the Lord's discourse and prayer at the last supper.

D. SOLEMNITIES OF THE ASCENSION AND PENTECOST

102. For the first reading the solemnity of the Ascension retains the account of the Ascension according to Acts. This text is complemented by the second reading from the apostolic reflections on Christ in exaltation at the right hand of the Father. For the gospel reading, each of the three Years has its own text in accord with the differences in the Synoptic Gospels.

In the evening Mass celebrated on the vigil of Pentecost four Old Testament texts are provided; any one of them may be used, in order to bring out the many aspects of Pentecost. The reading from the apostles shows the actual working of the Holy Spirit in the Church. The gospel reading recalls the promise of the Spirit made by Christ before his own glorification.

For the Mass on Pentecost itself, in accord with received usage, the account in Acts of the great occurrence on Pentecost is taken as the first reading. The texts from Paul bring out the effect of the action of the Holy Spirit in the life of the Church. The gospel reading is a remembrance of Jesus bestowing his Spirit on the disciples on Easter evening; other optional texts describe the action of the Spirit on the disciples and on the Church.

5. Ordinary Time

A. ARRANGEMENT AND CHOICE OF TEXTS

103. Ordinary Time begins on the Monday after the Sunday following 6 January; it lasts until the Tuesday before Lent inclusive. It begins again on the Monday after Pentecost Sunday and finishes before evening prayer I of the first Sunday of Advent.

The Order of Readings provides readings for thirty-four Sundays and the weeks following them. In some years, however, there are only thirty-three weeks of Ordinary Time. Further, some Sundays either belong to another season (the Sunday on which the feast of the Baptism of the Lord falls and Pentecost) or else are impeded by a solemnity that coincides with Sunday (for example, Holy Trinity or Christ the King).

104. For the correct arrangement in the use of the readings for Ordinary Time, the following are to be respected:

1. The Sunday on which the feast of the Baptism of the Lord falls replaces the first Sunday in Ordinary Time. Therefore the readings of the First Week of Ordinary Time begin on the Monday after the Sunday following 6 January. When the feast of the Baptism of the Lord is celebrated on Monday because Epiphany has been celebrated on the Sunday, the readings of the First Week begin on Tuesday.

2. The Sunday following the feast of the Baptism of the Lord is the Second Sunday of Ordinary Time. The remaining Sundays are numbered consecutively up to the Sunday preceding the beginning of Lent. The readings for the week in which Ash Wednesday falls are suspended after the Tuesday readings.

3. For the resumption of the readings of Ordinary Time after Pentecost Sunday:

—When there are thirty-four Sundays in Ordinary Time, the week to be used is the one that immediately follows the last week used before Lent.[115]

—When there are thirty-three Sundays in Ordinary Time, the first week that would have been used after Pentecost is omitted in order to reserve for the end of the year the eschatological texts that are assigned to the last two weeks.[116]

B. SUNDAY READINGS

1) Gospel readings

105. On the Second Sunday of Ordinary Time the gospel continues to center on the manifestation of the Lord, which Epiphany celebrates through the traditional passage about the wedding feast at Cana and two other passages from John.

Beginning with the Third Sunday, there is a semicontinuous reading of the Synoptic Gospels. This reading is arranged in such a way that as the Lord's life and preaching unfold the teaching proper to each of these Gospels is presented.

This distribution also provides a certain coordination between the meaning of each Gospel and the progress of the liturgical year. Thus after Epiphany the readings are on the beginning of the Lord's preaching and they fit in well with Christ's baptism and the first events in which he manifests himself. The liturgical year leads quite naturally to a termination in the eschatological theme proper to the last Sundays, since the chapters of the Synoptics that precede the account of the passion treat this eschatological theme rather extensively.

After the Sixteenth Sunday in Year B, five readings are incorporated from John 6 (the discourse on the bread of life). This is the proper place for these readings because the multiplication of the loaves from John takes the place of the same account in Mark. In the semicontinuous reading of Luke for Year C, the introduction of this Gospel has been prefixed to the first text (that is, on the Third Sunday). This passage expresses the author's intention very beautifully and there seemed to be no better place for it.

2. Old Testament readings

106. These readings have been chosen to correspond to the gospel passages in order to avoid an excessive diversity between the readings of different Masses and above all to bring out the unity between the Old and New Testament. The relationship between the readings of the same Mass is shown by a precise choice of the headings prefixed to the individual readings.

To the degree possible, the readings were chosen in such a way that they would be short and easy to grasp. But care has been taken to ensure that many Old Testament texts of major significance would be read on Sundays. Such readings are distributed not according to logical order but on the basis of what the gospel reading requires. Still, the treasury of the word of God will be opened up in such a way that nearly all the principal pages of the Old Testament will become familiar to those taking part in the Mass on Sundays.

3. Readings from the apostles

107. There is a semicontinuous reading of the Letters of Paul and James. (The Letters of Peter and John are read during the Easter and Christmas seasons.)

Because it is quite long and deals with such diverse issues, the First Letter to the Corinthians has been spread over the three years of the cycle at the beginning of Ordinary Time. It also was thought best to divide Hebrews into two parts; the first part is read in Year B and the second part in Year C.

Only readings that are short and readily grasped by the people have been chosen.

Table II at the end of this Introduction[117] indicates the distribution of letters of the apostles over the three-year cycle of the Sundays of Ordinary Time.

C. READINGS FOR SOLEMNITIES OF THE LORD DURING ORDINARY TIME

108. On the solemnities of Holy Trinity, Corpus Christi, and the Sacred Heart, the texts chosen correspond to the principal themes of these celebrations.

The readings of the Thirty-Fourth and last Sunday of Ordinary Time celebrate Christ the King. He was prefigured by David and heralded as king amid the humiliations of his passion and cross; he reigns in the Church and will come again at the end of time.

D. WEEKDAY READINGS

109. 1) The *gospels* are so arranged that Mark is read first (First to Ninth Week), then Matthew (Tenth to Twenty-first Week), then Luke (Twenty-second to Thirty-fourth Week). Mark 1–12 are read in their entirety, with the exception only of the two passages of Mark 6 that are read on weekdays in other seasons. From Matthew and Luke the readings comprise all the matters not contained in Mark. From all three Synoptics or from two of them, as the case may be, all those passages are read that either are distinctively presented in each Gospel or are needed for a proper understanding of its progression. Jesus' eschatological discourse as contained in its entirety in Luke is read at the end of the liturgical year.

110. 2) The first *reading* is taken in periods of weeks first from the Old then from the New Testament; the number of weeks depends on the length of the biblical books read.

Rather large selections are read from the New Testament books in order to give the substance, as it were, of each of the letters of the apostles.

From the Old Testament there is room only for select passages that, as far as possible, bring out the character of the individual books. The historical texts have been chosen in such a way as to provide an overall view of the history of salvation before the Lord's incarnation. But lengthy narratives could hardly be presented; sometimes verses have been selected that make for a reading of moderate length. In addition, the religious significance of the historical events is sometimes brought out by means of certain texts from the wisdom books that are placed as prologues or conclusions to a series of historical readings.

Nearly all the Old Testament books have found a place in the Order of Readings for weekdays in the Proper of Seasons. The only omissions are the shortest of the prophetic books (Obadiah and Zephaniah) and the poetic book (Song of Solomon). Of those narratives written to edify and requiring a rather long reading to be understood, Tobit and Ruth are included, but Esther and Judith are omitted. (Texts from these two books are assigned to Sundays and weekdays at other times of the year.)

Table III at the end of this Introduction[118] lists the way the books of the Old and the New Testament are distributed over the weekdays in Ordinary Time in the course of two years.

At the end of the liturgical year the readings are from Daniel and

Revelation, the books that correspond to the eschatological character of this period.

CHAPTER VI
ADAPTATIONS, TRANSLATIONS, AND FORMAT
OF THE ORDER OF READINGS

1. Adaptations and translations

111. In the liturgical assembly the word of God must always be read either from the Latin texts prepared by the Holy See or from vernacular translations approved by the conferences of bishops for liturgical use, according to existing norms.[119]

112. The Lectionary for Mass must be translated integrally in all its parts, including the Introduction. If the conference of bishops has judged it necessary and useful to add certain adaptations, these are to be incorporated after their confirmation by the Holy See.[120]

113. The size of the Lectionary will necessitate editions in more than one volume, no particular division of the volumes is prescribed. But each volume is to contain the explanatory texts on the structure and purpose of the section it contains.

The ancient custom is recommended of having separate books, one for the gospels and the other for the readings for the Old and the New Testament.

It may also be useful to publish separately a Sunday lectionary, which could also contain selected excerpts from the sanctoral cycle, and a weekday lectionary. A practical basis for dividing the Sunday lectionary is the three-year cycle, so that all the readings for each year are presented in sequence.

But there is freedom to adopt other arrangements that may be devised and seem to have pastoral advantages.

114. The texts for the chants are always to be adjoined to the readings, but separate books containing the chants alone are permitted. It is recommended that the texts be printed with divisions into stanzas.

115. Whenever a text consists of different parts, the typography must make this structure of the text clear. It is likewise recommended that even nonpoetic texts be printed with division into sense lines to assist the proclamation of the readings.

116. Where there are long and short forms of a text, they are to be

printed separately so that each can be read and with ease. But if such a separation does not seem feasible, a way is to be found to ensure that each text can be proclaimed without mistakes.

117. In vernacular editions the texts are not to be printed without the headings prefixed. If it seems advisable, an introductory note on the general meaning of the passage may be added to the heading. This note is to carry some distinctive symbol or is to be set in different type to show clearly that it is an optional text.[121]

118. It would be useful for every volume to have an index of the passages of the Bible, modeled on the biblical index of the present volume.[122] This will provide ready access to texts of the lectionaries for Mass that may be needed or helpful for specific occasions.

2. Format of individual readings

For each reading the present volume carries the textual reference, the heading, and the *incipit*.

A. TEXT REFERENCES

119. The text reference (that is, chapter and verse) is always given according to the Neo-Vulgate edition, except for the psalms.[123] But a second reference according to the original text (Hebrew, Aramaic, or Greek) has been added wherever there is a discrepancy. Depending on the decrees of the competent authorities for the individual languages, vernacular versions may retain the enumeration corresponding to the version of the Bible approved for liturgical use by the same authorities. Exact references to chapter and verses, however, must always appear and may be given in the text or in the margin.

120. These references provide liturgical books with the source of the "announcement" *(inscriptio)* of the text that must be read in the celebration, but which is not printed in this volume. This "announcement" of the text will observe the following norms, but they may be altered by decree of the competent authorities on the basis of what is customary and useful for different places and languages.

121. 1) The formula to be used is always: "A *reading* from the Book of . . .," "A *reading* from the Letter of . . .," or "A *reading* from the Gospel of . . .," and not: "The *beginning* of . . ." (unless this seems advisable in particular instances) or: "*Continuation* of . . ."

122. 2) The traditionally accepted titles for books are to be retained, with the following exceptions:

a. Where there are two books with the same name, the title is to be:

The First Book, The Second Book (e.g., of Kings, of Maccabees) or The First Letter, The Second Letter.

b. The title more common in current usage is to be accepted for the following books:
I and II Samuel instead of I and II Kings;
I and II Kings instead of III and IV Kings;
I and II Chronicles instead of I and II Paralipomenon;
Books of Ezra and Nehemiah instead of I and II Ezra.

c. The distinguishing titles for the wisdom books are: Book of Job, Book of Proverbs, Book of Ecclesiastes or Qoheleth, Song of Songs, Book of Wisdom, Book of Ecclesiasticus or Sirach.

d. For all the books that are included among the prophets in the Neo-Vulgate, the formula is to be: "A reading from the Book of Isaiah, or of Jeremiah or of Baruch" and: "A reading from the Prophecy of Ezekiel, of Daniel, of Hosea, of Malachi," even in the case of books not universally regarded as in fact prophetic.

e. The title is to be Book of Lamentations and Letter to the Hebrews, with no mention of Jeremiah and Paul.

B. HEADING

123. There is a *heading* prefixed to each text, chosen carefully (usually from the words of the text itself) in order to point out the main theme of the reading and, when necessary, to make the connection between the readings of the same Mass clear.

C. INCIPIT

124. In this Order of Readings the first element of the *incipit* is the customary introductory phrase, "At that time," "In those days," "Brothers and Sisters," "Dearly Beloved," or "Thus says the Lord." These words are not given when the text itself provides sufficient indication of the time or the persons involved or where such phrases would not fit in with the very nature of the texts. For the individual languages, such phrases may be changed or dropped by decree of the competent authorities.

After the first words of the *incipit* the Order of Readings gives the proper *beginning of the reading,* with some words deleted or supplied for intelligibility, inasmuch as the text is separated from its context. When the text for a reading is made up of nonconsecutive verses and this has required changes in wording, these are appropriately indicated.

D. FINAL ACCLAMATION

125. In order to facilitate the congregation's acclamation, the words for the reader, *This is the word of the Lord,* or similar words suited to local custom, are to be printed at the end of the reading for use by the reader.

TABLES

TABLE I

Seasonal Table of Principal Celebrations of the Liturgical Year

YEAR	SUNDAY CYCLE	WEEKDAY CYCLE	ASH WEDNESDAY	EASTER	ASCENSION	PENTECOST
1985	B	I	20 Feb	7 April	16 May	26 May
1986	C	II	12 Feb	30 March	8 May	18 May
1987	A	I	4 March	19 April	28 May	7 June
1988	B	II	17 Feb	3 April	12 May	22 May
1989	C	I	8 Feb	26 March	4 May	14 May
1990	A	II	28 Feb	15 April	24 May	3 June
1991	B	I	13 Feb	31 March	9 May	19 May
1992	C	II	4 March	19 April	28 May	7 June
1993	A	I	24 Feb	11 April	20 May	30 May
1994	B	II	16 Feb	3 April	12 May	22 May
1995	C	I	1 March	16 April	25 May	4 June
1996	A	II	21 Feb	7 April	16 May	26 May
1997	B	I	12 Feb	30 March	8 May	18 May
1998	C	II	25 Feb	12 April	21 May	31 May
1999	A	I	17 Feb	4 April	13 May	23 May
2000	B	II	8 March	23 April	1 June	11 June

| WEEKS OF ORDINARY TIME | | | | |
| BEFORE LENT | | AFTER EASTER SEASON | | 1ST SUNDAY |
ENDING	IN WEEK NO.	BEGINNING	IN WEEK NO.	OF ADVENT
19 Feb	6	27 May	8	1 Dec
11 Feb	5	19 May	7	30 Nov
3 March	8	8 June	10	29 Nov
16 Feb	6	23 May	8	27 Nov
7 Feb	5	15 May	6	3 Dec
27 Feb	8	4 June	9	2 Dec
12 Feb	5	20 May	7	1 Dec
3 March	8	8 June	10	29 Nov
23 Feb	7	31 May	9	28 Nov
15 Feb	6	23 May	8	27 Nov
28 Feb	8	5 June	9	3 Dec
20 Feb	7	27 May	8	1 Dec
11 Feb	5	19 May	7	30 Nov
24 Feb	7	1 June	9	29 Nov
16 Feb	6	24 May	8	28 Nov
7 March	9	12 June	10	3 Dec

TABLE II

Arrangement of the Second Reading on the Sundays of Ordinary Time

SUNDAY	YEAR A	YEAR B	YEAR C
2	1 Corinthians 1–4	1 Corinthians 6–11	1 Corinthians 12–15
3	"	"	"
4	"	"	"
5	"	"	"
6	"	"	"
7	"	2 Corinthians	"
8	"	"	"
9	Romans	"	Galatians
10	"	"	"
11	"	"	"
12	"	"	"
13	"	"	"
14	"	"	"
15	"	Ephesians	Colossians
16	"	"	"
17	"	"	"
18	"	"	"
19	"	"	Hebrews 11–12
20	"	"	"
21	"	"	"
22	"	James	"
23	"	"	Philemon
24	"	"	1 Timothy
25	Philippians	"	"
26	"	"	"
27	"	Hebrews 2–10	2 Timothy
28	"	"	"
29	1 Thessalonians	"	"
30	"	"	"
31	"	"	2 Thessalonians
32	"	"	"
33	"	"	"

TABLE III

Arrangement of the First Reading on the Weekdays of Ordinary Time

WEEK	YEAR I	YEAR II
1	Hebrews	1 Samuel
2	"	"
3	"	2 Samuel
4	"	2 Samuel; 1 Kings 1–16
5	Genesis 1–11	1 Kings 1–16
6	"	James
7	Sirach (Ecclesiasticus)	"
8	"	1 Peter; Jude
9	Tobit	2 Peter; 2 Timothy
10	2 Corinthians	1 Kings 17–22
11	"	1 Kings 17–22; 2 Kings
12	Genesis 12–50	2 Kings; Lamentations
13	"	Amos
14	"	Hosea; Isaiah
15	Exodus	Isaiah; Micah
16	"	Micah; Jeremiah
17	Exodus; Leviticus	Jeremiah
18	Numbers; Deuteronomy	Jeremiah; Nahum; Habakkuk
19	Deuteronomy; Joshua	Ezekiel
20	Judges; Ruth	"
21	1 Thessalonians	2 Thessalonians; 1 Corinthians
22	1 Thessalonians; Colossians	1 Corinthians
23	Colossians; 1 Timothy	"
24	1 Timothy	"
25	Ezra; Haggai; Zechariah	Proverbs, Qoheleth (Ecclesiastes)
26	Zechariah; Nehemiah; Baruch	Job
27	Jonah; Malachi; Joel	Galatians
28	Romans	Galatians; Ephesians
29	"	Ephesians
30	"	"
31	"	Ephesians; Philippians
32	Wisdom	Titus; Philemon; 2 and 3 John
33	1 and 2 Maccabees	Revelation
34	Daniel	"

NOTES

1. See CSL 7, 24, 33, 35, 48, 51, 52, 56; DV 21, 25, 26; AG 6; PO 18.
2. See MQ, no. V; EN 28, 43, 47; CTr 23, 27, 48; DC 10.
3. See EM 10; LI 2; GCD 10–12, 25; GI 9, 11, 24, 33, 60, 62, 316, 320; ID 1, 2, 3.
4. See Lectionary for Mass, Introduction (1969) nos. 1–7; decree of promulgation: AAS 61 (1969) 548–549.
5. See CSL 35, 56; EN 28, 47; DC 10, 11, 12.
6. For example, the terms: *word of God, sacred Scripture, Old and New Testament, reading(s) of the word of God, reading(s) from sacred scripture, celebration(s) of the word of God,* etc.
7. Thus the same text may be read or used for diverse reasons on diverse occasions and celebrations of the liturgical year; this has to be remembered in the homily, pastoral exegesis, and catechesis.
8. See Lk 4: 16–21; 24:25–35 and 44–49.
9. In the celebration of the Mass, for example, there is *proclamation, reading,* etc. (see GI 21, 23, 95, 131, 146, 234, 235). There are also other celebrations of the word of God in the Roman Pontifical, Roman Ritual and Liturgy of the Hours.
10. See CSL 7, 33; Mk 16:19–20; Mt 28:20.
11. See CSL 7.
12. See Heb 4:12.
13. See Augustine, *Quaestionum in Heptateuchum,* bk. 2, 73: PL 34, 623; DV 16.
14. See Jerome, *Commentarii in Isaiam prophetam* prologue: PL 24, 17A; DV 25.
15. See 2 Cor 1:20–22.
16. See CSL 10.
17. See 2 Thes 3:1.
18. See RM, opening prayers A, B and C in Mass for the Universal Church.
19. See RM, opening prayer for the Twenty-first Sunday in Ordinary Time.
20. See DV 8.
21. See Jn 14: 15–17, 25–26; 15:26–16:15.
22. See PO 4.
23. See CSL 51; PO 18; DV 21; AG 6; GI 8.
24. CSL 56.
25. GI 33.
26. See LI 2; DC 10; ID 1.
27. CSL 33.
28. See LMIn 111.
29. See *Missale Romanum* ex Decreto Sacrosancti Oecumenici Concilii Vaticani II instaurantum, *Ordo cantus Missae* (ed. typ., 1972) Praenotanda, nos. 4, 6, 10.
30. See GI 11.
31. See GI 272; LMIn 32–34.
32. See GI 35, 95.
33. See GI 82–84.
34. See GI 94, 131.
35. See RM, Order of Mass, "Liturgy of the Word: The Gospel."
36. See GI 36.
37. Paul VI, apostolic constitution, *Laudis canticum,* The Liturgy of the Hours; see CSL 24, 90; MS 39.
38. See LMIn 89–90.
39. See GI 18, 39.
40. See GI 272; LMIn 32ff.
41. See GI 39.
42. See GI 37–39; *Ordo cantus Missae, Praenotanda,* nos. 7–9; *Graduale Romanum* (1974), *Praenotanda,* no. 7, *Graduale Simplex* (2d *ed. typ.,* 1975), *Praenotanda,* no. 16.
43. See CSL 52; IOe 54.
44. See GI 42.
45. See CSL 35,2.
46. See CSL 6, 47.
47. See Paul VI, encyclical, *Mysterium fidei,* 3 Sept 1965: AAS 57 (1965) 753: AG 9; EN 43.
48. See CSL 35,2; GI 41.
49. CSL 10.
50. See CTr 48.
51. See GI 165.
52. See GI 42; EM 28.
53. See AP 6g; DMC 48.
54. See GI 42, 338; RR, Rite of Marriage

(1969), 22, 42, 57 and Rite of Funerals (1969), 41, 64.

55. See GI 97.
56. See GI 139.
57. See GI 23.
58. See GI 43.
59. See GI 45.
60. See GI 99.
61. See GI 47.
62. See LMIn, note 23.
63. See GI 272.
64. See SCL 122.
65. See *Roman Pontifical*, Ordination of Deacons, Priests and Bishops (1968): of deacons, 24; of deacons and priests, 21; of a deacon, 24; of a bishop, 25; of bishops, 25.
66. See LMIn 78–91.
67. See GI 318–320; 324–325.
68. See GI 313.
69. See GI 42; ID 3.
70. See GI 11.
71. See GI 68.
72. See GI 33, 47.
73. PO 4.
74. CSL 33.
75. GI 9.
76. CSL 7.
77. CSL 9.
78. See Rom 1:16.
79. See DV 21.
80. *Ibid.*
81. See Jn 14:15–26; 15:26–16:4, 5–15.
82. See AG 6, 15; DV 26.
83. See CSL 24; GCD 25.
84. See CSL 56; ID 1.
85. See CSL 24, 35.
86. See GI 34.
87. See GI 96.
88. See GI 47, 61, 132; ID 3.
89. GI 66.
90. See MQ, no. V.
91. See ID 2, 18; DMC 22, 24, 27.
92. See GI 47, 66, 151.
93. GI 66.
94. See GI 37a, 67.

95. See GI 68.
96. See Paul VI, apostolic constitution, *RM*.
97. See CSL 35, 51.
98. See Paul VI, apostolic constitution, *RM*.
99. See CSL 9, 33; IOe 7; CTr 23.
100. See CSL 35,4; IOe 37–38.
101. See AP 6; DMC 41–47; Paul VI, apostolic exhortation *Marialis cultus*, 2 Feb 1974, no. 12: AAS 66 (1974) 125–126.
102. Each of the years is designated by a letter, A, B or C.
    The following is the procedure to determine which year is A, B, or C. The letter C designates a year whose number is divisible into three equal parts, as though the cycle had taken its beginning from the first year of the Christian era. Thus the year 1 would have been Year A; year 2, Year B; year 3, Year C, (as would years, 6, 9 and 12). Thus, year 1980 was Year C; 1981, Year A; 1982, Year B; and 1983, Year C. Each cycle runs in accord with the plan of the liturgical year, that is, it begins with the first week of Advent which falls in the preceding year of the civil calendar. The distinguishing characteristic for the years in each cycle is based in a sense on the principal note of the synoptic gospel (Matthew, Mark or Luke) used for the semicontinuous reading of Ordinary Time.
103. See GI 36–40.
104. GI 313.
105. See GI 318; ID 1.
106. For example: in Lent the continuity of the Old Testament readings corresponds to the unfolding of the history of salvation; the Sundays in Ordinary Time provide the semicontinuous reading of one of the letters of the apostles. In these cases it is right that the priest choose one or other of the readings in a systematic way over a series of Sundays so that he may set up a coherent plan for catechesis. It is not right to read indiscriminately on one day from the Old Testament, on another from the

letter of an apostle, without any orderly plan for subsequent texts.

107. See GI 319.

108. See GI 316c; CSL 51.

109. See GI 318.

110. See RR, Rite of Penance (1974), introduction, no. 13.

111. See GI 320.

112. See GI 313.

113. See Lectionary for Mass, nos. 173–174.

114. See Lectionary for Mass, no. 224.

115. So when there are six weeks before Lent, the seventh week begins on the Monday after Pentecost. The solemnity of the Holy Trinity replaces the Sunday of Ordinary Time.

116. When there are five weeks before Lent, the Monday after Pentecost begins with the seventh week of Ordinary Time and the sixth week is dropped.

117. See LMIn, Table II.

118. See LMIn, Table III.

119. See Consilium, instruction *De Popularibus interpretationibus conficiendis*, 25 Jan 1969: Notitiae 5 (1969) 3–12; CDW, *Epistola ad Praesides Conferentiarum Episcoporum de linguis vulgaribus in S. Liturgiam inducendis:* Notitiae 12 (1976) 300–302.

120. See LI 11; GI 325.

121. See GI 11, 29, 68a, 139.

122. See Lectionary for Mass, index of readings.

123. The references for the psalms follow the order of the *Liber Psalmorum,* Pontifical Commission for the Neo-Vulgate.

GENERAL NORMS
FOR THE
LITURGICAL YEAR
AND
CALENDAR

March 1969

BACKGROUND

This 1969 document is concerned with the church's keeping of the feasts and seasons. It establishes the original feast day, our Sunday, in its place of primacy, and goes on to explain the system for ranking other days. In speaking of the year, the first consideration is the Easter Triduum, around which are kept the seasons of Eastertime and Lent. These seasons are centered on the paschal mystery and its presence in the initiation practices of the church. The document also notes the structure of the Advent and Christmas seasons and goes into great detail on the calendar of the local church.

The *General Norms* might well be studied in conjunction with the *Lectionary for Mass: Introduction*, especially chapter 5 of that document, "Description of the Order of Readings," in which the character of each season is discussed in light of its scriptures.

This document also includes the day-by-day calendar of feasts (this can be found in the sacramentary as well).

OUTLINE

GENERAL NORMS FOR THE LITURGICAL YEAR
AND THE CALENDAR

CHAPTER I
THE LITURGICAL YEAR

1.   Christ's saving work is celebrated in sacred memory by the Church on fixed days throughout the year. Each week on the day called the Lord's Day the Church commemorates the Lord's resurrection. Once a year at Easter the Church honors this resurrection and passion with the utmost solemnity. In fact through the yearly cycle the Church unfolds the entire mystery of Christ and keeps the anniversaries of the saints.

During the different seasons of the liturgical year, the Church, in accord with traditional discipline, carries out the formation of the faithful by means of devotional practices, both interior and exterior, instruction, and works of penance and mercy.[1]

2.   The principles given here may and must be applied to both the Roman Rite and all others; but the practical rules are to be taken as pertaining solely to the Roman Rite, except in matters that of their nature also affect the other rites.[2]

TITLE I: LITURGICAL DAYS

I. The Liturgical Day in General

3.   Each day is made holy through the liturgical celebrations of the people of God, especially through the eucharistic sacrifice and the divine office.

The liturgical day runs from midnight to midnight, but the observance of Sunday and solemnities begins with the evening of the preceding day.

II. Sunday

4.   The Church celebrates the paschal mystery on the first day of the week, known as the Lord's Day or Sunday. This follows a tradition handed down from the apostles and having its origin from the day of Christ's resurrection. Thus Sunday must be ranked as the first holy day of all.[3]

5.   Because of its special importance, the Sunday celebration gives way only to solemnities or feasts of the Lord. The Sundays of the seasons of Advent, Lent, and Easter, however, take precedence over all solemnities and feasts of the Lord. Solemnities occurring on these Sundays are observed on the Saturday preceding.

6.   By its nature, Sunday excludes any other celebration's being permanently assigned to that day, with these exceptions:

    a.   Sunday within the octave of Christmas is the feast of the Holy Family;

    b.   Sunday following 6 January is the feast of the Baptism of the Lord;

    c.   Sunday after Pentecost is the solemnity of the Holy Trinity;

    d.   The last Sunday in Ordinary Time is the solemnity of Christ the King.

7.   In those places where the solemnities of Epiphany, Ascension, and Corpus Christi are not observed as holy days of obligation, they are assigned to a Sunday, which is then considered their proper day in the calendar. Thus:

    a.   Epiphany, to the Sunday falling between 2 January and 8 January;

    b.   Ascension, to the Seventh Sunday of Easter;

    c.   the solemnity of Corpus Christi, to the Sunday after Trinity Sunday.

III. Solemnities, Feasts, and Memorials

8.   As it celebrates the mystery of Christ in yearly cycle, the Church also venerates with a particular love Mary, the Mother of God, and sets before the devotion of the faithful the memory of the martyrs and other saints.[4]

9.   The saints of universal significance have celebrations obligatory throughout the entire Church. Other saints either are listed in the General Calendar for optional celebration or are left to the veneration of some particular Church, region, or religious family.[5]

10.   According to their importance, celebrations are distinguished from each other and named as follows: solemnities, feasts, memorials.

11.   Solemnities are counted as the principal days in the calendar and their observance begins with evening prayer I of the preceding day. Some also have their own vigil Mass for use when Mass is celebrated in the evening of the preceding day.

12. The celebration of Easter and Christmas, the two greatest solemnities, continues for eight days, with each octave governed by its own rules.

13. Feasts are celebrated within the limits of the natural day and accordingly do not have evening prayer I. Exceptions are feasts of the Lord that fall on a Sunday in Ordinary Time and in the Christmas season and that replace the Sunday office.

14. Memorials are either obligatory or optional. Their observance is integrated into the celebration of the occurring weekday in accord with the norms set forth in the General Instruction of the Roman Missal and the Liturgy of the Hours.

Obligatory memorials occurring on Lenten weekdays may only be celebrated as optional memorials.

Should more than one optional memorial fall on the same day, only one may be celebrated; the others are omitted.

15. On Saturdays in Ordinary Time when there is no obligatory memorial, an optional memorial of the Blessed Virgin Mary is allowed.

IV. Weekdays

16. The days following Sunday are called weekdays. They are celebrated in different ways according to the importance each one has.

a. Ash Wednesday and the days of Holy Week, from Monday to Thursday inclusive, have precedence over all other celebrations.

b. The weekdays of Advent from 17 December to 24 December inclusive and all the weekdays of Lent have precedence over obligatory memorials.

c. All other weekdays give way to solemnities and feasts and are combined with memorials.

TITLE II: THE YEARLY CYCLE

17. By means of the yearly cycle the Church celebrates the whole mystery of Christ, from his incarnation until the day of Pentecost and the expectation of his coming again.[6]

I. Easter Triduum

18. Christ redeemed us all and gave perfect glory to God principally through his paschal mystery: dying he destroyed our death and rising he

restored our life. Therefore the Easter triduum of the passion and resurrection of Christ is the culmination of the entire liturgical year.[7] Thus the solemnity of Easter has the same kind of preeminence in the liturgical year that Sunday has in the week.[8]

19.   The Easter triduum begins with the evening Mass of the Lord's Supper, reaches its high point in the Easter Vigil, and closes with evening prayer on Easter Sunday.

20.   On Good Friday[9] and, if possible, also on Holy Saturday until the Easter Vigil,[10] the Easter fast is observed everywhere.

21.   The Easter Vigil, during the holy night when Christ rose from the dead, ranks as the "mother of all vigils."[11] Keeping watch, the Church awaits Christ's resurrection and celebrates it in the sacraments. Accordingly, the entire celebration of this vigil should take place at night, that is, it should either begin after nightfall or end before the dawn of Sunday.

II. Easter Season

22.   The fifty days from Easter Sunday to Pentecost are celebrated in joyful exultation as one feast day, or better as one "great Sunday."[12]

These above all others are the days for the singing of the Alleluia.

23.   The Sundays of this season rank as the paschal Sundays, and after Easter Sunday itself, are called the Second, Third, Fourth, Fifth, Sixth, and Seventh Sundays of Easter. The period of fifty sacred days ends on Pentecost Sunday.

24.   The first eight days of the Easter season make up the octave of Easter and are celebrated as solemnities of the Lord.

25.   On the fortieth day after Easter the Ascension is celebrated, except in places where, not being a holy day of obligation, it has been transferred to the Seventh Sunday of Easter (see no. 7).

26.   The weekdays after the Ascension until the Saturday before Pentecost inclusive are a preparation for the coming of the Holy Spirit.

III. Lent

27.   Lent is a preparation for the celebration of Easter. For the Lenten liturgy disposes both catechumens and the faithful to celebrate the paschal mystery: catechumens, through the several stages of Christian initiation; the faithful, through reminders of their own baptism and through penitential practices.[13]

28.   Lent runs from Ash Wednesday until the Mass of the Lord's Supper exclusive.

The Alleluia is not used from the beginning of Lent until the Easter Vigil.

29.   On Ash Wednesday, a universal day of fast,[14] ashes are distributed.

30.   The Sundays of this season are called the First, Second, Third, Fourth, and Fifth Sundays of Lent. The Sixth Sunday, which marks the beginning of Holy Week, is called Passion Sunday (Palm Sunday).

31.   Holy Week has as its purpose the remembrance of Christ's passion, beginning with his Messianic entrance into Jerusalem.

At the chrism Mass on Holy Thursday morning the bishop, concelebrating Mass with his body of priests, blesses the oils and consecrates the chrism.

IV. Christmas Season

32.   Next to the yearly celebration of the paschal mystery, the Church holds most sacred the memorial of Christ's birth and early manifestations. This is the purpose of the Christmas season.

33.   The Christmas season runs from evening prayer I of Christmas until the Sunday after Epiphany or after 6 January, inclusive.

34.   The Mass of the vigil of Christmas is used in the evening of 24 December, either before or after evening prayer I.

On Christmas itself, following an ancient tradition of Rome, three Masses may be celebrated: namely, the Mass at Midnight, the Mass at Dawn, and the Mass during the Day.

35.   Christmas has its own octave, arranged as follows:

a.   Sunday within the octave is the feast of the Holy Family;

b.   26 December is the feast of Saint Stephen, First Martyr;

c.   27 December is the feast of Saint John, Apostle and Evangelist;

d.   28 December is the feast of the Holy Innocents;

e.   29, 30, and 31 December are days within the octave;

f.   1 January, the octave day of Christmas, is the solemnity of Mary, Mother of God. It also recalls the conferral of the holy Name of Jesus.

36.   The Sunday falling between 2 January and 5 January is the Second Sunday after Christmas.

37. Epiphany is celebrated on 6 January, unless (where it is not observed as a holy day of obligation) it has been assigned to the Sunday occurring between 2 January and 8 January (see no. 7).

38. The Sunday falling after 6 January is the feast of the Baptism of the Lord.

V. Advent

39. Advent has a twofold character: as a season to prepare for Christmas when Christ's first coming to us is remembered; as a season when that remembrance directs the mind and heart to await Christ's Second Coming at the end of time. Advent is thus a period for devout and joyful expectation.

40. Advent begins with evening prayer I of the Sunday falling on or closest to 30 November and ends before evening prayer I of Christmas.

41. The Sundays of this season are named the First, Second, Third, and Fourth Sundays of Advent.

42. The weekdays from 17 December to 24 December inclusive serve to prepare more directly for the Lord's birth.

VI. Ordinary Time

43. Apart from those seasons having their own distinctive character, thirty-three or thirty-four weeks remain in the yearly cycle that do not celebrate a specific aspect of the mystery of Christ. Rather, especially on the Sundays, they are devoted to the mystery of Christ in all its aspects. This period is known as Ordinary Time.

44. Ordinary time begins on Monday after the Sunday following 6 January and continues until Tuesday before Ash Wednesday inclusive. It begins again on Monday after Pentecost and ends before evening prayer I of the First Sunday of Advent.

This is also the reason for the series of liturgical texts found in both the Roman Missal and *The Liturgy of the Hours* (Vol. III–IV), for Sundays and weekdays in this season.

VII. Rogation and Ember Days

45. On rogation and ember days the practice of the Church is to offer prayers to the Lord for the needs of all people, especially for the productivity of the earth and for human labor, and to give him public thanks.

46.   In order to adapt the rogation and ember days to various regions and the different needs of the people, the conference of bishops should arrange the time and plan of their celebration.

Consequently, the competent authority should lay down norms, in view of the local conditions, on extending such celebrations over one or several days and on repeating them during the year.

47.   On each day of these celebrations the Mass should be one of the votive Masses for various needs and occasions that is best suited to the intentions of the petitioners.

CHAPTER II
THE CALENDAR
TITLE I: CALENDAR AND CELEBRATIONS TO BE ENTERED

48.   The arrangement for celebrating the liturgical year is governed by the calendar: the General Calendar, for use in the entire Roman Rite, or a particular calendar, for use in a particular Church or in families of religious.

49.   In the General Calendar the entire cycle of celebrations is entered: celebrations of the mystery of salvation as found in the Proper of Seasons, of those saints having universal significance who must therefore be celebrated by everyone or of saints who show the universality and continuity of holiness within the people of God.

Particular calendars have more specialized celebrations, arranged to harmonize with the general cycle.[15] The individual Churches or families of religious should show a special honor to those saints who are properly their own.

Particular calendars, drawn up by the competent authority, must be approved by the Apostolic See.

50.   The drawing up of a particular calendar is to be guided by the following considerations:

a.   The Proper of Seasons (that is, the cycle of seasons, solemnities, and feasts that unfold and honor the mystery of redemption during the liturgical year) must be kept intact and retain its rightful preeminence over particular celebrations.

b.   Particular celebrations must be coordinated harmoniously with universal celebrations, with care for the rank and precedence indicated for each in the Table of Liturgical Days. Lest particular calendars be enlarged disproportionately, individual saints may have only one feast in the liturgical year. For persuasive pastoral reasons there may be another celebration in the form of an optional memorial marking the transfer or discovery of the bodies of patrons or founders of Churches or of families of religious.

c. Feasts granted by indult may not duplicate other celebrations already contained in the cycle of the mystery of salvation, nor may they be multiplied out of proportion.

51. Although it is reasonable for each diocese to have its own calendar and propers for the Mass and office, there is no reason why entire provinces, regions, countries, or even larger areas may not have common calendars and propers, prepared with the cooperation of all the parties involved.

This principle may also be followed in the case of the calendars for several provinces of religious within the same civil territory.

52. A particular calendar is prepared by inserting in the General Calendar special solemnities, feasts, and memorials proper to that calendar:

a. in a diocesan calendar, in addition to celebrations of its patrons and the dedication of the cathedral, the saints and the blessed who bear some special connection with that diocese, for example, as their birthplace, residence over a long period, or place of death;

b. in the calendar of religious, besides celebrations of their title, founder, or patron, those saints and blesseds who were members of that religious family or had some special relationship with it;

c. in a calendar for individual churches, celebrations proper to a diocese or religious community, those celebrations that are proper to that church and are listed in the Table of Liturgical Days and also the saints who are buried in that church. Members of religious communities should join with the community of the local Church in celebrating the anniversary of the dedication of the cathedral and the principal patrons of the place and of the larger region where they live.

53. When a diocese or religious family has the distinction of having many saints and blessed, care must be taken not to overload the calendar of the entire diocese or institute. Consequently:

a. The first measure that can be taken is to have a common feast of all the saints and the blessed of a given diocese or religious family or of some category.

b. Only the saints and blessed of particular significance for an entire diocese or religious family may be entered in the calendar with an individual celebration.

c. The other saints or blessed are to be celebrated only in those places with which they have closer ties or where their bodies are buried.

54. Proper celebrations should be entered in the calendar as obligatory or optional memorials, unless other provisions have been made for them in the Table of Liturgical Days or there are special historical or pastoral reasons. But there is no reason why some celebrations may not be observed with greater solemnity in some places than in the rest of the diocese or religious community.

55. Celebrations entered in a particular calendar must be observed by all who are bound to follow that calendar. Only with the approval of the Apostolic See may celebrations be removed from a calendar or changed in rank.

TITLE II: THE PROPER DATE FOR CELEBRATIONS

56. The Church's practice has been to celebrate the saints on the date of their death ("birthday"), a practice it would be well to follow when entering proper celebrations in particular calendars.

Even though proper celebrations have special importance for individual local Churches or religious families, it is of great advantage that there be as much unity as possible in the observance of solemnities, feasts, and obligatory memorials listed in the General Calendar.

In entering proper celebrations in a particular calendar, therefore, the following are to be observed:

a. Celebrations listed in the General Calendar are to be entered on the same date in a particular calendar, with a change in rank of celebration if necessary.

This also applies to diocesan or religious calendars when celebrations proper to an individual church alone are added.

b. Celebrations for saints not included in the General Calendar should be assigned to the date of their death. If the date of death is not known, the celebrations should be assigned to a date associated with the saint on some other grounds, such as the date of ordination or of the discovery or transfer of the saint's body; otherwise it is celebrated on a date unimpeded by other celebrations in that particular calendar.

c. If the date of death or other appropriate date is impeded in the General Calendar or in a particular calendar by another obligatory celebration, even of lower rank, the celebrations should be assigned to the closest date not so impeded.

d. If, however, it is a question of celebrations that cannot be transferred to another date because of pastoral reasons, the impeding celebration should itself be transferred.

e. Other celebrations, called feasts granted by indult, should be entered on a date more pastorally appropriate.

f. The cycle of the liturgical year should stand out with its full preeminence, but at the same time the celebration of the saints should not be permanently impeded. Therefore, dates that most of the time fall during Lent and the octave of Easter, as well as the weekdays between 17 December and 31 December, should remain free of any particular celebration, unless it is a question of optional memorials, feasts found in the Table of Liturgical Days under no. 8 a, b, c, d, or solemnities that cannot be transferred to another season.

The solemnity of Saint Joseph (19 March), except where it is observed as a holy day of obligation, may be transferred by the conference of bishops to another day outside Lent.

57. If some saints or blessed are listed in the calendar on the same date, they are always celebrated together whenever they are of equal rank, even though one or more of them may be more proper to that calendar. If one or other of these saints or blessed is to be celebrated with a higher rank, that office alone is observed and the others are omitted, unless it is appropriate to assign them to another date in the form of an obligatory memorial.

58. For the pastoral advantage of the people, it is permissible to observe on the Sundays in Ordinary Time those celebrations that fall during the week and have special appeal to the devotion of the faithful, provided the celebrations take precedence over these Sundays in the Table of Liturgical Days. The Mass for such celebrations may be used at all the Masses at which a congregation is present.

59. Precedence among liturgical days relative to the celebration is governed solely by the following table.

TABLE OF LITURGICAL DAYS
ACCORDING TO THEIR ORDER OF PRECEDENCE

I

1. Easter triduum of the Lord's passion and resurrection.

2. Christmas, Epiphany, Ascension, and Pentecost.
   Sundays of Advent, Lent, and the Easter season.
   Ash Wednesday.
   Weekdays of Holy Week from Monday to Thursday inclusive.
   Days within the octave of Easter.

3. Solemnities of the Lord, the Blessed Virgin Mary, and saints listed in the General Calendar.
   All Souls.

4. Proper solemnities, namely:
   a. Solemnity of the principal patron of the place, that is, the city or state.
   b. Solemnity of the dedication of a particular church and the anniversary.
   c. Solemnity of the title of a particular church.
   d. Solemnity of the title, or of the founder, or of the principal patron of a religious order or congregation.

II

5. Feasts of the Lord in the General Calendar.

6. Sundays of the Christmas season and Sundays in Ordinary Time.

7. Feasts of the Blessed Virgin Mary and of the saints in the General Calendar.

8. Proper feasts, namely:
   a. Feast of the principal patron of the diocese.
   b. Feast of the anniversary of the dedication of the cathedral.
   c. Feast of the principal patron of a region or province, or a country, or of a wider territory.
   d. Feast of the title, founder, or principal patron of an order or congregation and of a religious province, without prejudice to the directives in no. 4.
   e. Other feasts proper to an individual church.
   f. Other feasts listed in the calendar of a diocese or of a religious order or congregation.

9. Weekdays of Advent from 17 December to 24 December inclusive.
Days within the octave of Christmas.
Weekdays of Lent.

III

10. Obligatory memorials in the General Calendar.

11. Proper obligatory memorials, namely:

a. Memorial of a secondary patron of the place, diocese, region, or province, country or wider territory, or of an order or congregation and of a religious province.

b. Obligatory memorials listed in the calendar of a diocese, or of an order or congregation.

12. Optional memorials; but these may be celebrated even on the days listed in no. 9, in the special manner described by the General Instruction of the Roman Missal and of the Liturgy of the Hours.

In the same manner obligatory memorials may be celebrated as optional memorials if they happen to fall on the Lenten weekdays.

13. Weekdays of Advent up to 16 December inclusive.

Weekdays of the Christmas season from 2 January until the Saturday after Epiphany.

Weekdays of the Easter season from Monday after the octave of Easter until the Saturday before Pentecost inclusive.

Weekdays in Ordinary Time.

---

60. If several celebrations fall on the same day, the one that holds the highest rank according to the preceding Table of Liturgical Days is observed. But a solemnity impeded by a liturgical day that takes precedence over it should be transferred to the closest day not listed in nos. 1–8 in the table of the precedence; the rule of no. 5 remains in effect. Other celebrations are omitted that year.

61. If the same day were to call for celebration of evening prayer of that day's office and evening prayer I of the following day, evening prayer of the day with the higher rank in the Table of Liturgical Days takes precedence; in cases of equal rank, evening prayer of the actual day takes precedence.

NOTES

1. See CSL 102–105.
2. See CSL 5.
3. See CSL 106.
4. See CSL 103–104.
5. See CSL 111.
6. See CSL 102.
7. See CSL 5.
8. See CSL 106.
9. See Paul VI, apostolic constitution, *Paenitemini* [=P], 17 Feb 1966, II, §3: AAS 58 (1966) 184.
10. See CSL 110.
11. Augustine, Sermo 219: PL 38, 1088.
12. Athanasius, *Epist. Fest.* 1: PG 26, 1366.
13. See CSL 109.
14. See P, II, §3.
15. See CDW, instruction, *Calendaria particularia,* 24 June 1970: AAS 62 (1970) 651–663.

DIRECTORY FOR MASSES
WITH CHILDREN

November 1973

BACKGROUND

The importance of this 1973 document goes far beyond its title (as might be guessed from the fact that it is always to be printed in the front matter of the sacramentary). The Introduction and first chapter are especially important in the approach they take to the place of ritual celebration in the life of the family and the local church. Nearly every sentence in the brief first chapter is worth reflection and discussion, not only for application to school or family Masses, but for grasping the role of ritual within the community.

Chapters 2 and 3 offer fine insight into the ministries and order of the Mass. Realism and humor are not lacking (as in #16: "Infants who as yet are unable or *unwilling* [italics added] to take part in the Mass . . . "). Most remarkable is the sense that the ministers and planners, once they grasp and respect the structure of the liturgy, will understand how that structure is to serve the assembly.

The document was published before the three English eucharistic prayers for Masses with children were available. The final part of #52 is speaking of this previous situation.

OUTLINE

DIRECTORY FOR MASSES WITH CHILDREN
November 1973

INTRODUCTION

1.   The Church must show special concern for baptized children who have yet to be fully initiated through the sacraments of confirmation and eucharist as well as for children who have only recently been admitted to holy communion. Today the circumstances in which children grow up are not favorable to their spiritual progress.[1] In addition parents sometimes scarcely fulfill the obligations they accepted at the baptism of their children to bring them up as Christians.

2.   In the upbringing of children in the Church a special difficulty arises from the fact that liturgical celebrations, especially the eucharist, cannot fully exercise their inherent pedagogical force upon children.[2] Although the vernacular may now be used at Mass, still the words and signs have not been sufficiently adapted to the capacity of children.

In fact, even in daily life children do not always understand all their experiences with adults but rather may find them boring. It cannot therefore be expected of the liturgy that everything must always be intelligible to them. Nonetheless, we may fear spiritual harm if over the years children repeatedly experience in the Church things that are barely comprehensible: recent psychological study has established how profoundly children are formed by the religious experience of infancy and early childhood, because of the special religious receptivity proper to those years.[3]

3.   The Church follows its Master, who "put his arms around the children . . . and blessed them" (Mk 10:16). It cannot leave children in the condition described. Vatican Council II had spoken in the *Constitution on the Liturgy* about the need of liturgical adaptation for various groups.[4] Soon afterwards, especially in the first Synod of Bishops held in Rome in 1967, the Church began to consider how participation by children could be easier. On the occasion of the Synod, the President of the Consilium for the Implementation of the *Constitution on the Liturgy* said explicitly that it could not be a matter of "creating some entirely special rite but rather of

retaining, shortening, or omitting some elements or of making a better selection of texts."[5]

4.   All the details of eucharistic celebration with a congregation were determined in the General Instruction of the revised Roman Missal published in 1969. Then this Congregation began to prepare a special Directory for Masses with Children, as a supplement to the General Instruction. This was done in response to repeated petitions from the entire Catholic world and with the cooperation of men and women specialists from almost every nation.

5.   Like the *General Instruction of the Roman Missal*, this Directory reserves some adaptations to the conference of bishops or to individual bishops.[6]

     Some adaptations of the Mass may be necessary for children in a given country but cannot be included in a general directory. In accord with the *Constitution on the Liturgy* art. 40, the conferences of bishops are to propose such adaptations to the Aposotlic See for introduction into the liturgy with its consent.

6.   The Directory is concerned with children who have not yet entered the period of preadolescence. It does not speak directly of children who are physically or mentally handicapped, because a broader adaptation is sometimes necessary for them.[7] Nevertheless, the following norms may also be applied to the handicapped, with the necessary changes.

7.   The first chapter of the Directory (nos. 8–15) gives a kind of foundation by considering the different ways in which children are introduced to the eucharistic liturgy. The second chapter briefly treats Masses with adults in which children also take part (nos. 16–19). Finally, the third chapter (nos. 20–54) treats at greater length Masses with children in which only some adults take part.

CHAPTER I

THE INTRODUCTION OF CHILDREN TO THE EUCHARISTIC
CELEBRATION

8.   A fully Christian life is inconceivable without participation in the liturgical services in which the faithful, gathered into a single assembly, celebrate the paschal mystery. Therefore, the religious initiation of children must be in harmony with this purpose.[8] The Church baptizes children and therefore, relying on the gifts conferred by this sacrament, it must be concerned that once baptized they grow in communion with

Christ and each other. The sign and pledge of that communion is participation in the eucharistic table, for which children are being prepared or led to a deeper realization of its meaning. This liturgical and eucharistic formation may not be separated from their general education, both human and Christian; indeed it would be harmful if their liturgical formation lacked such a basis.

9.   For this reason all who have a part in the formation of children should consult and work together toward one objective: that even if children already have some feeling for God and the things of God, they may also experience in proportion to their age and personal development the human values that are present in the eucharistic celebration. These values include the community activity, exchange of greetings, capacity to listen and to seek and grant pardon, expression of gratitude, experience of symbolic actions, a meal of friendship, and festive celebration.[9]

Eucharistic catechesis, dealt with in no. 12, should develop such human values. Then, depending on their age and their psychological and social situation, children will gradually open their minds to the perception of Christian values and the celebration of the mystery of Christ.[10]

10.   The Christian family has the greatest role in instilling these Christian and human values.[11] Thus Christian education, provided by parents and other educators, should be strongly encouraged in relation to the liturgical formation of children as well.

By reason of the duty in conscience freely accepted at the baptism of their children, parents are bound to teach them gradually how to pray. This they do by praying with them each day and by introducing them to prayers said privately.[12] If children, prepared in this way even from their early years, take part in the Mass with their family when they wish, they will easily begin to sing and to pray in the liturgical community and indeed will already have some initial idea of the eucharistic mystery.

If the parents are weak in faith but still wish their children to receive Christian formation, they should be urged at least to communicate to their children the human values mentioned already, and when the occasion arises, to participate in meetings of parents and in noneucharistic celebrations held with children.

11.   The Christian communities to which the individual families belong or in which the children live also have a responsibility toward children baptized in the Church. By giving witness to the Gospel, living communal charity, and actively celebrating the mysteries of Christ, the Christian community is an excellent school of Christian and liturgical formation for the children who live in it.

Within the Christian community, godparents or other persons noted for their dedicated service can, out of apostolic zeal, contribute greatly to the necessary catechesis in the case of families that fail in their obligation toward the children's Christian upbringing.

Preschool programs, Catholic schools, and various kinds of associations for children serve these same ends in a special way.

12.   Even in the case of children, the liturgy itself always exerts its own inherent power to instruct.[13] Yet within religious-education programs in the schools and parishes the necessary importance should be given to catechesis on the Mass.[14] This catechesis should be directed to the child's active, conscious, and authentic participation.[15] "Suited to children's age and capabilities, it should, by means of the main rites and prayers of the Mass, aim at conveying its meaning, including what relates to taking part in the Church's life."[16] This is especially true of the text of the eucharistic prayer and of the acclamations by which the children take part in this prayer.

The catechesis preparing children for first communion calls for special mention. In it they should learn not only the truths of faith regarding the eucharist but also how from first communion on—after being prepared according to their capacity by penance—they can as full members of Christ's Body take part actively with the people of God in the eucharist, sharing in the Lord's table and the community of their brothers and sisters.

13.   Various kinds of celebrations may also play a major role in the liturgical formation of children and in their preparation for the Church's liturgical life. By the very fact of such celebrations children easily come to appreciate some liturgical elements, for example, greetings, silence, and common praise (especially when this is sung together). But care must be taken that the instructive element does not become dominant in these celebrations.

14.   Depending on the capacity of the children, the word of God should have a greater and greater place in these celebrations. In fact, as the children's spiritual capacity develops, celebrations of the word of God in the strict sense should be held frequently, especially during Advent and Lent.[17] These will help greatly to develop in the children an appreciation of the word of God.

15.   While all that has been said remains true, the final purpose of all liturgical and eucharistic formation must be a greater and greater conformity to the Gospel in the daily life of the children.

CHAPTER II
MASSES WITH ADULTS IN WHICH CHILDREN ALSO PARTICIPATE

16.   In many places parish Masses are celebrated, especially on Sundays and holy days, at which a good many children take part along with the large number of adults. On such occasions the witness of adult believers can have a great effect upon the children. Adults can in turn benefit spiritually from experiencing the part that the children have within the Christian community. The Christian spirit of the family is greatly fostered when children take part in these Masses together with their parents and other family members.

Infants who as yet are unable or unwilling to take part in the Mass may be brought in at the end of Mass to be blessed together with the rest of the community. This may be done, for example, if parish helpers have been taking care of them in a separate area.

17.   Nevertheless, in Masses of this kind it is necessary to take great care that the children present do not feel neglected because of their inability to participate or to understand what happens and what is proclaimed in the celebration. Some account should be taken of their presence: for example, by speaking to them directly in the introductory comments (as at the beginning and the end of Mass) and at some point in the homily.

Sometimes, moreover, if the place itself and the nature of the community permit, it will be appropriate to celebrate the liturgy of the word, including a homily, with the children in a separate, but not too distant, room. Then, before the eucharistic liturgy begins, the children are led to the place where the adults have meanwhile celebrated their own liturgy of the word.

18.   It may also be very helpful to give some tasks to the children. They may, for example, bring forward the gifts or perform one or other of the songs of the Mass.

19.   If the number of children is large, it may at times be suitable to plan the Mass so that it corresponds more closely to the needs of the children. In this case the homily should be directed to them but in such a way that adults may also benefit from it. Wherever the bishop permits, in addition to the adaptations already provided in the Order of Mass, one or other of the particular adaptations described later in the Directory may be employed in a Mass celebrated with adults in which children also participate.

CHAPTER III
MASSES WITH CHILDREN IN WHICH ONLY A FEW ADULTS
PARTICIPATE

20.   In addition to the Masses in which children take part with their parents and other family members (which are not always possible everywhere), Masses with children in which only a few adults take part are recommended, especially during the week. From the beginning of the liturgical reform it has been clear to everyone that some adaptations are necessary in these Masses.[18]

Such adaptations, but only those of a more general kind, will be considered later (numbers 38–54).

21.   It is always necessary to keep in mind that these eucharistic celebrations must lead children toward the celebration of Mass with adults, especially the Masses at which the Christian community must come together on Sundays.[19] Thus, apart from adaptations that are necessary because of the children's age, the result should not be entirely special rites, markedly different from the Order of Mass celebrated with a congregation.[20] The purpose of the various elements should always correspond with what is said in the *General Instruction of the Roman Missal* on individual points, even if at times for pastoral reasons an absolute *identity* cannot be insisted upon.

OFFICES AND MINISTRIES IN THE CELEBRATION

22.   The principles of active and conscious participation are in a sense even more significant for Masses celebrated with children. Every effort should therefore be made to increase this participation and to make it more intense. For this reason as many children as possible should have special parts in the celebration: for example; preparing the place and the altar (see no. 29), acting as cantor (see no. 24), singing in a choir, playing musical instruments (see no. 32), proclaiming the readings (see nos. 24 and 27), responding during the homily (see no. 48), reciting the intentions of the general intercessions, bringing the gifts to the altar, and performing similar activities in accord with the usage of various peoples (see no. 34).

To encourage participation, it will sometimes be helpful to have several additions, for example, the insertion of motives for giving thanks before the priest begins the dialogue of the preface.

In all this, it should be kept in mind that external activities will be fruitless and even harmful if they do not serve the internal participation of the children. Thus religious silence has its importance even in Masses with children (see no. 37). The children should not be allowed to forget that all the forms of participation reach their high point in eucharistic communion, when the body and blood of Christ are received as spiritual nourishment.[21]

23. It is the responsibility of the priest who celebrates with children to make the celebration festive, familial, and meditative.[22] Even more than in Masses with adults, the priest is the one to create this kind of attitude, which depends on his personal preparation and his manner of acting and speaking with others.

The priest should be concerned above all about the dignity, clarity, and simplicity of his actions and gestures. In speaking to the children he should express himself so that he will be easily understood, while avoiding any childish style of speech.

The free use of introductory comments[23] will lead children to a genuine liturgical participation, but these should be more than mere explanatory remarks.

It will help him to reach the hearts of the children if the priest sometimes expresses the invitations in his own words, for example, at the penitential rite, the prayer over the gifts, the Lord's Prayer, the sign of peace, and communion.

24. Since the eucharist is always the action of the entire ecclesial community, the participation of at least some adults is desirable. These should be present not as monitors but as participants, praying with the children and helping them to the extent necessary.

With the consent of the pastor or rector of the church, one of the adults may speak to the children after the gospel, especially if the priest finds it difficult to adapt himself to the mentality of children. In this matter the norms soon to be issued by the Congregation for the Clergy should be observed.

Even in Masses with children attention is to be paid to the diversity of ministries so that the Mass may stand out clearly as the celebration of a community.[24] For example, readers and cantors, whether children or adults, should be employed. In this way a variety of voices will keep the children from becoming bored.

PLACE AND TIME OF CELEBRATION

25. The primary place for the eucharistic celebration for children is the church. Within the church, however, a space should be carefully chosen if available, that will be suited to the number of participants. It should be a place where the children can act with a feeling of ease according to the requirements of a living liturgy that is suited to their age.

If the church does not satisfy these demands, it will sometimes be suitable to celebrate the eucharist with children outside a place of worship. But in that case the place chosen should be appropriate and worthy of the celebration.[25]

26.   The time of day chosen for Masses with children should correspond to the circumstances of their lives so that they may be most open to hearing the word of God and to celebrating the eucharist.

27.   Weekday Mass in which children participate can certainly be celebrated with greater effect and less danger of boredom if it does not take place every day (for example, in boarding schools). Moreover, preparation can be more careful if there is a longer interval between diverse celebrations.

Sometimes it will be preferable to have common prayer, to which the children may contribute spontaneously, or else a common meditation, or a celebration of the word of God. These are ways of continuing the eucharistic celebrations already held and of leading to a deeper participation in subsequent celebrations.

28.   When the number of children who celebrate the eucharist together is very great, attentive and conscious participation becomes more difficult. Therefore, if possible, several groups should be formed; these should not be set up rigidly according to age but with regard for the children's progress in religious formation and catechetical preparation.

During the week such groups may be invited to the sacrifice of the Mass on different days.

PREPARATION FOR THE CELEBRATION

29.   Each eucharistic celebration with children should be carefully prepared beforehand, especially with regard to the prayers, songs, readings, and intentions of the general intercessions. This should be done in discussion with the adults and with the children who will have a special ministry in these Masses. If possible, some of the children should take part in preparing and ornamenting the place of celebration and preparing the chalice with the paten and the cruets. Presupposing the appropriate internal participation, such activity will help to develop the spirit of community celebration.

30.   Singing must be given great importance in all celebrations, but it is to be especially encouraged in every way for Masses celebrated with children, in view of their special affinity for music.[26] The culture of various peoples and the capabilities of the children present should be taken into account.

If possible, the acclamations should be sung by the children rather than recited, especially the acclamations that form part of the eucharistic prayer.

31.   To facilitate the children's participation in singing the Gloria, Credo, Sanctus, and Agnus Dei, it is permissible to use with the melodies appropriate vernacular texts, accepted by competent authority, even if these do not correspond exactly to the liturgical texts.[27]

32.   The use of "musical instruments can add a great deal" in Masses with children, especially if they are played by the children themselves.[28] The playing of instruments will help to sustain the singing or to encourage the reflection of the children; sometimes in their own fashion instruments express festive joy and the praise of God.

Care should always be taken, however, that the musical accompaniment does not overpower the singing or become a distraction rather than a help to the children. Music should correspond to the purpose intended for the different periods at which it is played during the Mass.

With these precautions and with due and special discretion, recorded music may also be used in Masses with children, in accord with norms established by the conferences of bishops.

GESTURES

33.   In view of the nature of the liturgy as an activity of the entire person and in view of the psychology of children, participation by means of gestures and posture should be strongly encouraged in Masses with children, with due regard for age and local customs. Much depends not only on the actions of the priest,[29] but also on the manner in which the children conduct themselves as a community.

If, in accord with the norms of the *General Instruction of the Roman Missal*,[30] a conference of bishops adapts the congregation's actions at Mass to the mentality of a people, it should take the special condition of children into account or should decide on adaptations that are for children only.

34. Among the actions that are considered under this heading, processions and other activities that involve physical participation deserve special mention.

The children's entering in procession with the priest can serve to help them to experience a sense of the communion that is thus being created.[31] The participation of at least some children in the procession with the Book of the Gospels makes clear the presence of Christ announcing the word to his people. The procession of children with the chalice and the gifts expresses more clearly the value and meaning of the preparation of the gifts. The communion procession, if properly arranged, helps greatly to develop the children's devotion.

35. The liturgy of the Mass contains many visual elements and these should be given great prominence with children. This is especially true of the particular visual elements in the course of the liturgical year, for example, the veneration of the cross, the Easter candle, the lights on the feast of the Presentation of the Lord, and the variety of colors and liturgical appointments.

In addition to the visual elements that belong to the celebration and to the place of celebration, it is appropriate to introduce other elements that will permit children to perceive visually the wonderful works of God in creation and redemption and thus support their prayer. The liturgy should never appear as something dry and merely intellectual.

36. For the same reason, the use of art work prepared by the children themselves may be useful, for example, as illustrations of a homily, as visual expressions of the intentions of the general intercessions, or as inspirations to reflection.

SILENCE

37. Even in Masses with children "silence should be observed at the designated times as part of the celebration"[32] lest too great a place be given to external action. In their own way children are genuinely capable of reflection. They need some guidance, however, so that they will learn how, in keeping with the different moments of the Mass (for example, after the homily or after communion[33]), to recollect themselves, meditate briefly, or praise God and pray to him in their hearts.[34]

Besides this, with even greater care than in Masses with adults, the liturgical texts should be proclaimed intelligibly and unhurriedly, with the necessary pauses.

38.   The general structure of the Mass, which "is made up as it were of the liturgy of the word and the liturgy of the eucharist," should always be maintained, as should certain rites to open and conclude the celebration.[35] Within individual parts of the celebration, the adaptations that follow seem necessary if children are truly to experience in their own way and according to the psychological patterns of childhood, "the mystery of faith . . . by means of rites and prayers."[36]

39.   Some rites and texts should never be adapted for children lest the difference between Masses with children and the Masses with adults become too pronounced.[37] These are "the acclamations and the responses to the priest's greeting,"[38] the Lord's Prayer, and the Trinitarian formulary at the end of the blessing with which the priest concludes the Mass. It is urged, moreover, that children should become accustomed to the Nicene Creed little by little, the right to use the Apostles' Creed indicated in no. 49 remaining intact.

A. Introductory Rite

40.   The introductory rite of Mass has as its purpose "that the faithful coming together take on the form of a community and prepare themselves to listen to God's word and celebrate the eucharist properly."[39] Therefore every effort should be made to create this disposition in the children and not to jeopardize it by any excess of rites in this part of Mass.

It is sometimes proper to omit one or other element of the introductory rite or perhaps to expand one of the elements. There should always be at least some introductory element, which is completed by the opening prayer. In choosing individual elements, care should be taken that each one be used from time to time and that none be entirely neglected.

B. Reading and Explanation of the Word of God

41.   Since readings taken from holy Scripture "form the main part of the liturgy of the word,"[40] even in Masses with children biblical reading should never be omitted.

42.   With regard to the number of readings on Sundays and holy days, the decrees of the conferences of bishops are to be observed. If three or even two readings appointed on Sundays or weekdays can be understood by children only with difficulty, it is permissible to read two or only one of them, but the reading of the gospel should never be omitted.

43. If all the readings assigned to the day seem to be unsuited to the capacity of the children, it is permissible to choose readings or a reading either from the Lectionary of the Roman Missal or directly from the Bible, but taking into account the liturgical seasons. It is recommended, moreover, that the individual conferences of bishops see to the composition of lectionaries for Masses with children.

If, because of the limited capabilities of the children, it seems necessary to omit one or other verse of a biblical reading, this should be done cautiously and in such a way "that the meaning of the text or the intent and, as it were, style of the Scriptures are not distorted."[41]

44. In the choice of readings the criterion to be followed is the quality rather than the quantity of the texts from the Scriptures. A shorter reading is not as such always more suited to children than a lengthy reading. Everything depends on the spiritual advantage that the reading can bring to the children.

45. In the biblical texts "God is speaking to his people . . . and Christ is present to the faithful through his own word."[42] Paraphrases of Scripture should therefore be avoided. On the other hand, the use of translations that may already exist for the catechesis of children and that are accepted by the competent authority is recommended.

46. Verses of psalms, carefully selected in accord with the understanding of children, or singing in the form of psalmody or the Alleluia with a simple verse should be sung between the readings. The children should always have a part in this singing, but sometimes a reflective silence may be substituted for the singing.

If only a single reading is chosen, the singing may follow the homily.

47. All the elements that will help explain the readings should be given great consideration so that the children may make the biblical readings their own and may come more and more to appreciate the value of God's word.

Among such elements are the introductory comments that may precede the readings[43] and that by explaining the context or by introducing the text itself help the children to listen better and more fruitfully. The interpretation and explanation of the readings from the Scriptures in the Mass on a saint's day may include an account of the saint's life, not only in the homily but even before the readings in the form of an introduction.

When the text of the readings lends itself to this, it may be helpful to have the children read it with parts distributed among them, as is provided for the reading of the Lord's passion during Holy Week.

48. The homily explaining the word of God should be given great prominence in all Masses with children. Sometimes the homily intended for children should become a dialogue with them, unless it is preferred that they should listen in silence.

49. If the profession of faith occurs at the end of the liturgy of the word, the Apostle's Creed may be used with children, especially because it is part of their catechetical formation.

C. Presidential Prayers

50. The priest is permitted to choose from the Roman Missal texts of presidential prayers more suited to children, so that he may truly associate the children with himself. But he is to take into account the liturgical season.

51. Since these prayers were composed for adult Christians, however, the principle simply of choosing from among them does not serve the purpose of having the children regard the prayers as an expression of their own life and religious experience.[44] If this is the case, the text of prayers of the Roman Missal may be adapted to the needs of children, but this should be done in such a way that, preserving the purpose of the prayer and to some extent its substance as well, the priest avoids anything that is foreign to the literary genre of a presidential prayer, such as moral exhortations or a childish manner of speech.

52. The eucharistic prayer is of the greatest importance in the eucharist celebrated with children because it is the high point of the entire celebration.[45] Much depends on the manner in which the priest proclaims this prayer[46] and on the way the children take part by listening and making their acclamations.

The disposition of mind required for this central part of the celebration and the calm and reverence with which everything is done must make the children as attentive as possible. Their attention should be on the real presence of Christ on the altar under the elements of bread and wine, on his offering, on the thanksgiving through him and with him and in him, and on the Church's offering, which is made during the prayer and by which the faithful offer themselves and their lives with Christ to the eternal Father in the Holy Spirit.

For the present, the four eucharistic prayers approved by the supreme authority for Masses with adults and introduced into liturgical use are to be employed until the Apostolic See makes other provision for Masses with children.

D. Rites before Communion

53.   When the eucharistic prayer has ended, the Lord's Prayer, the breaking of bread, and the invitation to communion should always follow,[47] that is, the elements that have the principal significance in the structure of this part of the Mass.

E. Communion and the Following Rites

54.   Everything should be done so that the children who are properly disposed and who have already been admitted to the eucharist may go to the holy table calmly and with recollection and thus take part fully in the eucharistic mystery. If possible, there should be singing, suited to the children, during the communion procession.[48]

The comments that precede the final blessing[49] are important in Masses with children. Before they are dismissed they need some repetition and application of what they have heard, but this should be done in a very few words. In particular, this is the appropriate time to express the connection between the liturgy and life.

At least sometimes, depending on the liturgical seasons and different occasions in the children's life, the priest should use more expanded forms of blessing, but at the end should always retain the Trinitarian formulary with the sign of the cross.[50]

*   *   *   *   *

55.   The contents of the Directory have as their purpose to help children readily and joyfully to encounter Christ together in the eucharistic celebration and to stand with him in the presence of the Father.[51] If they are formed by conscious and active participation in the eucharistic sacrifice and meal, they should learn day by day, at home and away from home, to proclaim Christ to others among their family and among their peers, by living the "faith, that works through love" (Gal 5:6).

This Directory was prepared by the Congregation for Divine Worship. On 22 October 1973, Pope Paul VI approved and confirmed it and ordered that it be published.

NOTES

1. See GCD 5.
2. See CSL 33.
, 3. See GCD 78.
4. See CSL 38; also AP.
5. First Synod of Bishops, Liturgy: *Notitiae* 3 (1967) 368.
6. See DMC 19, 32, 33.
7. See Order of Mass with children who are deafmutes for German-speaking countries, confirmed 26 June 1970 by CDW (prot. no. 1546/70).
8. See CSL 14, 19.
9. See GCD 25.
10. See Vatican Council II, Declaration on Christian Education, *Gravissimum educationis*, no. 2.
11. See *Ibid.*, 3.
12. See GCD 78.
13. See CSL 33.
14. See EM 14.
15. See GCD 25.
16. See EM 14; GCD 57.
17. See CSL 35,4
18. See DMC 3.
19. See CSL 42, 106.
20. See first Synod of Bishops, Liturgy: *Notitiae* 3 (1967) 368.
21. See GI 56.
22. See DMC 37.
23. See GI 11.
24. See CL 28.
25. See GI 253.
26. See GI 19.
27. See MS 55.
28. *Ibid.*, 62.
29. See DMC 23.
30. See GI 21.
31. See GI 24.
32. GI 23.
33. See EM 38.
34. See GI 23.
35. GI 8.
36. CSL 48.

37. See DMC 21.
38. GI 15.
39. GI 24.
40. GI 33.
41. Lectionary for Mass: Introduction, 1969 edition, no. 7d.
42. GI 33.
43. See GI 11.
44. See Consilium for the Implementation of the Constitution on the Sacred Liturgy, instruction on translations of liturgical texts for celebrations with a congregation, 25 Jan 1969, no. 20: *Notitiae* 5 (1969) 7.
45. GI 54.
46. See DMC 23, 37.
47. See DMC 23.
48. See MS 32.
49. See GI 11.
50. See DMC 39.
51. See Eucharistic prayer II.

MUSIC
IN
CATHOLIC WORSHIP

REVISED EDITION

1983

BACKGROUND

Music in Catholic Worship
and
Liturgical Music Today

In 1972 and in 1982 the Bishops' Committee on the Liturgy of the United States Catholic Conference issued important statements on the role of music in our liturgy. The first of these, *Music in Catholic Worship*, remains a touchstone for thinking about the function of music, its ministers, times and kinds. It establishes norms for evaluating the selection of music and priorities for leading every assembly to be at home with a repertoire of acclamations, litanies, psalms and songs.

The 1982 document, *Liturgical Music Today*, is something of an appendix which attempts to speak to circumstances and rites not covered in *Music in Catholic Worship*.

Careful reading, discussion, and the passing of years help the reader separate the lasting insights and directives from those notes which met a passing concern. That done, these texts can remain inspiration and evaluation for the liturgy.

OUTLINE

MUSIC IN CATHOLIC WORSHIP

THE THEOLOGY OF CELEBRATION

1.   We are Christians because through the Christian community we have met Jesus Christ, heard his word in invitation, and responded to him in faith. We gather at Mass that we may hear and express our faith again in this assembly and, by expressing it, renew and deepen it.

2.   We do not come to meet Christ as if he were absent from the rest of our lives. We come together to deepen our awareness of, and commitment to, the action of his Spirit in the whole of our lives at every moment. We come together to acknowledge the love of God poured out among us in the work of the Spirit, to stand in awe and praise.

3.   We are celebrating when we involve ourselves meaningfully in the thoughts, words, songs, and gestures of the worshipping community—when everything we do is wholehearted and authentic for us—when we mean the words and want to do what is done.

4.   People in love make signs of love, not only to express their love but also to deepen it. Love never expressed dies. Christians' love for Christ and for one another and Christians' faith in Christ and in one another must be expressed in the signs and symbols of celebration or they will die.

5.   Celebrations need not fail, even on a particular Sunday when our feelings do not match the invitation of Christ and his Church to worship. Faith does not always permeate our feelings. But the signs and symbols of worship can give bodily expression to faith as we celebrate. Our own faith is stimulated. We become one with others whose faith is similarly expressed. We rise above our own feelings to respond to God in prayer.

6.   Faith grows when it is well expressed in celebration. Good celebrations foster and nourish faith. Poor celebrations may weaken and destroy it.

7.   To celebrate the liturgy means to do the action or perform the sign in such a way that its full meaning and impact shine forth in clear and compelling fashion. Since liturgical signs are vehicles of communication

and instruments of faith, they must be simple and comprehensible. Since they are directed to fellow human beings, they must be humanly attractive. They must be meaningful and appealing to the body of worshippers or they will fail to stir up faith and people will fail to worship the Father.

8.   The signs of celebration should be short, clear, and unencumbered by useless repetition; they should be "within the people's powers of comprehension, and normally should not require much explanation."[1]

        If the signs need explanation to communicate faith, they will often be watched instead of celebrated.

9.   In true celebration each sign or sacramental action will be invested with the personal and prayerful faith, care, attention, and enthusiasm of those who carry it out.

PASTORAL PLANNING FOR CELEBRATION

10.   The responsibility for effective pastoral celebration in a parish community falls upon all those who exercise major roles in the liturgy. "The practical preparation for each liturgical celebration should be done in a spirit of cooperation by all parties concerned, under the guidance of the rector of the church, whether it be ritual, pastoral, or musical matters."[2] In practice this ordinarily means an organized "planning team" or committee which meets regularly to achieve creative and coordinated worship and a good use of the liturgical and musical options of a flexible liturgy.

11.   The power of a liturgical celebration to share faith will frequently depend upon its unity—a unity drawn from the liturgical feast or season or from the readings appointed in the lectionary as well as artistic unity flowing from the skillful and sensitive selection of options, music, and related arts. The sacred scriptures ought to be the source and inspiration of sound planning, for it is of the very nature of celebration that people hear the saving words and works of the Lord and then respond in meaningful signs and symbols. Where the readings of the lectionary possess a thematic unity, the other elements ought to be so arranged as to constitute a setting for and response to the message of the Word.

12.   The planning team or committee is headed by the priest (celebrant and homilist) for no congregation can experience the richness of a unified celebration if that unity is not grasped by the one who presides, as well as by those who have special roles. The planning group should include those with the knowledge and artistic skills needed in celebration: men and women trained in music, poetry, and art, and familiar with current

resources in these areas; men and women sensitive also to the present day thirst of so many for the riches of scripture, theology, and prayer. It is always good to include some members of the congregation who have not taken special roles in the celebrations so that honest evaluations can be made.

13.   The planning should go beyond the choosing of options, songs, and ministers to the composition of such texts as the brief introduction, general intercessions, and other appropriate comments as provided for in the *General Instruction of the Roman Missal.* How people are invited to join in a particular song may be as important as the choice of the song itself.

14.   In planning pastoral celebrations the congregation, the occasion, and the celebrant must be taken into consideration.

THE CONGREGATION

15.   "The pastoral effectiveness of a celebration will be heightened if the texts of readings, prayers, and songs correspond as closely as possible to the needs, religious dispostions, and aptitude of the participants."[3] A type of celebration suitable for a youth group may not fit in a retirement home; a more formal style effective in a parish church may be inappropriate in a home liturgy. The music used should be within the competence of most of the worshippers. It should suit their age level, cultural background, and level of faith.

16.   Variations in level of faith raise special problems. Liturgical celebration presupposes a minimum of biblical knowledge and a deep commitment of living faith. If these are lacking, there might arise the tendency to use the liturgy as a tool of evangelization. Greater liberty in the choice of music and style of celebration may be required as the participants are led toward that day when they can share their growing faith as members of the Christian community. Songs like the psalms may create rather than solve problems where faith is weak. Music, chosen with care, can serve as a bridge to faith as well as an expression of it.

17.   The diversity of people present at a parish liturgy gives rise to a further problem. Can the same parish liturgy be an authentic expression for a grade school girl, her college-age brother, their married sister with her young family, their parents and grandparents? Can it satisfy the theologically and musically educated along with those lacking in training? Can it please those who seek a more informal style of celebration? The planning team must consider the general makeup of the total community. Each Christian must keep in mind that to live and worship in community often demands a personal sacrifice. All must be willing to share likes and dislikes with others whose ideas and experiences may be quite unlike their own.

18.   Often the problem of diversity can be mitigated by supplementing the parish Sunday celebration with special celebrations for smaller homogeneous groups. "The needs of the faithful of a particular cultural background or of a particular age level may often be met by a music that can serve as a congenial, liturgically oriented expression of prayer."[4] The music and other options may then be more easily suited to the particular group celebrating. Celebration in such groups, "in which the genuine sense of community is more readily experienced, can contribute significantly to growth in awareness of the parish as community, especially when all the faithful participate in the parish Mass on the Lord's day."[5] Nevertheless, it would be out of harmony with the Lord's wish for unity in his Church if believers were to worship only in such homogeneous groupings.[6]

THE OCCASION

19.   The same congregation will want to celebrate in a variety of ways. During the course of the year the different mysteries of redemption are recalled in the Mass so that in some way they are made present.[7] Each feast and season has its own spirit and its own music. The penitential occasions demand more restraint. The great feasts demand more solemnity. Solemnity, however, depends less on the ornateness of song and magnificence of ceremonial than on worthy and religious celebration.[8]

20.   Generally a congregation or choir will want to sing more on the great feasts like Christmas and Easter and less in the season through the year. Important events in family and parish life will suggest fuller programs of song. Sundays will be celebrated with variety but always as befits the day of the Lord. All liturgies, from the very simple to the most ornate, must be truly pastoral and prayerful.

THE CELEBRANT

21.   No other single factor affects the liturgy as much as the attitude, style, and bearing of the celebrant: his sincere faith and warmth as he welcomes the worshipping community; his human naturalness combined with dignity and seriousness as he breaks the Bread of Word and Eucharist.

22.   The style and pattern of song ought to increase the effectiveness of a good celebrant. His role is enhanced when he is capable of rendering some of his parts in song, and he should be encouraged to do so. What he cannot sing well and effectively he ought to recite. If capable of singing, he ought, for the sake of people, to rehearse carefully the sung parts that contribute to their celebration.[9]

THE PLACE OF MUSIC IN THE CELEBRATION

MUSIC SERVES THE EXPRESSION OF FAITH

23.   Among the many signs and symbols used by the Church to celebrate its faith, music is of preeminent importance. As sacred song united to words it forms a necessary or integral part of the solemn liturgy.[10] Yet the function of music is ministerial; it must serve and never dominate. Music should assist the assembled believers to express and share the gift of faith that is within them and to nourish and strengthen their interior commitment of faith. It should heighten the texts so that they speak more fully and more effectively. The quality of joy and enthusiasm which music adds to community worship cannot be gained in any other way. It imparts a sense of unity to the congregation and sets the appropriate tone for a particular celebration.

24.   In addition to expressing texts, music can also unveil a dimension of meaning and feeling, a communication of ideas and intuitions which words alone cannot yield. This dimension is integral to the human personality and to growth in faith. It cannot be ignored if the signs of worship are to speak to the whole person. Ideally, every communal celebration of faith, including funerals and the sacraments of baptism, confirmation, penance, anointing, and matrimony, should include music and singing. Where it is possible to celebrate the Liturgy of the Hours in a community, it, too, should include music.

25.   To determine the value of a given musical element in a liturgical celebration a threefold judgment must be made: musical, liturgical, and pastoral.

THE MUSICAL JUDGMENT

26.   Is the music technically, aesthetically, and expressively good? This judgment is basic and primary and should be made by competent musicians. Only artistically sound music will be effective in the long run. To admit the cheap, the trite, the musical cliche often found in popular songs for the purpose of "instant liturgy" is to cheapen the liturgy, to expose it to ridicule, and to invite failure.

27.   Musicians must search for and create music of quality for worship, especially the new musical settings for the new liturgical texts. They must also do the research to find new uses for the best of the old music. They must explore the repertory of good music in other communions. They must find practical means of preserving and using our rich heritage of Latin chants and motets.[11]

In the meantime, however, the words of St. Augustine should not be forgotten: "Do not allow yourselves to be offended by the imperfect while you strive for the perfect."

28.   We do a disservice to musical values, however, when we confuse the judgment of music with the judgment of musical style. Style and value are two distinctive judgments. Good music of new styles is finding a happy home in the celebrations of today. To chant and polyphony we have effectively added the chorale hymn, restored reponsorial singing to some extent, and employed many styles of contemporary composition. Music in folk idiom is finding acceptance in eucharistic celebrations. We must judge value within each style.

"In modern times the Church has consistently recognized and freely admitted the use of various styles of music as an aid to liturgical worship. Since the promulgation of the *Constitution on the Liturgy* and more especially since the introduction of vernacular languages into the liturgy, there has arisen a more pressing need for musical compositions in idioms that can be sung by the congregation and thus further communal participation."[12]

29.   The musician has every right to insist that the music be good. But although all liturgical music should be good, not all good music is suitable to the liturgy. The musical judgment is basic but not final. There remain the liturgical and pastoral judgments.

THE LITURGICAL JUDGMENT

30.   The nature of the liturgy itself will help to determine what kind of music is called for, what parts are to be preferred for singing, and who is to sing them.

A. Structural Requirements

31.   The choice of sung parts, the balance between them, and the style of musical setting used should reflect the relative importance of the parts of the Mass (or other service) and the nature of each part. Thus elaborate settings of the entrance song, "Lord have Mercy" and "Glory to God" may make the proclamation of the word seem unimportant; and an overly elaborate offertory song with a spoken "Holy, Holy, Holy Lord" may make the eucharistic prayer seem less important.

B. Textual Requirements

32.   Does the music express and interpret the text correctly and make it more meaningful? Is the form of the text respected? In making these judgments the principal classes of texts must be kept in mind:

proclamations, acclamations, psalms and hymns, and prayers. Each has a specific function which must be served by the music chosen for a text.

In most instances there is an official text approved by the episcopal conference. "Vernacular texts set to music composed in earlier periods," however, "may be used in liturgical texts."[13] As noted elsewhere, criteria have been provided for the texts which may replace the processional chants of Mass. In these cases and in the choice of all supplementary music, the texts "must always be in conformity with Catholic doctrine; indeed they should be drawn chiefly from holy scripture and from liturgical sources."[14]

C. Role Differentiation

33.   "In liturgical celebrations each one, minister or layperson, who has an office to perform, should do all of, but only, those parts which pertain to that office by the nature of the rite and the principles of liturgy."[15] Special musical concern must be given to the role of the congregation, the cantor, the choir, and the instrumentalists.

D. The Congregation

34.   Music for the congregation must be within its members' performance capability. The congregation must be comfortable and secure with what they are doing in order to celebrate well.

E. The Cantor

35.   While there is no place in the liturgy for display of virtuosity for its own sake, artistry is valued, and an individual singer can effectively lead the assembly, attractively proclaim the Word of God in the psalm sung between the readings, and take his or her part in other responsorial singing. "Provision should be made for at least one or two properly trained singers, especially where there is no possibility of setting up even a small choir. The singer will present some simpler musical settings, with the people taking part, and can lead and support the faithful as far as is needed. The presence of such a singer is desirable even in churches which have a choir, for those celebrations in which the choir cannot take part but which may fittingly be performed with some solemnity and therefore with singing."[16] Although a cantor "cannot enhance the service of worship in the same way as a choir, a trained and competent cantor can perform an important ministry by leading the congregation in common sacred song and in responsorial singing."[17]

F. The Choir

36.   A well-trained choir adds beauty and solemnity to the liturgy and also assists and encourages the singing of the congregation. The Second

Vatican Council, speaking of the choir, stated emphatically: "Choirs must be diligently promoted," provided that "the whole body of the faithful may be able to contribute that active participation which is rightly theirs."[18]

"At times the choir, within the congregation of the faithful and as part of it, will assume the role of leadership, while at other times it will retain its own distinctive ministry. This means that the choir will lead the people in sung prayer, by alternating or reinforcing the sacred song of the congregation, or by enhancing it with the addition of a musical elaboration. At other times in the course of liturgical celebration the choir alone will sing works whose musical demands enlist and challenge its competence."[19]

G. The Organist and Other Instrumentalists

37.   Song is not the only kind of music suitable for liturgical celebration. Music performed on the organ and other instruments can stimulate feelings of joy and contemplation at appropriate times.[20] This can be done effectively at the following points: an instrumental prelude, a soft background to a spoken psalm, at the preparation of the gifts in place of singing, during portions of the communion rite, and the recessional.

In the dioceses of the United States, "musical instruments other than the organ may be used in liturgical services, provided they are played in a manner that is suitable to public worship."[21] This decision deliberately refrains from singling out specific instruments. Their use depends on circumstances, the nature of the congregation, etc.

38.   The *proper placing* of the organ and choir according to the arrangement and acoustics of the church will facilitate celebration. Practically speaking, the choir must be near the director and the organ (both console and sound). The choir ought to be able to perform without too much distraction; the acoustics ought to give a lively presence of sound in the choir area and allow both tone and word to reach the congregation with clarity. Visually it is desirable that the choir appear to be part of the worshipping community, yet a part which serves in a unique way. Locating the organ console too far from the congregation causes a time lag which tends to make the singing drag unless the organist is trained to cope with it. A location near the front pews will facilitate congregational singing.

THE PASTORAL JUDGMENT

39.   The pastoral judgment governs the use and function of every element of celebration. Ideally this judgment is made by the planning team or committee. It is the judgment that must be made in this particular situation, in these concrete circumstances. Does music in the celebration

enable these people to express their faith, in this place, in this age, in this culture?

40. The instruction of the Congregation for Divine Worship, issued September 5, 1970, encourages episcopal conferences to consider not only liturgical music's suitability to the time and circumstances of the celebration, "but also the needs of the faithful who will sing them. All means must be used to promote singing by the people. New forms should be used, which are adapted to the different mentalities and to modern tastes." The document adds that the music and the instruments "should correspond to the sacred character of the celebration and the place of worship."

41. A musician may judge that a certain composition or style of composition is good music, but this musical judgment really says nothing about whether and how this music is to be used in this celebration. The signs of the celebration must be accepted and received as meaningful for a genuinely human faith experience for these specific worshippers. This pastoral judgment can be aided by sensitivity to the cultural and social characteristics of the people who make up the congregation: their age, culture, and education. These factors influence the effectiveness of the liturgical signs, including music. No set of rubrics or regulations of itself will ever achieve a truly pastoral celebration of the sacramental rites. Such regulations must always be applied with a pastoral concern for the given worshipping community.

GENERAL CONSIDERATIONS OF LITURGICAL STRUCTURE

42. Those responsible for planning the music for eucharistic celebrations in accord with the three preceding judgments must have a clear understanding of the structure of the liturgy. They must be aware of what is of primary importance. They should know the nature of each of the parts of the liturgy and the relationship of each part to the overall rhythm of the liturgical action.

43. The Mass is made up of the liturgy of the word and the liturgy of the Eucharist. These two parts are so closely connected as to form one act of worship. The table of the Lord is both the table of God's Word and the table of Christ's Body, and from it the faithful are instructed and refreshed. In addition, the Mass has introductory and concluding rites.[22] The introductory and concluding rites are secondary.

THE INTRODUCTORY RITES

44. The parts preceding the liturgy of the word, namely, the entrance, greeting, penitential rite, Kyrie, Gloria, and opening prayer or collect, have the character of introduction and preparation. The purpose of these rites is to help the assembled people become a worshipping community and to prepare them for listening to God's word and celebrating the Eucharist.[23] Of these parts the entrance song and the opening prayer are primary. All else is secondary.

If Mass begins with the sprinkling of the people with blessed water, the penitential rite is omitted; this may be done at all Sunday Masses.[24] Similarly, if the psalms of part of the Liturgy of the Hours precede Mass, the introductory rite is abbreviated in accord with the *General Instruction on The Liturgy of the Hours.*[25]

THE LITURGY OF THE WORD

45. Readings from scripture are the heart of the liturgy of the word. The homily, responsorial psalms, profession of faith, and general intercessions develop and complete it. In the readings, God speaks to his people and nourishes their spirit; Christ is present through his word. The homily explains the readings. The chants and the profession of faith comprise the people's acceptance of God's Word. It is of primary importance that the people hear God's message of love, digest it with the aid of psalms, silence and the homily, and respond, involving themselves in the great covenant of love and redemption. All else is secondary.

THE PREPARATION OF THE GIFTS

46. The eucharistic prayer is preceded by the preparation of the gifts. The purpose of the rite is to prepare bread and wine for the sacrifice. The secondary character of the rite determines the manner of the celebration. It consists very simply of bringing the gifts to the altar, possibly accompanied by song, prayers to be said by the celebrant as he prepares the gifts and the prayer over the gifts. Of these elements, the bringing of the gifts, the placing of the gifts on the altar, and the prayer over the gifts are primary. All else is secondary.

THE EUCHARISTIC PRAYER

47. The eucharistic prayer, a prayer of thanksgiving and sanctification, is the center of the entire celebration. By an introductory dialogue the priest invites the people to lift their hearts to God in praise and thanks; he

unites them with himself in the prayer he addresses in their name to the Father through Jesus Christ. The meaning of the prayer is that the whole congregation joins itself to Christ in acknowledging the works of God and in offering the sacrifice.[26] As a statement of the faith of the local assembly it is affirmed and ratified by all those present through acclamations of faith: the first acclamation or Sanctus, the memorial acclamation, and the Great Amen.

THE COMMUNION RITE

48.   The eating and drinking of the Body and Blood of the Lord in a paschal meal is the climax of our eucharistic celebration. It is prepared for by several rites: the Lord's Prayer with embolism and doxology, the rite of peace, breaking of bread (and commingling) during the "Lamb of God," private preparation of the priest, and showing of the eucharistic bread. The eating and drinking are accompanied by a song expressing the unity of communicants and followed by a time of prayer after communion.[27] Those elements are primary which show forth signs that the first fruit of the Eucharist is the unity of the Body of Christ, Christians being loved by Christ and loving him through their love of one another. The principal texts to accompany or express the sacred action are the Lord's Prayer, the song during the communion procession, and the prayer after communion.

THE CONCLUDING RITE

49.   The concluding rite consists of the priest's greeting and blessing, which is sometimes expanded by the prayer over the people or another solemn form, and the dismissal which sends forth each member of the congregation to do good works, praising and blessing the Lord.[28]

A recessional song is optional. The greeting, blessing, dismissal, and recessional song or instrumental music ideally form one continuous action which may culminate in the priest's personal greetings and conversations at the church door.

APPLICATION OF THE PRINCIPLES OF CELEBRATION
TO MUSIC IN EUCHARISTIC WORSHIP

50.   Many and varied musical patterns are now possible within liturgical structure. Musicians and composers need to respond creatively and responsibly to the challenge of developing new music for today's celebrations.

51.   While it is possible to make technical distinctions in the forms of the Mass—all the way from the Mass in which nothing is sung to the Mass in which everything is sung—such distinctions are of little significance in themselves; almost unlimited combinations of sung and recited parts may be chosen. The important decision is whether or not this or that part may be or should be sung in this particular celebration and under these specific circumstances.[29] The former distinction between the ordinary and proper parts of the Mass with regard to musical settings and distribution of roles is no longer retained. For this reason the musical settings of the past are usually not helpful models for composing truly liturgical pieces today.

52.   Two patterns formerly served as the basis for creating and planning liturgy. One was "High Mass" with its five movements, sung Ordinary and fourfold sung Proper. The other was the four-hymn "Low Mass" format that grew out of the *Instruction of Sacred Music* of 1958. The four-hymn pattern developed in the context of a Latin Mass which could accommodate song in the vernacular only at certain points. It is now outdated, and the Mass has more than a dozen parts that may be sung, as well as numerous options for the celebrant. Each of these parts must be understood according to its proper nature and function.

A. Acclamations

53.   The acclamations are shouts of joy which arise from the whole assembly as forceful and meaningful assents to God's Word and Action. They are important because they make some of the most significant moments of the Mass (gospel, eucharistic prayer, Lord's Prayer) stand out. It is of their nature that they be rhythmically strong, melodically appealing, and affirmative. The people should know the acclamations by heart in order to sing them spontaneously. Some variety is recommended and even imperative. The challenge to the composer and people alike is

232   Music in Catholic Worship

one of variety without confusion.

54.   In the eucharistic celebration there are five acclamations which ought to be sung even at Masses in which little else is sung: Alleluia; "Holy, Holy, Holy Lord"; Memorial Acclamation; Great Amen; Doxology to the Lord's Prayer.

THE ALLELUIA

55.   This acclamation of paschal joy is both a reflection upon the Word of God proclaimed in the liturgy and a preparation for the gospel. All stand to sing it. After the cantor or choir sings the alleluia(s), the people customarily repeat it. Then a single proper verse is sung by the cantor or choir, and all repeat the alleluia(s). If not sung, the alleluia should be omitted.[30] A moment of silent reflection may be observed in its place. During Lent a brief verse of acclamatory character replaces the alleluia and is sung in the same way.

HOLY, HOLY, HOLY LORD

56.   This is the people's acclamation of praise concluding the preface of the eucharistic prayer. We join the whole communion of saints in acclaiming the Lord. Settings which add harmony or descants on solemn feasts and occasions are appropriate, but since this chant belongs to priest and people the choir parts must facilitate and make effective the people's parts.

THE MEMORIAL ACCLAMATION

57.   We support one another's faith in the paschal mystery, the central mystery of our belief. This acclamation is properly a memorial of the Lord's suffering and glorification, with an expression of faith in his coming. Variety in text and music is desirable.

THE GREAT AMEN

58.   The worshippers assent to the eucharistic prayer and make it their own in the Great Amen. To be most effective, the Amen may be repeated or augmented. Choirs may harmonize and expand upon the people's acclamation.

DOXOLOGY TO THE LORD'S PRAYER

59.   These words of praise, "For the Kingdom, the power and the glory are yours, now and forever," are fittingly sung by all, especially when the Lord's Prayer is sung. Here, too, the choir may enhance the acclamation with harmony.

B. Processional Songs

60.   The two processional chants—the entrance song and the communion song—are very important for creating and sustaining an awareness of community. Proper antiphons are given to be used with appropriate psalm verses. These may be replaced by the chants of the *Simple Gradual*, by other psalms and antiphons, or by other fitting songs.[31]

THE ENTRANCE SONG

61.   The entrance song should create an atmosphere of celebration. It helps put the assembly in the proper frame of mind for listening to the Word of God. It helps people to become conscious of themselves as a worshipping community. The choice of texts for the entrance song should not conflict with these purposes. In general, during the most important seasons of the Church year—Easter, Lent, Christmas, and Advent—it is preferable that most songs used at the entrance be seasonal in nature.[32]

THE COMMUNION SONG

62.   The communion song should foster a sense of unity. It should be simple and not demand great effort. It gives expression to the joy of unity in the body of Christ and the fulfillment of the mystery being celebrated. Because they emphasize adoration rather than communion, most benediction hymns are not suitable. In general, during the most important seasons of the Church year—Easter, Lent, Christmas, and Advent—it is preferable that most songs used at the communion be seasonal in nature. For the remainder of the Church year, however, topical songs may be used during the communion procession, provided these texts do not conflict with the paschal character of every Sunday."[33]

C. Responsorial Psalm

63.   This unique and very important song is the response to the first lesson. The new lectionary's determination to match the content of the psalms to the theme of reading is reflected in its listing of 900 refrains. The liturgy of the Word comes more fully to life if between the first two readings a cantor sings the psalm and all sing the response. Since most groups cannot learn a new response every week, seasonal refrains are offered in the lectionary itself and in the *Simple Gradual*. Other psalms and refrains may also be used, including psalms arranged in responsorial form and metrical and similar versions of psalms, provided they are used in accordance with the principles of the *Simple Gradual* and are selected in harmony with the liturgical season, feast or occasion. The choice of the texts which are not from the psalter is not extended to the chants between the readings.[34] To facilitate reflection, there may be a brief period of silence between the first reading and the responsorial psalm.

64.   The fourth category is the ordinary chants, which now may be treated as individual choices. One or more may be sung; the others, spoken. The pattern may vary according to the circumstances. These chants are the following:

LORD HAVE MERCY

65.   This short litany was traditionally a prayer of praise to the risen Christ. He has been raised and made "Lord," and we beg him to show his loving kindness. The sixfold Kyrie of the new order of Mass may be sung in other ways, for example, as a ninefold chant.[35] It may also be incorporated in the penitential rite, with invocations addressed to Christ. When sung, the setting should be brief and simple in order not to give undue importance to the introductory rites.

GLORY TO GOD

66.   This ancient hymn of praise is now given in a new poetic and singable translation. It may be introduced by celebrant, cantor, or choir. The restricted use of the Gloria, i.e., only on Sundays outside Advent and Lent and on solemnities and feasts,[36] emphasizes its special and solemn character. The new text offers many opportunities for alternation of choir and people in poetic parallelisms. The "Glory to God" also provides an opportunity for the choir to sing alone on festive occasions.

LORD'S PRAYER

67.   This prayer begins our immediate preparation for sharing in the Paschal Banquet. The traditional text is retained and may be set to music by composers with the same freedom as other parts of the Ordinary. All settings must provide for the participation of the priest and all present.

LAMB OF GOD

68.   The Agnus Dei is a litany-song to accompany the breaking of the bread in preparation for communion. The invocation and response may be repeated as the action demands. The final response is always "grant us peace." Unlike the "Holy, Holy, Holy Lord," and the Lord's Prayer, the "Lamb of God" is not necessarily a song of the people. Hence it may be sung by the choir, though the people should generally make the response.

PROFESSION OF FAITH

69.   This is a communal profession of faith in which ". . . the people who have heard the Word of God in the lesson and in the homily may assent and respond to it, and may renew in themselves the rule of faith as they begin to celebrate the Eucharist."[37] It is usually preferable that the Creed

be spoken in declamatory fashion rather than sung.[38] If it is sung, it might more effectively take the form of a simple musical declamation rather than an extensive and involved musical structure.

E. Supplementary Songs

70.   This category includes songs for which there are no specified texts nor any requirements that there should be a spoken or sung text. Here the choir may play a fuller role, for there is no question of usurping the people's part. This category includes the following:

THE OFFERTORY SONG

71.   The offertory song may accompany the procession and preparation of the gifts. It is not always necessary or desirable. Organ or instrumental music is also fitting at the time. When song is used, it need not speak of bread and wine or of offering. The proper function of this song is to accompany and celebrate the communal aspects of the procession. The text, therefore, can be any appropriate song of praise or of rejoicing in keeping with the season. The antiphons of the Roman Gradual, not included in the new Roman Missal, may be used with psalm verses. Instrumental interludes can effectively accompany the procession and preparation of the gifts and thus keep this part of the Mass in proper perspective relative to the eucharistic prayer which follows.

THE PSALM OR SONG AFTER COMMUNION

72.   The singing of a psalm or hymn of praise after the distribution of communion is optional. If the organ is played or the choir sings during the distribution of communion, a congregational song may well provide a fitting expression of oneness in the Eucharistic Lord. Since no particular text is specified, there is ample room for creativity.

THE RECESSIONAL SONG

73.   The recessional song has never been an official part of the rite; hence musicians are free to plan music which provides an appropriate closing to the liturgy. A song is one possible choice. However, if the people have sung a song after communion, it may be advisable to use only an instrumental or choir recessional.

LITANIES

74.   Litanies are often more effective when sung. The repetition of melody and rhythm draws the people together in a strong and unified response. In addition to the "Lamb of God," already mentioned, the general intercessions (prayer of the faithful) offer an opportunity for litanical singing, as do the invocations of Christ in the penitential rite.

75. Many new patterns and combinations of song are emerging in eucharistic celebrations. Congregations most frequently sing an entrance song, alleluia, "Holy, Holy, Holy Lord," memorial acclamation, Great Amen, and a song at communion (or a song after communion). Other parts are added in varying quantities, depending on season, degree of solemnity and musical resource. Choirs often add one or more of the following: a song before Mass, an Offertory song, the "Glory to God" on special occasions, additional communion songs or a song after communion or a recessional. They may also enhance the congregationally sung entrance song and acclamations with descants, harmony, and antiphonal arrangements. Harmony is desirable when, without confusing the people, it gives breadth and power to their voices in unison.

76. Flexibility is recognized today as an important value in liturgy. The musician with a sense of artistry and a deep knowledge of the rhythm of the liturgical action will be able to combine the many options into an effective whole. For the composer and performer alike there is an unprecedented challenge. They must enhance the liturgy with new creations of variety and richness and with those compositions from the time-honored treasury of liturgical music which can still serve today's celebrations. Like the wise householder in Matthew's Gospel, the church musician must be one "who can produce from his store both the new and the old."

77. The Church in the United States today needs the service of many qualified musicians as song leaders, organists, instrumentalists, cantors, choir directors, and composers. We have been blessed with many generous musicians who have given years of service despite receiving only meager financial compensation. For the art to grow and face the challenges of today and tomorrow, every diocese and parish should establish policies for hiring and paying living wages to competent musicians. Full-time musicians employed by the Church ought to be on the same salary scale as teachers with similar qualifications and workloads.[39]

78. Likewise, to insure that composers and publishers receive just compensation for their work, those engaged in parish music programs and those responsible for budgets must often be reminded that it is illegal and immoral to reproduce copyrighted texts and music by any means without written permission of the copyright owner. The fact that these duplicated materials are not for sale but for private use does not alter the legal or moral situation of copying without permission.[40]

MUSIC IN SACRAMENTAL CELEBRATIONS

79.   While music has traditionally been part of the celebration of weddings, funerals, and confirmation, the communal celebration of baptism, anointing, and penance has only recently been restored. The renewed rituals, following the *Constitution on the Sacred Liturgy*, provide for and encourage communal celebrations, which, according to the capability of the congregation, should involve song.[41]

80.   The rite of baptism is best begun by an entrance song;[42] the liturgy of the word is enhanced by a sung psalm and/or alleluia. Where the processions to and from the place of the liturgy of the word and the baptistry take some time, they should be accompanied by music. Above all, the acclamations—the affirmation of faith by the people, the acclamation immediately after the baptism, the acclamation upon completion of the rite—should be sung by the whole congregation.

81.   Whenever rites like the anointing of the sick or the sacrament of penance are celebrated communally, music is important. The general structure is introductory rite, liturgy of the word, sacrament, and dismissal. The introductory rite and liturgy of the word follow the pattern of the Mass. At the time of the sacrament an acclamation or song by all the people is desirable.

82.   Confirmation and marriage are most often celebrated within a Mass. The norms given above pertain. Great care should be taken, especially at marriages, that all the people are involved at the important moments of the celebration, that the same general principles of planning worship and judging music are employed as at other liturgies, and, above all, that the liturgy is a prayer for all present, not a theatrical production.

83.   Music becomes particularly important in the new burial rites. Without it the themes of hope and resurrection are very difficult to express. The entrance song, the acclamations, and the song of farewell or commendation are of primary importance for the whole congregation. The choral and instrumental music should fit the paschal mystery theme.[43]

CONCLUSION

84.   There is vital interest today in the Mass as prayer, and in this understanding of the Mass lies a principle of synthesis which is essential to good liturgical worship. When all strive with one accord to make the Mass a prayer, a sharing and celebration of faith, the result is unity. Styles of music, choices of instruments, forms of celebration—all converge in a single purpose: that men and women of faith may proclaim and share that faith in prayer and Christ may grow among us all.

NOTES

1. CSL 34.
2. MS 5e; GI 73.
3. GI 313.
4. BCLN, 18 April 1966.
5. BCLN, 17 Feb 1967.
6. AP.
7. GI 1; cf. CSL 102.
8. MS 11.
9. MS 8.
10. Cf. CSL 112.
11. Cf. CSL 114, 116.
12. BCLN, 18 April 1966.
13. National Conference of Catholic Bishops, [=NCCB] Nov 1967.
14. CSL 121.
15. CSL 28.
16. MS 21.
17. BCLN, 18 April 1966.
18. CSL 114.
19. BCLN, 18 April 1966.
20. Cf. CSL 120; MS 63–65; LI 3c.
21. NCCB, Nov 1967; cf. CSL 120.
22. GI 8.
23. GI 24.
24. Cf. RM, Blessing and Sprinkling of Holy Water, 1.
25. The Liturgy of the Hours, General Instruction, 93–98.
26. GI 54.
27. GI 56.
28. GI 57.
29. Cf. GI 19; MS 28, 36.
30. GI 39. The first edition of this document had the word "may" instead of "should." This change has been made in the second edition in light of the norm found in LMI 23.
31. GI 56.
32. NCCB, Nov. 1969.
33. *Ibid.*
34. NCCB, Nov 1968; cf. GI 6.
35. Cf. GI 30.
36. GI 31.
37. GI 43.
38. NCCB, Nov 1967.
39. BCLN, 18 April 1966.
40. BCLN, April 1969.
41. Cf. CSL 27.
42. Baptism 5, 32, 35.
43. Rite of Funerals, 1.

LITURGICAL MUSIC
TODAY

1982

OUTLINE

LITURGICAL MUSIC TODAY
1982

INTRODUCTION

1.   Liturgical music today exhibits signs of great vitality and creativity. During the nearly twenty years that have passed since the promulgation of the *Constitution on the Sacred Liturgy* of the Second Vatican Council, the ministerial role of liturgical music has received growing acceptance and greater appreciation by the Christian people. The sung prayer of our assemblies, often timid and weak but a few years ago, has taken on the characteristics of confidence and strength. In the liturgical ministry of music, more and more capable persons are assuming roles of leadership as cantors, instrumentalists and members of choirs. New musical compositions are appearing in great numbers and the quality of their craftsmanship and beauty is improving. All these developments serve as signs of hope for the present and future of liturgical music.

2.   Ten years ago the Bishops' Committee on the Liturgy published *Music in Catholic Worship*, itself the revision of an earlier statement.[1] That document has proven to be very useful in setting out the principles for Church music in the reformed liturgy. It has served well over these years.

3.   Since the Roman liturgical books were still in the process of revision ten years ago, the Committee recognizes that there are subjects that *Music in Catholic Worship* addressed only briefly or not at all, such as music within sacramental rites and in the Liturgy of the Hours. Morever, the passage of time has raised a number of unforeseen issues in need of clarification and questions revealing new possibilities for liturgical music. We take this opportunity to note these developments. This statement, therefore, should be read as a companion to *Music in Catholic Worship* and *Environment and Art in Catholic Worship*.[2]

4.   The introduction of *Music in Catholic Worship* includes these words: " . . . mere observance of a pattern or rule of sung liturgy will not create a living and authentic celebration of worship in Christian congregations. That is the reason why statements such as this must take the form of recommendation and attempts at guidance."[3] These words continue to be

true. Guidelines, far from being absolute, need to be adapted to particular circumstances. But first they must be read, reflected upon, and valued for the insights they contain. And ultimately they will be successful to the extent that they are implemented, to the extent that the context out of which they grow is communicated and understood.

5.   These guidelines concern the Church's liturgy, which is inherently musical. If music is not valued within the liturgy, then this statement will have little to offer. On the other hand, if music is appreciated as a necessarily normal dimension of every experience of communal worship, then what follows may help to promote continued understanding of the liturgy, dialogue among those responsible for its implementation, and music itself as sung prayer.

GENERAL PRINCIPLES

THE STRUCTURE OF THE LITURGY

6.   A sacrament is celebrated either within Mass or with a liturgy of the word. This is the larger context for making judgments about what will be sung. This consideration will help to preserve the integrity of the entire liturgical prayer experience while, at the same time preventing the celebration from being top heavy in one or other part, and ensuring a good flow throughout.

7.   In all liturgical celebrations proper use should be made of the musical elements within the liturgy of the word, i.e., responsorial psalm, gospel acclamation, and sometimes an acclamation after the homily or profession of faith. *Music in Catholic Worship* treated these sung prayers in its discussion of eucharistic celebrations.[4] What was said there is applicable to all other liturgical celebrations which include a liturgy of the word. Further efforts are needed to make the assembly's response in song the normal pastoral practice in the celebration of God's Word.

THE PLACE OF SONG

8.   The structure of the liturgical unit will disclose the elements to be enhanced by music. For example, the liturgy of baptism or confirmation is placed between the liturgy of the word and the liturgy of the eucharist when celebrated at Mass. Each rite is composed of a number of elements, some of which lend themselves to singing. The first place to look for guidance in the use and choice of music is the rite itself. Often the rubrics contained in the approved liturgical books will indicate the place for song, and will also prescribe or suggest an appropriate text to be set musically.

Thus, in confirmation, the ritual recommends singing at the end of the renewal of baptismal promises and during the anointing.[5] In baptism, the acclamations after the profession of faith and after the baptism itself demand song, since they are by nature musical forms.[6]

9.   The various functions of sung prayer must be distinguished within liturgical rites. Sometimes song is meant to accompany ritual actions. In such cases the song is not independent but serves, rather, to support the prayer of the assembly when an action requires a longer period of time or when the action is going to be repeated several times. The music enriches the moments and keeps it from becoming burdensome. Ritual actions which employ such use of song include: the enrollment of names at the Election of Catechumens;[7] the processions in the celebration of baptism;[8] the vesting and sign of peace at an ordination;[9] the presentation of the Bible at the institution of a reader;[10] the anointings with chrism at confirmation[11] and ordination.[12]

10.   At other places in the liturgical action the sung prayer itself is a constituent element of the rite. While it is being prayed, no other ritual action is being performed. Such would be: the song of praise, which may be sung after communion;[13] the litany of saints at celebrations of Christian initiation,[14] ordination,[15] religious profession,[16] or the dedication of a church;[17] the proclamation of praise for God's mercy at the conclusion of the rite of reconciliation;[18] acclamations to conclude the baptismal profession of faith,[19] blessing of water,[20] or the thanksgiving over oil.[21] Even more important is the solemn chanting of the prayer of consecration by the bishop at ordinations,[22] or of the prayer of dedication of a church.[23] In each of these cases the music does not serve as a mere accompaniment, but as the integral mode by which the mystery is proclaimed and presented.

11.   Beyond determining the moments when song is needed, the musical form employed must match its liturgical function. For instance, at the end of the baptismal profession of faith the assembly may express its assent by an acclamation. In place of the text provided ("This is our faith . . . ") another appropriate formula or suitable song may be substituted.[24] An acclamation—a short, direct and strong declarative statement of the community's faith—will usually be more suitable for this than the several verses of a metrical hymn. The hymn form, appropriate in other contexts, may not work here because its form is usually less compact, less intense.

PASTORAL CONCERNS

12.   The pastoral judgment discussed in *Music in Catholic Worship* must always be applied when choosing music. Sacramental celebrations are significant moments in an individual's life, but just as importantly they are constitutive events of the community's life in Christ. The music selected must express the prayer of those who celebrate, while at the same time guarding against the imposition of private meanings on public rites. Individual preference is not, of itself, a sufficient principle for the choice of music in the liturgy. It must be balanced with liturgical and musical judgments and with the community's needs. Planning is a team undertaking, involving the presider, the musicians and the assembly.

PROGRESSIVE SOLEMNITY

13.   Music should be considered a normal and ordinary part of any liturgical celebration. However, this general principle is to be interpreted in the light of another one, namely, the principle of progressive solemnity.[25] This latter principle takes into account the abilities of the assembly, the relative importance of the individual rites and their constituent parts, and the relative festivity of the liturgical day. With regard to the Liturgy of the Hours, formerly a sung office meant a service in which everything was sung. Today the elements which lend themselves to singing (the psalms and canticles with their antiphons, the hymns, responsories, litanies and prayers, and the acclamations, greetings and responses) should be sung in accordance with the relative solemnity of the celebration. This principle likewise applies to the music sung in all other liturgical celebrations.

LANGUAGE AND MUSICAL IDIOMS

14.   Different languages may be used in the same celebration.[26] This may also be said of mixing different musical idioms and media. For example, pastoral reasons might suggest that in a given liturgical celebration some music reflect classical hymnody, with other music drawn from gospel or "folk" idioms, from contemporary service music, or from the plainsong or polyphonic repertoires. In the same celebration music may be rendered in various ways: unaccompanied; or accompanied by organ, piano, guitar or other instruments.

15.   While this principle upholding musical plurality has pastoral value, it should never be employed as a license for including poor music. At the same time, it needs to be recognized that a certain musical integrity within a liturgical prayer or rite can be achieved only by unity in the musical composition. Thus, it is recommended that for the acclamations in the

eucharistic prayer one musical style be employed.

MUSIC IN THE EUCHARIST

16.   The function of the various chants within the Eucharistic Liturgy has already been set out in *Music in Catholic Worship*, as well as above. Additional notes follow regarding specific elements.

ACCLAMATIONS

17.   The acclamations (gospel acclamation, doxology after the Lord's Prayer, and eucharistic acclamations—including the special acclamations of praise in the *Eucharistic Prayers of Masses with Children*[27]) are the preeminent sung prayers of the eucharistic liturgy. Singing these acclamations makes their prayer all the more effective. They should, therefore, be sung, even at weekday celebrations of the Eucharist. The gospel acclamation, moreover, must always be sung.[28]

PROCESSIONAL CHANTS

18.   Processional chants accompany an action. In some cases they have another function. The entrance song serves to gather and unite the assembly and set the tone for the celebration as much as to conduct the ministers into the sanctuary. The communion processional song serves a similiar purpose. Not only does it accompany movement, and thus give order to the assembly, it also assists each communicant in the realization and achievement of "the joy of all" and the fellowship of those "who join their voices in a single song."[29]

19.   While the responsorial form of singing is especially suitable for processions, the metrical hymn can also fulfill the function of the entrance song. If, however, a metrical hymn with several verses is selected, its form should be respected. The progression of text and music must be allowed to play out its course and achieve its purpose musically and poetically. In other words, the hymn should not be ended indiscriminately at the end of the procession. For this same reason, metrical hymns may not be the most suitable choices to accompany the preparation of the gifts and altar at the Eucharist, since the music should not extend past the time necessary for the ritual.

LITANIES

20.   The Lamb of God achieves greater significance at Masses when a larger sized eucharistic bread is broken for distribution and, when

communion is given under both kinds, chalices must be filled. The litany is prolonged to accompany this action of breaking and pouring.[30] In this case one should not hesitate to add tropes to the litany so that the prayerfulness of the rite may be enriched.

21.   The litany of the third form of the penitential rite at Mass increasingly is being set to music for deacon (or cantor) and assembly, with the people's response made in Greek or English. This litany functions as a "general confession made by the entire assembly"[31] and as praise of Christ's compassionate love and mercy. It is appropriately sung at more solemn celebrations and in Advent and Lent when the Gloria is omitted.[32] Similar litanic forms of song could be employed when the rite of sprinkling replaces the penitential rite.

MUSIC IN THE CELEBRATION OF
OTHER SACRAMENTS AND RITES

CHRISTIAN INITIATION

22.   As parish communities become more accustomed to initiate adults in stages, the opportunities for sung prayer within the *Rite of Christian Initiation of Adults* should become more apparent. The ritual book gives attention to the following: in the rite of becoming a catechumen, before the invitation to sponsors to present the candidates, and during their subsequent entry into the church building; in the rite of election, during the enrollment of names; in the Lenten scrutinies, after the prayer of exorcism; at the Easter Vigil celebration, an acclamation following baptism, song between the celebration of baptism and confirmation, and an acclamation during the anointing with chrism.[33]

23.   In the *Rite of Baptism of Children*, there is even greater emphasis on the sung prayer of the assembly: during the procession to the place where the Word of God will be celebrated; after the homily or after the short litany; during the procession to the place of baptism; an acclamation after the profession of faith and after each baptism; an acclamation or baptismal song during the procession to the altar.[34]

24.   At confirmation, the *Roman Pontifical* calls for song after the profession of faith and during the anointings with chrism.[35]

25.   Each of the various rites of initiation includes a liturgy of the word and is often followed by the Eucharist. Thus, in planning music for the celebration, proper emphasis should be given to each of the two or three primary liturgical rites. For instance, in the celebration of the baptism of a child, the assembly should not sing only at the times noted in ritual for that

sacrament while singing nothing during the celebration of the Word. Rather, a proper balance would require that singing be an essential element throughout the entire prayer experience.

26.   Composers of church music are encouraged to create musical settings of the acclamations from Sacred Scripture, the hymns in the style of the New Testament, and the songs from ancient liturgies which are included in the approved ritual books.[36] Much service music, set to texts in English, Spanish, and other vernacular languages, is still required for the full experience of these liturgical celebrations of initiation. Simpler musical settings would be especially welcome for use at celebrations where no musical accompanist is present.

RECONCILIATION

27.   Communal celebrations of reconciliation (Forms 2 and 3 of the sacrament, as well as non-sacramental penance services) normally require an entrance song or song of gathering; a responsorial psalm and a gospel acclamation during the liturgy of the word; an optional hymn after the homily; and a hymn of praise for God's mercy following the absolution.[37] The litany within the General Confession of Sins (alternating between the deacon or cantor and the assembly) or another appropriate song may also be sung, as well as the Lord's Prayer. Singing or soft instrumental music may be used during the time of individual confessions, especially when there is a large number of people present for the celebration.

CHRISTIAN MARRIAGE

28.   Weddings present particular challenges and opportunities to planners. It is helpful for a diocese or a parish to have a definite (but flexible) policy regarding wedding music. This policy should be communicated early to couples as a normal part of their preparation in order to avoid last minute crises and misunderstandings. Both musician and pastor should make every effort to assist couples to understand and share in the planning of their marriage liturgy. Sometimes the only music familiar to the couple is a song heard at a friend's ceremony and one not necessarily suitable to the sacrament. The pastoral musician will make an effort to demonstrate a wider range of possibilities to the couple, particularly in the choice of music to be sung by the entire assembly present for the liturgy.

29.   Particular decisions about choice and placement of wedding music should grow out of the three judgments proposed in *Music in Catholic Worship*. The liturgical judgment: Is the music's text, form, placement and

style congruent with the nature of liturgy?[38] The musical judgment: Is the music technically, aesthetically and expressively good irrespective of musical idiom or style?[39] The pastoral judgment: Will it help this assembly to pray?[40] Such a process of dialogue may not be as easy to apply as an absolute list of permitted or prohibited music, but in the long run it will be more effective pastorally.

CHRISTIAN BURIAL

30. Funerals, because of often difficult pastoral situations in which some family members and friends are overburdened with grief, unchurched or otherwise unable to enter into the liturgy, have frequently received little or no attention musically. In this respect, funerals may be the least successfully reformed of our liturgical rites.

31. It is the pastoral responsibility of parishes to provide liturgical music at all Masses of Christian Burial. Attempts to involve the congregation more actively are to be encouraged. Appropriate participation aids should be prepared and provided for members of the praying assembly.

32. Many parishes have found it helpful to form choirs of retired parishioners or others who are at home on weekdays, whose unique ministry it is to assist the grieving members of a funeral assembly by leading the sung prayer of the funeral liturgy. Where this is not possible, a cantor is able to perform a similar ministry. In all cases a serious effort should be made to move beyond the practice of employing a "funeral singer" to perform all the sung parts of the liturgy. Reconsideration should be given to the location of the singer, that person's role, and the kind of music that is sung. The cantor ought not individually sing or recite the congregational prayers as a substitute for the assembly. The same norms applicable to music at any Mass apply equally to the Mass of Christian Burial.[41]

33. The principle of progressive solemnity, already mentioned, applies especially to the rites of Christian Burial. A few things sung well (the acclamations, responsorial psalm, entrance and communion processionals, and song of farewell during the final commendation) should be given priority at funerals and may be drawn from a parish's common musical repertoire.

34.   A growing number of parishes celebrate at least some part of the Liturgy of the Hours, usually Evening Prayer, during one or more of the liturgical seasons. The question of singing in the office is treated in the *General Instruction on the Liturgy of the Hours* and should be consulted along with *Study Text VII*.[42] The following observations expand on what is written there.

METHODS OF SINGING THE PSALMS

35.   The psalms and canticles are songs; therefore are most satisfying when sung. The *General Instruction* lists several ways in which the psalms may be sung: responsorially, antiphonally or straight through *(in directum.)*[43] Music may be of the formula type (e.g., psalm tones) or composed for each psalm or canticle.

A. Responsorial

36.   The responsorial form of psalm singing appears to have been the original style for congregational use and still remains as the easiest method for engaging the congregation in the singing of psalms. In this model the psalmist or choir sings the verses of the psalm and the assembly responds with a brief antiphon (refrain). For pastoral or musical reasons, the *General Instruction* permits the substitution of other approved texts for these refrains.[44]

B. Antiphonal

37.   In the antiphonal style, the praying assembly is divided into two groups. The text of the psalm is shared between them; generally the same musical configuration (e.g., a psalm tone) is used by both. A refrain is ordinarily sung before and after the psalm by the whole body. This method of singing has its roots in the choir and monastic traditions. Today where it is used by the congregation, care must be taken that the latter can be at ease with this form of sung prayer.

C. Through-composed

38.   In a through-composed setting (*in directum*), the musical material is ordinarily not repeated, unless the psalm calls for it. The music may be for soloist, soloist and choir or choir alone (e.g., an anthem). Only rarely will this form be found in settings designed for congregational use. The purpose of the *in directum* setting should be to complement the literary structure of the psalm and to capture its emotions.

D. Metrical Psalms

39. The *General Instruction on the Liturgy of the Hours* makes no mention of the practice of singing the psalms in metrical paraphrases. This manner of psalm singing developed with some of the Reformation churches. Due to its four hundred year tradition, a large and important repertoire of metrical psalms in English is available today. Poets and composers continue to add to this resource of psalm settings.

40. While metrical psalmody may be employed fruitfully in the Church's liturgy (for instance, when a hymn is part of one of the rites), introduction of this musical form into the psalmody of the Liturgy of the Hours profoundly affects and alters the praying of the psalms as a ritual. Thus, metrical psalms should not be used as substitutes either for the responsorial psalm in a liturgy of the word of one of the rites or for the psalms in the Liturgy of the Hours.

FORMULA TONES

41. Formula tones (Gregorian plainsong tones, Anglican chants, faux-bourdons) are readily available and adaptable to modern use. Care should be taken in setting vernacular texts that the verbal accent pattern is not distorted by the musical cadence. These tones grew out of the paired half-line pattern of the Vulgate psalter. Modern translations of the psalms, however, have restored the Hebrew pattern of strophes (stanzas) of three, four, five or more lines. The sense unit in a strophe will frequently run beyond the musical pattern of the classical formula tone and will often require some repetition and even some accommodation for half-lines.

42. Another kind of formula tone has more recently been developed (e.g. the Gelineau and Bevenot systems) which is based on the strophe as a unit. These tones are longer and make provisions for irregularities in the number of lines. They more naturally fit the Grail psalter, which is the approved translation of the psalms for the Liturgy of the Hours.

43. Where formula tones are employed for the hours of the office, especially with a parish congregation, variety should be sought in the use of other forms of sung prayer, particularly the responsorial style. The Old Testament Canticle in Morning Prayer and the New Testament Canticle in Evening Prayer are especially suitable for this latter method of singing.

44.   The principle mentioned earlier concerning the mixing of different musical idioms has special application in a sung celebration of the Liturgy of the Hours. Psalms may be sung in the manners discussed above. Certain psalms, however, might be sung by a choir alone. A few might lend themselves to recitation. The nature and literary form of the psalm itself should suggest the way it is to be prayed. Likewise, in the same office some parts may be rendered unaccompanied, others accompanied by organ, piano, guitar or other instruments.

45.   Naturally, the hymns in the Liturgy of the Hours should be sung.[45] The responsories also lend themselves to singing, but as yet the number of published settings is few.[46] The readings are not usually chanted.[47] The introductory versicles and greetings can be easily learned and sung. The Lord's Prayer and the intercessions at Morning and Evening Prayer, either in the form of a litany with a fixed response (by far the easiest and most effective method for praying the intercessions) or as versicles and responses, are suited to singing.[48]

OTHER MATTERS

MUSIC AND THE LITURGICAL YEAR

46.   The mystery of God's love in Christ is so great that a single celebration cannot exhaust its meaning. Over the course of the centuries the various seasons and feasts have developed to express the richness of the paschal mystery and of our need to celebrate it. While the liturgy celebrates but one "theme," the dying and rising of Christ, and while Sunday is the original Christian feast, even so the liturgical year shows forth this mystery like so many facets of a resplendent jewel.[49]

47.   Music has been a unique means of celebrating this richness and diversity and of communicating the rhythm of the church year to the assembly. Music enhances the power of the readings and prayer to capture the special quality of the liturgical seasons. What would Christmas be without its carols? How diminished would the fifty-day Easter feast be without the solemn, joyful Alleluia song?

48.   Great care must be shown in the selection of music for seasons and feasts. Contemporary culture seems increasingly unwilling either to prepare for or to prolong Christian feasts and seasons. The Church's pastors and ministers must be aware of cultural phenomena which run counter to the liturgical year or even devalue our feasts and seasons, especially through consumerism. The season of Advent should be

preserved in its integrity, Christmas carols being reserved for the Christmas season alone. Hymns which emphasize the passion and death of Christ should be used only in the last week of the Lenten season. Easter should not be allowed to end in a day, but rather, the fifty days of its celebration should be planned as a unified experience.

MUSIC OF THE PAST

49.   *The Constitution on the Sacred Liturgy* sets forth the principles for the recent reform of the liturgy. At the same time it called the heritage of sacred music "a treasure of inestimable vaiue."[50] These purposes, while not opposed to each other, do exist in a certain tension. The restoration of active participation in the liturgy, the simplification of the rites, and the use of the vernacular have meant a massive change in the theory and practice of church music, a shift already detailed in *Music in Catholic Worship* and the present statement.

50.   Some have viewed this situation with profound regret. For some, the setting aside of the Latin repertoire of past centuries has been a painful experience, and a cause of bitter alienation. "Now is the time for healing."[51] It is also the time to make realistic assessments of what place the music of the past can still have in the liturgies of today.

51.   On the eve of the Council few parishes were performing the authentic repertoire recommended by Saint Pius X in his famous *motu proprio* on music.[52] Rather, most parishes generally used only a few of the simple chant Masses along with modern imitations of Renaissance motets and Masses. Moreover, the great music of the past was seldom the music of the ordinary parish church. Most often it was a product of the cathedrals and court chapels.

52.   However, singing and playing the music of the past is a way for Catholics to stay in touch with and preserve their rich heritage. A place can be found for this music, a place which does not conflict with the assembly's role and the other demands of the rite. Such a practice no longer envisions the performance of "Masses" as set pieces, but looks more to the repertoire of motets, antiphons and anthems which can be harmonized more easily with the nature of the renewed liturgy and with its pastoral celebration.[53]

53.   At Mass that place will typically include the time during the preparation of the gifts and the period after communion. A skillful director will also be able to find suitable choral repertoire to use as a prelude to the Mass, at the end of it, and at the Glory to God. *Jubilate Deo*, the basic collection of simple Gregorian chants, should also be employed as a source for the assembly's participation.

54.   Just as the great liturgical music of the past is to be remembered, cherished and used, so also the rich diversity of the cultural heritage of the many peoples of our country today must be recognized, fostered and celebrated. The United States of America is a nation of nations, a country in which people speak many tongues, live their lives in diverse ways, celebrate events in song and music in the folkways of their cultural, ethnic and racial roots.

55.   Liturgical music today must be as diverse and multi-cultural as the members of the assembly. Pastors and musicians must encourage not only the use of traditional music of other languages, but also the composition of new liturgical music appropriate to various cultures. Likewise the great musical gifts of the Hispanic, Black and other ethnic communities in the Church should enrich the whole Church in the United States in a dialogue of cultures.

INSTRUMENTAL MUSIC

56.   The liturgy prefers song to instrumental music. "As a combination of sacred music and words it forms a necessary or integral part of the solemn liturgy."[54] Yet the contribution of instrumentalists is also important, both in accompanying the singing and in playing by themselves.

57.   Church music legislation of the past reflected a culture in which singing was not only primary, but was presumed to be unaccompanied (chant and polyphony). The music of today, as indeed musical culture today, regularly presumes that the song is accompanied. This places instruments in a different light. The song achieves much of its vitality from the rhythm and harmony of its accompaniment. Instrumental accompaniment is a great support to an assembly in learning new music and in giving full voice to its prayer and praise in worship.

58.   Instrumental music can also assist the assembly in preparing for worship, in meditating on the mysteries, and in joyfully progressing in its passage from liturgy to life. Instrumental music, used in this way, must be understood as more than an easily dispensable adornment to the rites, a decoration to dress up a ceremony. It is rather ministerial, helping the assembly to rejoice, to weep, to be of one mind, to be converted, to pray. There is a large repertoire of organ music which has always been closely associated with the liturgy. Much suitable music can be selected from the repertoires of other appropriate instruments as well.

59.   The proper place of silence must not be neglected, and the temptation must be resisted to cover every moment with music.[55] There are times when instrumental interlude is able to bridge the gap between two parts of a ceremony and help to unify the liturgical action. But music's function is always ministerial and must never degenerate into idle background music.

RECORDED MUSIC

60.   The liturgy is a complexus of signs expressed by living human beings. Music, being preeminent among those signs, ought to be "live." While recorded music, therefore, might be used to advantage outside the liturgy as an aid in the teaching of new music, it should, as a general norm, never be used within the liturgy to replace the congregation, the choir, the organist or other instrumentalists.

61.   Some exceptions to this principle should be noted, however. Recorded music may be used to accompany the community's song during a procession out-of-doors and, when used carefully, in Masses with children.[56] Occasionally it might be used as an aid to prayer, for example, during long periods of silence in a communal celebration of reconciliation. It may never become a substitute for the community's song, however, as in the case of the responsorial psalm after a reading from Scripture or during the optional hymn of praise after communion.

62.   A prerecorded sound track is sometimes used as feature of contemporary "electronic music" composition. When combined with live voices and/or instruments, it is an integral part of the performance and, therefore, is a legitimate use of prerecorded music.

MUSIC MINISTRY

63.   The entire worshiping assembly exercises a ministry of music. Some members of the community, however, are recognized for the special gifts they exhibit in leading the musical praise and thanksgiving of Christian assemblies. These are the pastoral musicians, whose ministry is especially cherished by the Church.

64.   What motivates the pastoral musician? Why does he or she give so much time and effort to the service of the church at prayer? The only answer can be that the church musician is first a disciple and then a minister. The musician belongs first of all to the assembly; he or she is a worshiper above all. Like any member of the assembly, the pastoral musician needs to be a believer, needs to experience conversion, needs to hear the Gospel and so proclaim the praise of God. Thus, the pastoral

Liturgical Music Today

musician is not merely an employee or volunteer. He or she is a minister, someone who shares faith, serves the community, and expresses the love of God and neighbor through music.

65. Additional efforts are needed to train men and women for the ministry of music. Colleges and universities offering courses of studies in liturgical music, as well as a growing number of regional and diocesan centers for the formation of liturgical ministers, are encouraged to initiate or to continue programs which develop musical skills and impart a thorough understanding of the liturgy of the Church.

66. The musician's gift must be recognized as a valued part of the pastoral effort, and for which proper compensation must be made.[57] Clergy and musicians should strive for mutual respect and cooperation in the achievement of their common goals.

67. As the assembly's principal liturgical leaders, priests and deacons must continue to be mindful of their own musical role in the liturgy. Priests should grow more familiar with chanting the presidential prayers of the Mass and other rites. Deacons, too, in the admonitions, exhortations, and especially in the litanies of the third penitential rite and in the general intercessions of the Mass, have a significant musical role to play in worship.

68. Among music ministers, the cantor has come to be recognized as having a crucial role in the development of congregational singing. Besides being qualified to lead singing, he or she must have the skills to introduce and teach new music, and to encourage the assembly. This must be done with sensitivity so that the cantor does not intrude on the communal prayer or become manipulative. Introductions and announcements should be brief and avoid a homiletic style.

69. The cantor's role is distinct from that of the psalmist, whose ministry is the singing of the verses of the responsorial psalm and communion psalm. Frequently the two roles will be combined in one person.

70. A community will not grow in its ability either to appreciate or express its role in musical liturgy if each celebration is thought of as a discrete moment. A long-range plan must be developed which identifies how music will be used in the parish and how new music will be learned. The abilities of the congregation should never be misjudged. Some cannot or will not sing, for whatever reason. Most will take part and will enjoy learning new music if they have effective leaders.

COPYRIGHT

71.   In the last decade pastors and musicians have become more aware of the legal and moral·implications of copyright.[58] As a result parishes and institutions are now more sensitive to the need composers, poets and publishers have to receive a just compensation for their creative work. Publishers have cooperated in making their requirements known and their music available to reprint at reasonable rates, an effort for which they deserve the thanks of the Church in the United States.

72.   Additional education regarding copyright needs to continue. At the same time, parishes and other institutions should annually budget sufficient monies for the purchase of music necessary for the proper celebration of the liturgy. The need for much copying would then be lessened.

CONCLUSION

73.   The past decade has shown important signs of growth. The eagerness of many congregations to make a beginning in singing has been matched by a second harvest of musical compositions. As time goes by, new generations will come to accept, as a matter of course, what was brand new and very strange only a few years ago, namely, that all should join in the songs and prayers of the liturgy.

74.   The Church in the United States continues on its journey of liturgical renewal and spiritual growth. It is the hope of the Bishops' Committee on the Liturgy that this statement will be a further encouragement in our progress along that course. The words of Saint Augustine remind us of our pilgrimage: "You should sing as wayfarers do—sing but continue your journey. Do not be lazy, but sing to make your journey more enjoyable. Sing, but keep going."[59]

NOTES

1. MCW; BCL, "The Place of Music in Eucharistic Celebrations," Nov 1967.
2. See *The Liturgy Documents* for this text.
3. MCW, introduction.
4. MCW 45, 55, 63.
5. Rite of Confirmation 23, 29.
6. Baptism 59, 60.
7. RCIA 146.
8. Baptism 42, 52, 67.
9. Ordination of a Deacon, 25; Ordination of a Priest, 27; Ordination of a Bishop, 35.
10. Institution of a Reader, 7.
11. Rite of Confirmation, 46.
12. Ordination of a Priest, 25.
13. GI 56j.
14. RCIA 214; Baptism 48.
15. Ordination of a Deacon, 18; of a Priest, 17; of a Bishop, 21.
16. Consecration to a Life of Virginity, 20, 59.
17. Dedication of a Church and an Altar, 58.
18. Rite of Penance, 56.
19. Baptism 59.
20. RCIA 389; Baptism 223–234.
21. Pastoral Care of the Sick, 75b.
22. Ordination of a Deacon, 21; of a Priest, 22; of a Bishop, 26.
23. Dedication of a Church and an Altar, 62.
24. Baptism 96.
25. The Liturgy of the Hours, General Instruction [= GILOTH], 273.
26. GILOTH 276.
27. Eucharistic Prayers for Masses with Children and for Masses of Reconciliation, provisional text.
28. LMIn, 23. "The Alleluia or the verse before the gospel must be sung and during it, all stand. It is not to be sung by the cantor who intones it or by the choir, but by the whole congregation together."
29. GI 56i.
30. GI 56e.
31. GI 29.
32. GI 31.
33. RCIA, 74, 90, 146, 164, 171, 178, 221, 227, 231.
34. Baptism 42, 47, 52, 59, 60, 67.
35. Rite of Confirmation, 23, 29.
36. RCIA, 390; Baptism 225–245. See also "A Letter to Composers of Liturgical Music from the Bishops' Committee on the Liturgy" in BCL *Newsletter* XVI (Dec 1980) 237® 239.
37. Rite of Penance, 56. The ritual recommends the Canticle of Mary (Lk 1:46–55), Psalm 136 or another psalm listed in 206 as especially fitting as a song of praise.
38. MCW 30–38.
39. MCW 26–29.
40. MCW 39–41.
41. Rite of Funerals, 23–25, especially 25,5.
42. GILOTH 267–284; BCL, *Study Text VII: The Liturgy of the Hours* (Washington: USCC, 1981).
43. GILOTH 279, 121–123.
44. GILOTH 274.
45. GILOTH 280.
46. GILOTH 281–282.
47. GILOTH 283.
48. GILOTH 284.
49. GNLY 4; CSL 104ff.
50. CSL 112.
51. BCL, *A Commemorative Statement* (Nov 1978), in BCL *Newsletter* XIV (Dec 1978) 143.
52. Pius X, motu proprio, *Tra Le Sollecitudini* (22 Nov 1903).
53. MS 53.
54. CSL 112.
55. GI 23; GILOTH 202; Paul VI, apostolic exhortation, *Evangelica Testificatio* (29 June 1971) 46.
56. *Notitiae* 127 (Feb 1977) 94; DMC, 32.
57. MCW 77; BCL, A Commemorative Statement (Nov 1978) in BCL *Newsletter* XIV (Dec 1978) 143–144.

58. BCL *Newsletter* III, 12 (Dec 1967) 109; *Ibid.* V, 5 (May 1969) 177; *Ibid.* XVI (Jan 1980) 197; FDLC Liturgical Arts Committee, Copyright Update: Reprint Permission Policies of Publishers of Liturgical Music and Sacred Scripture (Washington: FDLC, 1982).

59. St. Augustine, Sermo 256, 3 (PL 38:1193).

ENVIRONMENT AND ART
IN
CATHOLIC WORSHIP

1978

BACKGROUND

Like *Music in Catholic Worship*, this is the work of the United States Bishops' Committee on the Liturgy. It was published in 1978 and is widely recognized as a landmark document. Its first concern is fundamentals: the liturgy is celebrated by the people assembled, and it is this assembly—the church—that is the primary environment of our liturgy. This assembly needs those arts with which we celebrate. Only in that context can we speak of the building (the house of the church), of gestures and movement, and finally of furnishings and the objects used in liturgy. To all of these we bring the insights of the introduction and the requirements established in the first two chapters.

It would be a mistake to turn to this document only when there is a question of church renovation or commissioning new vestments. *Environment and Art in Catholic Worship* is a standard. It offers a vision of parish liturgy that should be regularly pondered and discussed by all charged with liturgical responsibilities.

OUTLINE

ENVIRONMENT AND ART IN CATHOLIC WORSHIP

INTRODUCTION

1.   Faith involves a good tension between human modes of expressive communications and God himself, whom our human tools can never adequately grasp. God transcends. God is mystery. God cannot be contained in or confined by any of our words or images or categories.

2.   While our words and art forms cannot contain or confine God, they can, like the world itself, be icons, avenues of approach, numinous presences, ways of touching without totally grasping or seizing. Flood, fire, the rock, the sea, the mountain, the cloud, the political situations and institutions of succeeding periods—in all of them Israel touched the face of God, found help for discerning a way, moved toward the reign of justice and peace. Biblical faith assures us that God covenants a people through human events and calls the covenanted people to shape human events.

3.   And then in Jesus, the Word of God is flesh: "This is what we proclaim to you: what was from the beginning, what we have heard, what we have seen with our eyes, what we have looked upon and our hands have touched—we speak of the word of life."[1]

4.   Christians have not hesitated to use every human art in their celebration of the saving work of God in Jesus Christ, although in every historical period they have been influenced, at times inhibited, by cultural circumstances. In the resurrection of the Lord, all things are made new. Wholeness and healthiness are restored, because the reign of sin and death is conquered. Human limits are still real and we must be conscious of them. But we must also praise God and give God thanks with the human means we have available. God does not need liturgy; people do, and people have only their own arts and styles of expression with which to celebrate.

5.   Like the covenant itself, the liturgical celebrations of the faith community (Church) involve the whole person. They are not purely religious or merely rational and intellectual exercises, but also human experiences calling on all human faculties: body, mind, senses, imagination, emotions, memory. Attention to these is one of the urgent needs of contemporary liturgical renewal.

6.   Historically, music has enjoyed a preeminence among the arts of public worship, and there is no clear evidence to justify denying it the same place today. The Bishops' Committee on the Liturgy, therefore, published guidelines *(Music in Catholic Worship, 1972)* encouraging attention to music, both instrumental and choral/vocal. This companion booklet, *Environment and Art in Catholic Worship,* offers guidelines to encourage the other arts necessary for a full experience in public worship. The two booklets, therefore, should be used together, complementing one another, by those responsible for planning and conducting liturgical celebrations. For that reason, music is excluded from the specific concerns of the following pages.

7.   If we maintain that no human words or art forms can contain or exhaust the mystery of God's love, but that all words and art forms can be used to praise God in the liturgical assembly, then we look for criteria to judge music, architecture, and the other arts in relation to public worship.[2]

8.   The reason for offering principles to guide rather than blueprints to follow was stated clearly by the Council fathers: "The Church has not adopted any particular style of art as her very own; it has admitted styles from every period according to the natural talents and circumstances of peoples, and the needs of the various rites. Thus, in the course of the centuries, she has brought into being a treasury of art which must be carefully preserved. The art of our own days, coming from every race and region, shall also be given free scope in the Church, provided that it adorns the sacred buildings and holy rites with due reverence and honor; thereby it is enabled to contribute its own voice to that wonderful chorus of praise . . ."[3]

I. THE WORSHIP OF GOD AND ITS REQUIREMENTS

LITURGY AND TRADITION

9.   Liturgy has a special and unique place in the life of Christians in the local churches, their communities of faith. Each Church gathers regularly to praise and thank God, to remember and make present God's great deeds, to offer common prayer, to realize and celebrate the kingdom of peace and justice. That action of the Christian assembly is liturgy.

10.   Common traditions carried on, developed and realized in each community make liturgy an experience of the Church which is both local and universal. The roots as well as the structure of its liturgical celebrations are biblical and ecclesial, asserting a communion with believers of all times and places. This tradition furnishes the symbol language of that action, along with structures and patterns refined

through the centuries of experience, and gives the old meanings new life in our time, our place, with our new knowledge, talents, competencies, arts. Therefore, this celebration is that of a community at a given place and time, celebrated with the best of its resources, talents and arts in the light of our own tradition.[4]

A CLIMATE OF HOSPITALITY

11.   As common prayer and ecclesial experience, liturgy flourishes in a climate of hospitality: a situation in which people are comfortable with one another, either knowing or being introduced to one another; a space in which people are seated together, with mobility, in view of one another as well as the focal points of the rite, involved as participants and *not* as spectators.[5]

THE EXPERIENCE OF MYSTERY

12.   The experience of mystery which liturgy offers is found in its God-consciousness and God-centeredness. This involves a certain beneficial tension with the demands of hospitality, requiring a manner and an environment which invite contemplation (seeing beyond the face of the person or the thing, a sense of the holy, the numinous, mystery). A simple and attractive beauty in everything that is used or done in liturgy is the most effective invitation to this kind of experience. One should be able to sense something special (and nothing trivial) in everything that is seen and heard, touched and smelled, and tasted in liturgy.

13.   Incarnation, the paschal mystery and the Holy Spirit in us are faith's access to the transcendence, holiness, otherness of God. An action like liturgy, therefore, has special significance as a means of relating to God, or responding to God's relating to us. This does not mean that we have "captured" God in our symbols. It means only that God has graciously loved us on our own terms, in ways corresponding to our condition. Our response must be one of depth and totality, of authenticity, genuineness, and care with respect to everything we use and do in liturgical celebration.

THE OPENING UP OF SYMBOLS

14.   Every word, gesture, movement, object, appointment must be real in the sense that it is our own. It must come from the deepest understanding of ourselves (not careless, phony, counterfeit, pretentious, exaggerated, etc.). Liturgy has suffered historically from a kind of minimalism and an overriding concern for efficiency, partly because sacramental causality and efficacy have been emphasized at the expense of sacramental significance. As our symbols tended in practice to shrivel up and petrify, they became much more manageable and efficient. They still "caused," were still "efficacious" even though they had often ceased to signify in the richest, fullest sense.

15. Renewal requires the opening up of our symbols, especially the fundamental ones of bread and wine, water, oil, the laying on of hands, until we can experience all of them as authentic and appreciate their symbolic value.

THE PERSONAL – COMMUNAL EXPERIENCE

16. A culture which is oriented to efficiency and production has made us insensitive to the symbolic function of persons and things. Also, the same cultural emphasis on individuality and competition has made it more difficult for us to appreciate the liturgy as a *personal-communal* experience. As a consequence, we tend to identify anything private and individual as "personal." But, by inference, anything communal and social is considered impersonal. For the sake of good liturgy, this misconception must be changed.

17. To identify liturgy as an important *personal-communal* religious experience is to see the virtue of simplicity and commonness in liturgical texts, gestures, music, etc. This is easier said than done. But it does require a persevering effort to respect the Church's mind in terms of its common feelings and simplicity, for example, by not drowning the action in a flood of words or by not making the action more complex than necessary in order to signify the gospel essentials.

THE SACRED

18. An important part of contemporary Church renewal is the awareness of the community's recognition of the sacred. Environment and art are to foster this awareness. Because different cultural and subcultural groups in our society may have quite different styles of artistic expression, one cannot demand any universal sacred forms.[6]

QUALITY AND APPROPRIATENESS

19. This is not that liturgy makes no demand upon architecture, music and the other arts. To be true to itself and to protect its own integrity, liturgy must make demands. Basically, its demands are two: *quality* and *appropriateness*. Whatever the style or type, no art has a right to a place in liturgical celebration if it is not of high quality and if it is not appropriate.[7]

20. *Quality* is perceived only by contemplation, by standing back from things and really trying to see them, trying to let them speak to the beholder. Cultural habit has conditioned the contemporary person to look at things in a more pragmatic way: "What is it worth?" "What will it do?" Contemplation sees the hand stamp of the artist, the honesty and care that went into an object's making, the pleasing form and color and texture. Quality means love and care in the making of something, honesty and genuineness with any materials used, and the artist's special gift in

producing a harmonious whole, a well-crafted work. This applies to music, architecture, sculpture, painting, pottery making, furniture making, as well as to dance, mime or drama—in other words, to any art form that might be employed in the liturgical environment or action.

21.   *Appropriateness* is another demand that liturgy rightfully makes upon any art that would serve its action. The work of art must be appropriate in two ways: 1) it must be capable of bearing the weight, awe, reverence, and wonder which the liturgical action expresses; 2) it must clearly *serve* (and not interrupt) ritual action which has its own structure, rhythm and movement.

22.   The first point rules out anything trivial and self-centered, anything fake, cheap or shoddy, anything pretentious or superficial. That kind of appropriateness, obviously, is related to quality. But it demands more than quality. It demands a kind of transparency, so that we see and experience both the work of art and something beyond it.

23.   The second point (to serve) refers both to the physical environment of public worship and to any art forms which might be employed as part of the liturgical action (e.g., ritual movement, gestures, audio-visuals, etc.).

THE SERVING ENVIRONMENT

24.   By environment we mean the larger space in which the action of the assembly takes place. At its broadest, it is the setting of the building in its neighborhood, including outdoor spaces. More specifically it means the character of a particular space and how it affects the action of the assembly. There are elements in the environment, therefore, which contribute to the overall experience, e.g., the seating arrangement, the placement of liturgical centers of action, temporary decoration, light, acoustics, spaciousness, etc. The environment is appropriate when it is beautiful, when it is hospitable, when it clearly invites and needs an assembly of people to complete it.

Furthermore, it is appropriate when it brings people close together so that they can see and hear the entire liturgical action, when it helps people feel involved and become involved. Such an environment works with the liturgy, not against it.

THE SERVICE OF THE ARTS

25.   If an art form is used in liturgy it must aid and serve the action of liturgy since liturgy has its own structure, rhythm and pace: a gathering, a building up, a climax, and a descent to dismissal. It alternates between persons and groups of persons, between sound and silence, speech and song, movement and stillness, proclamation and reflection, word and action. The art form must never seem to interrupt, replace, or bring the

course of liturgy to a halt. If one uses film, for example, in such a way that one seems to be saying, "We will stop the liturgy for a few moments now in order to experience this art form," then that use is inappropriate. If, however, an art form is used to enhance, support and illumine a part or parts of the liturgical action or the whole action, it can be both appropriate and rewarding.

26.   A major and continuing educational effort is required among believers in order to restore respect for competence and expertise in all the arts and a desire for their best use in public worship. This means winning back to the service of the Church professional people whose places have long since been taken by "commercial" producers, or volunteers who do not have the appropriate qualifications. Both sensitivity to the arts and willingness to budget resources for these are the conditions of progress so that quality and appropriateness can be real.

II. THE SUBJECT OF LITURGICAL ACTION:
THE CHURCH

27.   To speak of environmental and artistic requirements in Catholic worship, we have to begin with ourselves—we who are the Church, the baptized, the initiated.

THE ASSEMBLY OF BELIEVERS
28.   Among the symbols with which liturgy deals, none is more important than this assembly of believers. It is common to use the same name to speak of the building in which those persons worship, but that use is misleading. In the words of ancient Christians, the building used for worship is called *domus ecclesiae,* the house of the Church.

THE ACTION OF THE ASSEMBLY
29.   The most powerful experience of the sacred is found in the celebration and the persons celebrating, that is, it is found in the action of the assembly: the living words, the living gestures, the living sacrifice, the living meal. This was at the heart of the earliest liturgies. Evidence of this is found in their architectural floor plans which were designed as general gathering spaces, spaces which allowed the whole assembly to be part of the action.

30.   Because liturgical celebration is the worship action of the entire Church, it is desirable that persons representing the diversity of ages, sexes, ethnic and cultural groups in the congregation should be involved in planning and ministering in the liturgies of the community. Special competencies in music, public readings, and any other skills and arts

related to public worship should be sought, respected and used in celebration. Not only the planners and ministers, however, are active in the liturgy. The entire congregation is an active component. There is no audience, no passive element in the liturgical celebration. This fact alone distinguishes it from most other public assemblies.

31.   The assembly's celebration, that is, celebration in the midst of the faith community, by the whole community, is the normal and normative way of celebrating any sacrament or other liturgy. Even when the communal dimension is not apparent, as sometimes in communion for the sick or for prisoners, the clergy or minister function within the context of the entire community.

32.   The action of the assembly is also unique since it is not merely a "celebration of life," reflecting all of the distinctions stemming from color, sex, class, etc. Quite the contrary, liturgy requires the faith community to set aside all those distinctions and divisions and classifications. By doing this the liturgy celebrates the reign of God, and as such maintains the tension between what is (the status quo of our daily lives) and what must be (God's will for human salvation—liberation and solidarity). This uniqueness gives liturgy its key and central place in Christian life as seen from the perspective of an actual community. Just as liturgy makes its own demands on the environment and the arts, so, too, does the assembly. When the assembly gathers with its own varied background, there is a commonness demanded which stems from our human condition. The commonality here seeks the best which people can bring together rather than what is compromised or less noble. For the assembly seeks its own expression in an atmosphere which is beautiful, amidst actions which probe the entire human experience. This is what is most basic and most noble. It is what the assembly seeks in order to express the heart of the Church's liturgy.

CONTEMPORARY

33.   Contemporary art forms belong to the liturgical expressions of the assembly as surely as the art forms of the past. The latter are part of our common memory, our communion (which extends over time as well as over geographical boundaries). Contemporary art is our own, the work of artists, of our time and place, and belongs in our celebrations as surely as we do. If liturgy were to incorporate only the acceptable art of the past, conversion, commitment and tradition would have ceased to live. The assembly should, therefore, be equally unhesitating in searching out, patronizing and using the arts and media of past and present. Because it is symbolic communication, liturgy is more dependent on past tradition than many human activities are. Because it is the action of a contemporary assembly, it has to clothe its basically traditional structures with the living flesh and blood of our times and our arts.

34.   Because the assembly gathers in the presence of God to celebrate his saving deeds, liturgy's climate is one of awe, mystery, wonder, reverence, thanksgiving and praise. So it cannot be satisfied with anything less than the *beautiful* in its environment and all its artifacts, movements, and appeals to the senses.[8] Admittedly difficult to define, the beautiful is related to the sense of the numinous, the holy. Where there is evidently no care for this, there is an environment basically unfriendly to mystery and awe, an environment too casual, if not careless, for the liturgical action. In a world dominated by science and technology, liturgy's quest for the beautiful is a particularly necessary contribution to full and balanced human life.

THE HUMAN EXPERIENCE

35.   To gather intentionally in God's presence is to gather our total selves, our complete persons—a "living sacrifice." Other human activities tend to be more incomplete, specialized, and to claim one or the other facet of ourselves, lives, talents, roles. Liturgy is total, and therefore must be much more than a merely rational or intellectual exercise. Valid tradition reflects this attention to the whole person. In view of our culture's emphasis on reason, it is critically important for the Church to reemphasize a more total approach to the human person by opening up and developing the non-rational elements of liturgical celebration: the concerns for feelings of conversion, support, joy, repentance, trust, love, memory, movement, gesture, wonder.

SINFUL

36.   The Church is a church of sinners, and the fact that God forgives, accepts and loves sinners places the liturgical assembly under a fundamental obligation to be honest and unpretentious, without deceit or affectation, in all it does. If all distinctions have been stripped away, then basic honesty has to be carried through in all the words, gestures and movements, art forms, objects, furnishings of public worship. Nothing which pretends to be other than it is has a place in celebration, whether it is a person, cup, table or sculpture.

SERVANT

37.   Different ministries in such an assembly do not imply "superiority" or "inferiority." Different functions are necessary in the liturgy as they are in any human, social activity. The recognition of different gifts and talents and the ordination, institution or delegation for the different services required (priest, reader, acolyte, musician, usher, etc.) is to facilitate worship. These are services to the assembly and those who perform them are servants of God who render services to the assembly. Those who perform such ministries are indeed servants of the assembly.

38. The liturgical assembly, as presented, is Church, and as Church is servant to the world. It has a commitment to be sign, witness, and instrument of the reign of God. That commitment must be reflected and implemented not only in the individual lives of its members but also in the community's choices and in its is use of its money, property and other resources. Liturgical buildings and spaces should have the same witness value. Their planning should involve representatives of oppressed and disadvantaged parts of the communities in which they are located.

III. A HOUSE FOR THE CHURCH'S
LITURGICAL CELEBRATIONS

39. The congregation, its liturgical action, the furniture and the other objects it needs for its liturgical action—these indicate the necessity of a space, a place, a hall, or a building for the liturgy. It will be a place for praying and singing, for listening and speaking—a place for human interaction and active participation—where the mysteries of God are recalled and celebrated in human history. The servant nature of the Church in relation to the rest of the community in its area (and in the world) invites it to consider the broader needs of the community, especially in the community's deprived, handicapped and suffering members, and therefore to consider a breadth of possible uses of its buildings.

PRIMARY DEMAND: THE ASSEMBLY

40. In no case, however, should this mean a lack of attention to the requirements of the liturgical celebration or a yielding of the primary demands that liturgy must make upon the space: the gathering of the faith community in a participatory and hospitable atmosphere for word and eucharist, for initiation and reconciliation, for prayer and praise and song.

41. Such a space acquires a sacredness from the sacred action of the faith community which uses it. As a place, then, it becomes quite naturally a reference and orientation point for believers. The historical problem of the church as a *place* attaining a dominance over the faith community need not be repeated as long as Christians respect the primacy of the living assembly.

42. The norm for designing liturgical space is the assembly and its liturgies. The building or cover enclosing the architectural space is a shelter or "skin" for a liturgical action. It does not have to "look like" anything else, past or present. Its integrity, simplicity and beauty, its physical location and landscaping should take into account the neighborhood, city and area in which it is built.

43.   Many local Churches must use spaces designed and built in a former period, spaces which may now be unsuitable for the liturgy. In the renovation of these spaces for contemporary liturgical use, there is no substitute for an ecclesiology that is both ancient and modern in the fullest sense. Nor is there any substitute for a thorough understanding of ritual needs in human life and the varied liturgical tradition of the Church. With these competencies, a renovation can respect both the best qualities of the original structure and the requirements of contemporary worship.

TEAMWORK

44.   Whether designing a new space for the liturgical action or renovating an old one, teamwork and preparation by the congregation (particularly its liturgy committee), clergy, architect and consultant (liturgy and art) are essential.[9] A competent architect should have the assistance of a consultant in liturgy and art both in the discussion stages of the project (dialogue with congregation and clergy as well as among themselves) and throughout the stages of design and building. Recent competitions in the design of buildings for liturgy have indicated the advantages of such consultation.

45.   The congregation, or local Church, commonly acting through its delegates, is a basic and primary component in the team. The congregation's work is to acquaint the architect and consultant with its own self-image as Church and its sense of the larger community in which it exists. It is important for the congregation and clergy to recognize the area of their own competence. This will also define the limits beyond which they should not go. Respect for the competence of others in their respective fields is essential for good teamwork.

46.   If a community has selected competent and skilled persons, they will receive from the architect and the consultant a design which will stimulate and inspire, as well as serve the assembly's needs as they have been described. When financial benefactors are involved, they have the same part in this process as the congregation and the clergy, subject to the same prior requirements of good liturgy.

47.   A good architect will possess both the willingness to learn from the congregation and sufficient integrity not to allow the community's design taste or preference to limit the freedom necesary for a creative design. The architect will look to the congregation and clergy for an understanding of the character and purpose of the liturgical assembly. With that rapport, it is the architect's task to design the space, using contemporary materials and modes of construction, in dialogue with consultants who are expert in the areas of liturgical art, rites, acoustics and other specialized issues.

48.   The liturgical-artistic consultant is an invaluable partner of the architect, for the purposes of space can be imagined and the place creatively designed only by a competent designer (architect) who is nourished with liturgy's tradition, its current shape, together with the appropriate furniture and other objects used. The feeling of liturgical action is as crucial as the craft of the designer in producing a worthy space and place.

49.   One of the primary requirements of the space is visibility of all in the assembly: others in the congregation as well as the principal focal point of the ritual action.

50.   Visibility speaks more to the quality of view than merely the mechanics of seeing. A space must create a sense that what is seen is proximate, important and personal. The arrangement of the space should consider levels of priority in what is seen, allowing visual flow from one center of liturgical action to another. Furthermore, the sense and variety of light, artificial or natural, contribute greatly to what is seen.

51.   Audibility of all (congregation and ministers) is another primary requirement. A space that does not require voice amplification is ideal. Where an amplifying system is necessary, provision for multiple microphone jacks should be made (e.g., at the altar, ambo, chair, font, space immediately in front of the congregation, and a few spots through the congregation). Since the liturgical space must accommodate both speech and song, there must be a serious acoustical consideration of the conflicting demands of the two. The services of an acoustical engineer can enable architect and builder to be aware of certain disadvantages in rooms that are exclusively "dry" or "live." A room designed to deaden all sounds is doomed to kill liturgical participation.

THE SCALE OF A SPACE

52.   The liturgical space should have a "good feeling" in terms of human scale, hospitality and graciousness. It does not seek to impress, or even less, to dominate, but its clear aim is to facilitate the public worship and common prayer of the faith community.

UNITY OF SPACE

53.   Special attention must be given to the unity of the entire liturgical space. Before considering the distinction of roles within the liturgy, the space should communicate an integrity (a sense of oneness, of wholeness) and a sense of being the gathering place of the initiated community. Within that one space there are different areas corresponding to different roles and functions, but the wholeness of the total space should be

strikingly evident.

54. Planning for a convergence of pathways to the liturgical space in a concourse or foyer or other place adequate for gathering before or after liturgies is recommended. In some climates this might be outdoors. Such a gathering-space can encourage introductions, conversations, the sharing of refreshments after a liturgy, the building of the kind of community sense and feeling recognized now to be a prerequisite of good celebration.

IV. THE ARTS AND THE
BODY LANGUAGE OF LITURGY

55. Liturgical celebration, because of its public and corporate nature, and because it is an expression of the total person within a community, involves not only the use of a common language and ritual tradition, but also the use of a common place, common furnishings, common art forms and symbols, common gestures, movements and postures. But when one examines the quality of these common elements, one finds that an uncommon sensitivity is demanded. For these common elements create a tremendous impact on the assembly visually, environmentally and bodily. This section and those following will offer a basic orientation and some principles with regard to each of these elements. We will begin with the sense of the person in the space: the bodily movement.

PERSONAL GESTURES

56. The liturgy of the Church has been rich in a tradition of ritual movement and gestures. These actions, subtly, yet really, contribute to an environment which can foster prayer or which can distract from prayer. When the gestures are done in common, they contribute to the unity of the worshipping assembly. Gestures which are broad and full in both a visual and tactile sense, support the entire symbolic ritual. When the gestures are done by the presiding minister, they can either engage the entire assembly and bring them into an even greater unity, or if done poorly, they can isolate.[10]

POSTURE

57. In an atmosphere of hospitality, posture will never be a marshalled, forced uniformity. It is important that the liturgical space can accommodate certain common postures: sitting for preparations, for listening, for silent reflection; standing for the gospel, solemn prayer, praise and acclamation; kneeling for adoration, penitential rites. Those who suffer from handicaps of one sort or another must be carefully planned for so that they can participate in the liturgy without unnecessary strain or burden.

58.   Attentiveness, expressed in posture and eye contact, is a requirement for full participation and involvement in the liturgy. It is part of one's share in the life of the community and something one owes the rest of the assembly. Because of this, a space and its seating should be so designed that one can see the places of the ritual action, but further, that these spaces cannot be so distant that eye contact is impossible, for eye contact is important in any act of ministry—in reading, preaching, in leading the congregation in music and prayer. Not only are the ministers to be visible to all present, but among themselves the faithful should be able to have visual contact, being attentive to one another as they celebrate the liturgy.

PROCESSIONS

59.   Beyond seeing what is done, because good liturgy is a ritual action, it is important that worship space allow for movement.[11] Processions and interpretations through bodily movement (dance) can become meaningful parts of the liturgical celebration if done by truly competent persons in the manner that benefits the total liturgical action. A procession should move from one place to another with some purpose (not simply around the same space), and should normally include the congregation, sometimes with stops of stations for particular prayers, readings, or actions. The design of the space and arrangement of the seating should allow this sort of movement. There should be concern for the quality, the gracefulness, and the surety of this movement. Seating arrangements which prohibit the freedom of action to take place, are inappropriate.

60.   In the general movement of the liturgical rite, the role of the one who presides is critical and central. The area of presiding should allow that person to be attentive to and present to the entire congregation, the other ministers, and each part of the liturgical action, even if not personally leading the action at that moment. The place should allow one to conduct the various ministers in their specific activity and roles of leadership, as well as the congregation in its common prayer.

61.   In the above instances, audibility and visibility to all in the assembly are minimal requirements. The chair, the lectern and the altar should be constructed so that all can see and hear the person of the reader or one who presides.

EASE OF MOVEMENT

62.   The proper use of furniture and other objects which have a symbolic function is important in ritual action. These objects are next in importance to the people themselves and their total environment. They are part of a total rite which everyone present should be able to

experience as fully as possible. Thus, their placement and use should allow for ease of movement.

V. FURNISHINGS
FOR LITURGICAL CELEBRATION

63. Because the Sunday eucharistic assembly is the most fundamental ecclesial symbol, the requirements of that celebration will have the strongest claim in the provision of furnishings for liturgy. Consequently, any liturgical space must take into consideration not only the general requirements of the assembly but also the need for a feeling of contact with altar, ambo and celebrant's chair.

64. This primacy of the eucharistic assembly, however, should not discourage a liturgical life of greater richness and variety in the local Church. In planning construction, renovation or refurnishing of liturgical spaces, baptism and the other sacraments, morning and evening prayer, services of the word, prayer meetings and other community events should be kept in mind.

65. When multi-functional use of the space is indicated by the needs either of the faith community or of the surrounding city, town or rural area which the faith community services, a certain flexibility or movability should be considered even for the essential furnishings. Great care, however, should be taken in the design and care of movable furnishings that none of the dignity, noble and simple beauty proper to such objects is sacrificed. There is no reason why a movable altar or ambo need have a flimsy, cheap or disposable appearance.

66. Normally the furnishings used in a liturgical celebration of any kind should be placed before the celebration begins and remain stationary during the celebration. Ritual action is not enhanced by the moving of furniture during a rite. A careful arrangement of furnishings is an integral part of liturgical planning.

DIGNITY AND BEAUTY

67. Consultation with persons who are experts, at least one in liturgy and one in the arts, is not a luxury but a necessity for those responsible for furnishing the liturgical space. Each piece of furniture has its own requirements, but at least two criteria are applicable to all of them, in fact, to any object used in any way in liturgy: 1) None should be made in such a way that it is far removed from the print of the human hand and human craft. When mass-produced items are chosen, care must be taken that

they are truly suitable. Dignity and beauty in materials used, in design and form, in color and texture—these are concerns of artists for their work, for the furniture they build, and are not, unfortunately, the evident concerns of many mass manufacturers and merchandisers. 2) All furnishings taken together should possess a unity and harmony with each other and with the architecture of the place.

BENCHES OR CHAIRS

68.   Benches or chairs for seating the assembly should be so constructed and arranged that they maximize feelings of community and involvement.[12] The arrangement should facilitate a clear view not only of the one who presides and the multiple focal points of reading, preaching, praying, music and movement during the rite, but also of other members of the congregation. This means striving for a seating pattern and furniture that do not constrict people, but encourage them to move about when it is appropriate.

69.   Benches or chairs for the seating of those engaged in the ministry of music, instrumental or choral, should be so constructed and arranged that they have the advantages described above for congregational seating and also that they are clearly part of the assembly.[13] Yet, the ministers of music should be able to sing and play facing the rest of the assembly in order to elicit the participation of the community without distracting from the central action of the liturgy. The same should be said of an individual cantor or song leader.

THE CHAIR

70.   Chairs or benches for the presiding minister or other ministers, should be so constructed and arranged that they are clearly part of the one assembly, yet conveniently situated for the exercise of their respective offices. The importance of the personal symbol and function of the one who presides in liturgical celebration should not be underrated or underplayed, because it is essential for good celebration. The chair of that person should be clearly in a presiding position, although it should not suggest either domination or remoteness.[14]

THE ALTAR

71.   The altar, the holy table, should be the most noble, the most beautifully designed and constructed table the community can provide.[15] It is the common table of the assembly, a symbol of the Lord, at which the presiding minister stands and upon which are placed the bread and wine and their vessels and the book. It is never used as a table of convenience or as a resting place for papers, notes, cruets, or anything else. It stands free, approachable from every side, capable of being encircled. It is desirable

that candles, cross, any flowers or other decoration in the area should not be so close to the altar as to constitute impediments to anyone's approach or movement around the common table.

72.   The altar is designed and constructed for the action of a community and the functioning of a single priest—not for concelebrants. The holy table, therefore, should not be elongated, but square or slightly rectangular, an attractive, impressive, dignified, noble table, constructed with solid and beautiful materials, in pure and simple proportions. Its symbolic function, of course, is rendered negligible when there are other altars in sight. The liturgical space has room for but one.

73.   The location of the altar will be central in any eucharistic celebration, but this does not mean it must be spatially in the center or on a central axis. In fact, an off-center location may be a good solution in many cases. Focus and importance in any celebration move with the movement of the rite. Placement and elevation must take into account the necessity of visibility and audibility for all.

THE AMBO

74.   The ambo or lectern is a standing desk for reading and preaching (although preaching can be done from the chair or elsewhere).[16] One main ambo should be reserved for these functions and therefore not used by commentators, song leaders, etc. Like the altar, it should be beautifully designed, constructed of fine materials, and proportioned carefully and simply for its function. The ambo represents the dignity and uniqueness of the Word of God and of reflection upon that Word.

75.   A very simple lectern, in no way competing or conflicting with the main ambo, and placed for the necessary visibility and audibility, can be used by a cantor, song leader, commentator, and reader of the announcements. It should be located for easy communication with both musicians and congregation.

BAPTISTRY

76.   To speak of symbols and of sacramental signification is to indicate that immersion is the fuller and more appropriate symbolic action in baptism.[17] New baptismal fonts, therefore, should be constructed to allow for the immersion of infants, at least, and to allow for the pouring of water over the entire body of a child or adult. Where fonts are not so constructed, the use of a portable one is recommended.

77.   The place of the font, whether it is in an area near the main entrance of the liturgical space or one in the midst of the congregation, should facilitate full congregational participation, regularly in the Easter Vigil.[18] If

the baptismal space is in a gathering place or entry way, it can have living, moving water, and include provision for warming the water for immersion. When a portable font is used, it should be placed for maximum visibility and audibility, without crowding or obscuring the altar, ambo and chair.

78.   The *celebration* of the eucharist is the focus of the normal Sunday assembly. As such, the major space of a church is designed for this *action*. Beyond the celebration of the eucharist, the Church has had a most ancient tradition of reserving the eucharistic bread. The purpose of the this reservation is to bring communion to the sick and to be the object of private devotion. Most appropriately, this reservation should be designated in a space designed for individual devotion. A room or chapel specifically designed and separate from the major space is important so that no confusion can take place between the celebration of the eucharist and reservation.[19] Active and static aspects of the same reality cannot claim the same human attention at the same time. Having the eucharist reserved in a place apart does not mean it has been relegated to a secondary place of no importance. Rather, a space carefully designed and appointed can give proper attention to the reserved sacrament.

79.   This space should offer easy access from the porch areas, garden or street as well as the main space. The devotional character of the space should create an atmosphere of warmth while acknowledging the mystery of the Lord. It should support private meditation without distractions. If iconography or statuary are present, they should not obscure the primary focus of reservation.

THE TABERNACLE

80.   The tabernacle, as a receptacle for the reservation of the eucharist, should be solid and unbreakable, dignified and properly ornamented.[20] It may be placed in a wall niche, on a pillar, eucharistic tower. It should not be placed on an altar for the altar is a place for action not for reservation. There should be only one tabernacle in a church building. A lamp should burn continously near it.

RECONCILIATION CHAPEL

81.   A room or rooms for the reconciliation of individual penitents may be located near the baptismal area (when that is at the entrance) or in another convenient place.[21] Furnishings and decoration should be simple and austere, offering the penitent a choice between face-to-face encounter or the anonymity provided by a screen, with nothing superfluous in evidence beyond a simple cross, table and bible. The

purpose of this room is primarily for the celebration of the reconciliation liturgy; it is not a lounge, counseling room, etc. The word "chapel" more appropriately describes this space.

SACRISTY

82.   A sacristy or vesting space should be located to favor the procession of cross, candles, book and ministers through the midst of the congregation to the altar area.

MUSICAL INSTRUMENTS

83.   Because choir, instrumentalists and organ often function as an ensemble, they need to be located together in such a way that the organist can see the other musicians and the liturgical action directly or by means of a simple mirror.[22] Organ consoles can be detached from the pipework and their connection supplied by flexible means. This allows for movable consoles, which may be an advantage, especially when the liturgical space serves other functions as well. However, self-contained organs, where console and pipework are united in a single element, are a possibility also, and can be designed so that the whole organ is movable. Organs designed for liturgical rather than concert purposes need not be very large; they should not be grandiose or visually dominating. But they should be superior musically, and as with all artifacts, the instrument and its casework should be authentic, beautiful and coherent with its environment. Proper space must also be planned for other musical instruments used in liturgical celebrations.

VI. OBJECTS USED IN LITURGICAL CELEBRATION

84.   Like the furniture, all other objects used in liturgical celebrations should be designed or selected in consultation with experts in both liturgy and art. Each should be not only suitable for its purpose but also capable of making a visual or other sensory contribution to the beauty of the action. The two principles cited above are applicable to everything employed in liturgy.

DUPLICATED AND MINIMIZED

85.   There is a cultural tendency to minimize symbols and symbolic gestures and to cover them with a heavy curtain of texts, words and commentary. As a result there are two other problems in our use of objects in worship.

86.   One problem is the tendency to duplicate signs and objects, a practice which seems to have multiplied in proportion to the symbols' diminution. (The converse is also true: the multiplication of the symbols causes their very diminution.) A symbol claims human attention and consciousness with a power that seems to be adversely affected by overdose. For example, the multiplication of crosses in a liturgical space or as an ornamentation on objects may lessen rather than increase attention to that symbol.

87.   A second common problem in the use of symbolic objects is a tendency to "make up" for weak primary symbols by secondary ones. It is not uncommon for example, to make extensive and expensive efforts to enrich and enliven a Sunday eucharistic celebration without paying any attention to the bread that is used or to the sharing of the cup. Bread and wine are primary eucharistic symbols, yet peripheral elements frequently get more attention. It is important to focus on central symbols and to allow them to be expressed with full depth of their vision. This may mean solutions which are less efficient and pragmatic.

THE CROSS

88.   A cross is a basic symbol in any Christian liturgical celebration. The advantage of a processional cross with a floor standard, in contrast to one that is permanently hung or affixed to a wall, is that it can be placed differently according to the celebration and the other environmental factors.[23] While it is permissible for the cross to rest on the altar, it is preferable that it be elsewhere, not only for non-eucharistic liturgies but also so that in eucharistic celebrations the altar is used only for bread and wine and book.

CANDLESTICKS AND CANDLES

89.   The same can be said of candlesticks and candles. When they are floor-standing, they can be arranged differently from time to time. The number can be varied according to the season and feast and the solemnity of the celebration. Like the cross, the candles should be visible without impeding the sight of the altar, ambo, chair and action.[24]

90.   The Easter Candle and its standard call for very special dimensions and design. They occupy a central location in the assembly during the Easter season and a place at the baptismal font thereafter.[25]

BOOKS

91.   Any book which is used by an officiating minister in a liturgical celebration should be of a large (public, noble) size, good paper, strong design, handsome typography and binding.[26] The Book of the Gospels or lectionary, of course, is central and should be handled and carried in a

special way. The other liturgical books of the Church, which contain the rites of our public worship tradition, are also worthy of venerable treatment and are a significant part of the liturgical environment. Each should be visually attractive and impressive. The use of pamphlets and leaflets detracts from the visual integrity of the total liturgical action. This applies not only to books used by ministers at the altar, chair and font, but also to those used in any other public or semipublic rite.

92.   When a liturgical book is employed at a place other than altar or ambo, the book should be held by an assistant or acolyte so that the hands and body of the one who reads are free.

VESTMENTS

93.   The wearing of ritual vestment by those charged with leadership in a ritual action is an appropriate symbol of their service as well as a helpful aesthetic component of the rite.[27] That service is a function which demands attention from the assembly and which operates in the focal area of the assembly's liturgical action. The color and form of the vestments and their difference from everyday clothing invite an appropriate attention and are part of the ritual experience essential to the festive character of a liturgical celebration.[28]

94.   The more these vestments fulfill their function by their color, design and enveloping form, the less they will need the signs, slogans and symbols which an unkind history has fastened on them. The tendency to place symbols upon symbols seems to accompany the symbolic deterioration and diminution already discussed.[29]

95.   Vesture may also be used appropriately on an altar or ambo or other objects at times, especially for festive occasions, not as "frontals" or "facades," but as decorative covering which respects the integrity and totality of the particular object.[30] The fabrics used in these instances should be chosen because of the quality of design, texture and color.

VESSELS

96.   In a eucharistic celebration, the vessels for the bread and wine deserve attention and care.[31] Just as in other types of celebration those objects which are central in the rite are a natural focus. When the eucharistic assembly is large, it is desirable not to have the additional plates and cups necessary for communion on the altar. A solution is to use one large breadplate and either one large chalice or a large flagon until the breaking of the bread. At the fraction, any other chalices or plates needed are brought to the altar. While the bread is broken on sufficient plates for sharing, the ministers of the cups pour from the flagon into the communion chalices. The number and design of such vessels will depend

on the size of the community they serve. To eat and drink is the essence of the symbolic fullness of this sacrament. Communion under one kind is an example of the minimizing of primary symbols.

97.   Like the plates and chalices or flagons, all other vessels and implements used in the liturgical celebration should be of such quality and design that they speak of the importance of the ritual action. Pitchers, vessels for holy oils, bowls, cruets, sprinklers, censers, baskets for collection, etc.—all are presented to the assembly in one way or another and speak well or ill of the deed in which the assembly is engaged.

IMAGES

98.   Images in painting or sculpture, as well as tapestries, cloth hangings, banners and other permanent or seasonal decorations should be introduced into the liturgical space upon consultation with an art consultant.[32] Like the furniture and other objects used in worship, they become part of the environment and are subject to its criteria of quality and appropriateness. In addition, their appropriateness must take into account the current renewed emphasis on the action of the assembly. If instead of serving and aiding that action, they threaten it or compete with it, then they are unsuitable.

99.   In a period of Church and liturgical renewal, the attempt to recover a solid grasp of Church and faith and rites involves the rejection of certain embellishments which have in the course of history become hindrances. In many areas of religious practice, this means a simplifying and refocusing on primary symbols. In building, this effort has resulted in more austere interiors, with fewer objects on the walls and in the corners.

DECORATIONS

100. Many new or renovated liturgical spaces, therefore, invite temporary decoration for particular celebrations, feasts and seasons. Banners and hangings of various sorts are both popular and appropriate, as long as the nature of these art forms is respected. They are creations of forms, colors, and textures, rather than signboards to which words must be attached. Their purpose is to appeal to the senses and thereby create an atmosphere and a mood, rather than to impress a slogan upon the minds of observers or deliver a verbal message.

101. Although the art and decoration of the liturgical space will be that of the local culture, identifying symbols of particular cultures, groups, or nations are not appropriate as permanent parts of the liturgical environment. While such symbols might be used for a particular occasion or holiday, they should not regularly constitute a part of the environment of common prayer.

102. Flowers, plants and trees—genuine, of course—are particularly apt for the decoration of liturgical space, since they are of nature, always discreet in their message, never cheap or tawdry or ill-made. Decoration should never impede the approach to or the encircling of the altar or any of the ritual movement and action, but there are places in most liturgical spaces where it is appropriate and where it can be enhancing. The whole space is to be considered the arena of decoration, not merely the sanctuary.

103. Suitable decoration need not and should not be confined to the altar area, since the unity of the celebration space and the active participation of the entire assembly are fundamental principles. The negative aspect of this attention to the whole space invites a thorough housecleaning in which superfluities, things that have no use or are no longer used, are removed. Both beauty and simplicity demand careful attention to each piece of furniture, each object, each decorative element, as well as to the whole ensemble, so that there is no clutter, no crowding. These various objects and elements must be able to breathe and function without being smothered by excess.

AUDIOVISUALS

104. It is too early to predict the effect of contemporary audiovisual media—films, video tape, records, tapes—on the public worship of Christians. It is safe to say that a new church building or renovation project should make provision for screens and/or walls which will make the projection of films, slides, and filmstrips visible to the entire assembly, as well as an audio system capable for fine electronic reproduction of sound.[33]

105. There seems to be a parallel between the new visual media and the traditional function of stained glass. Now that the easily printed word has lost its grip on popular communication, the neglect of audiovisual possibilities is a serious fault. Skill in using these media in ways which will not reduce the congregation to an audience or passive state can be gained only by experience.

106. Such media, of course should never be used to replace essential congregational action. At least two ways in which they may be used to enhance celebration and participation are already apparent: 1) visual media may be used to create an environment for the liturgical action, surrounding the rite with appropriate color and form; 2) visual and audio media may be used to assist in the communication of appropriate content, a use which requires great delicacy and a careful, balanced integration into the liturgy taken as a whole.

VII. CONCLUSION

107. When the Christian community gathers to celebrate its faith and vision, it gathers to celebrate what is most personally theirs and most nobly human and truly Church. The actions of the assembly witness the great deeds God has done; they confirm an age-old covenant. With such vision and depth of the assembly can the environment be anything less than a vehicle to meet the Lord and to encounter one another? The challenge of our environment is the final challenge of Christ: We must make ready until he returns in glory.

NOTES

1. 1 Jn 1.
2. Among the official conciliar and postconciliar documents which specifically address these questions are: CSL, chap. 6, 7; CR, Instruction for the Proper Implementation of the Constitution on the Sacred Liturgy, chap. 6; GI, chap. 5, 6.
3. CSL 123.
4. GI introduction, 6–15.
5. GI 4, 5.
6. CSL 123.
7. GI 254.
8. GI 253.
9. CSL 126; GI 258.
10. The DMC bases the importance of the development of gestures, postures and actions in the liturgy on the fact that liturgy, by its nature, is the activity of the entire person (see no. 33).
11. See RR, Holy Communion and Worship of the Eucharist Outside Mass [= EOM], 101–108; DMC 34.
12. GI 273.
13. GI 274.
14. GI 271.
15. GI 259–270; GIapp 263.
16. GI 272.
17. Baptism, introduction.
18. *Ibid.*, 25.
19. GI 276.
20. GI 277.
21. Rite of Penance, 12, 18b; BCLN, p. 450.
22. GI 274, 275; MCW 38.
23. GI 84, 270; GIapp 270.
24. GI 269; EOM, 85.
25. Baptism, 25.
26. BCLN, p. 417.
27. GI 297–310; GIapp 305–306.
28. GI 308; GIapp 308.
29. GI 306.
30. GI 268.
31. GI 289–296.
32. CSL 125; GI 278.
33. See DMC 35–36.

TOPICAL INDEX

ABLUTIONS
after communion or after Mass, GI 120
of fingers, when necessary, GI 237
of place where consecrated species has fallen, GI 239
of sacred vessels, GI 238

ACCLAMATION
element of eucharistic prayer, GI 55

ACCLAMATIONS
CSL 30
after consecration, GI 17
before gospel, LMIn 90–91
between readings, GI 89
in eucharistic prayer, LMT 15
in Masses with children, DMC 30
music of, MCW 53–59
part of liturgy, GI 15

preeminent sung prayers, LMT 17

ACOLYTE
CSL 29
GI 65, 58
function of Mass, GI 142–147
cf. MINISTER

ACOUSTICS
EAW 51

ACTIONS
of congregation, GI app 21
in Mass, GI 20–22
in Masses with children, DMC 33–34

ACTIVE PARTICIPATION
CSL 26–32
assembly's music ministry, LMT 63
in Masses for children, DMC 22

BIBLE READINGS
cf. READINGS

BIBLE SERVICES
CSL 35
principles for celebration of word of God, LMIn 1–10
their role in liturgical formation of children, DMC 13

BISHOPS
adaptations beyond the DMC, DMC 5
and diocesan liturgy, CSL 42
approval of words of new songs, GI 26, 56i
as high priest, CSL 41
celebration, GIapp 59
consideration for each people, region and congregation GI 6
control of liturgy, CSL 22, 39–41
decision of manner of giving peace, GI 56b
decision on postures, GI 21
dealing with sacred art, GI 256
directs all celebrations of eucharist, GI 59
judges appropriateness of concelebration and communion under two species, GI 153, 242
makes rules concelebration, GI 155
Mass he presides over, GI 74
permission for changes in vestments, GI 304, 308f
permission for new materials in vestments, GI 288
permission for special readings on certain days, GI 325
permission for women to read, GI 66
permission to honor altar and gospel book in different manner, GI 232
permission to select Masses for different needs, GI 331
rite of ordination, CSL 76
should preside, GI 59
suppression of one of feast day's three readings, GI 318
cf. CONFERENCE OF BISHOPS

BLESSING
in concluding Mass, GI 57
of altars, GI 265
of people, GI 124
of sacred vessels, GI 296

BODILY MOVEMENTS
EAW 55–62

BODY
physical attitude should show interior, GI 20
cf. POSTURES

BOOKS
for liturgy of the word, LMIn 35–37
preparation of, GI 79–80
revision of liturgical, CSL 25, 31, 38, 40

BOW
of head, GI 234
of body, GI 84, 234

BREAD
eucharistic symbol, EAW 87
larger sized, LMT 20
made of wheat flour without leaven, GI 282
should look like bread — a single piece, if possible, GI 283
cf. SPECIES OF EUCHARIST

BREAKING OF BREAD
meaning, GI 56

BUILDING(S)
austerity, EAW 99
breadth of possible uses, EAW 39
church, CSL 124, 128
domus ecclesiae, EAW 28
cf. LITURGICAL SPACE

BURIAL OF DEAD
revision of rites, CSL 81–82

CALENDAR
GNLY 48–61
and evening prayer, GNLY 61
celebrations to be entered, GNLY 48–55
determination of celebration rank, GNLY 55
for regions, countries, GNLY 51
need for unity in observance, GNLY 56
of Roman rite, GNLY 48
particular to diocese, GNLY 50
precedence of liturgical days, GNLY 59–61

CANDLES
GI 79, 84, 269

CANDLESTICKS
EAW 89

CANON
cf. EUCHARISTIC PRAYER

CANTOR
MCW 35

function, GI 36, 67, 80
in charge of congregational singing, GI
64, LMT 68–69
in liturgy of word, LMIn 53, 56
not at lectern, except for Gradual, GI
272

CATECHESIS
for first communion, DMC 12

CATECHUMENATE
CSL 64

CCD CLASSES
and liturgical formation, DMC 11

CELEBRANT
cf. PRIEST

CELEBRATIONS (LITURGICAL)
action of entire, church, EAW 30
biblical and ecclesial, EAW 10
by bishop, GIapp 59
common elements, EAW 55
communal, CSL 27
context of entire community, EAW 31
different forms, GI 74–231
different functions in, EAW 37
entire congregation an active
component, EAW 30
every action must be real, EAW 14
everything sensed as something
special, EAW 12
experience of the sacred, EAW 29
furnishings placed before ceremony,
EAW 66
governed by calendar, GNLY 48
heart of the earliest, EAW 29
local and universal experience,
common traditions, EAW 10
minimalism, EAW 14
music and progressive solemnity, LMT
13
nonrational elements, EAW 35
normal and normative way, EAW 31
objects used in, EAW 84–106
of the word of God, LMIn 1–10

paraliturgical, their role in liturgical
formation, DMC 12
participants, not spectators, EAW 11
planning and ministering liturgies,
EAW 30
proper music, LMT 7
qualities, EAW 13
recognition of gifts and talents, EAW
37
structure, rhythm, pace, EAW 25
theology of, MCW 1–9
the whole person involved in, EAW 5,
35
two Masses or other liturgical
celebrations

CENSERS
EAW 97

CHAIR
preparations for Mass with
congregation, GI 80
priest there at beginning of Mass, GI 86
location, GI 271

CHAIRS
EAW 68–70

CHALICE
EAW 96

on credence table, GI 80
brought to altar at offertory, GI 100
in offertory ceremony, GI 103
cf. VESSELS

CHALICE VEIL
white, on credence table, GI 80

CHANTS (ORDINARY)
MCW 64–69

CHANTS BETWEEN READINGS
GI app 36
in Mass, description and rite, GI 36–40

CHASUBLE
proper vestment for Mass and
accompanying ceremonies, GI 299
when it may be left off for Mass, GI
161

CHILDREN
and adults at Mass, DMC 16–19
and eucharist, DMC 8–15

CHOIR
CSL 29, 114
GI 63, 274
MCW 36

  liturgical space for, EAW 83
  of retirees for funerals, LMT 32

CHRISM MASS
GNLY 31

CHRIST
EAW 3, 4, 107

  church follows his example, GI 281
  church is his body, GI 297
  eucharist in memory of him, GI 48
  he sanctifies world, GI 1
  Mass is his act, GI 1, 4
  presence in liturgical actions, CSL 7
  present by his word, GI 9
  priest represents him, GI 10
  priests are minister of his gospel, GI
    341
  redemptive work of, CSL 5–6
  sacrifice of eucharist is his Passover, GI
    235

CHRISTMAS SEASON
GNLY 32–38

  readings, LMIn 95–96
  vestment colors, GI 308

CHURCH
CSL 2, 4, 9, 14, 26, 41, 43, 53, 83, 102, 104, 112,
122, 123

  a sacrament, CSL 2, 5
  as dominant place, EAW 41
  concern for children and their
    participation in Mass, DMC 1–7
  servant nature of, EAW 39
  servant to the world, EAW 38
  subject of liturgical action, EAW 27–38

CHURCH BUILDING
CSL 122–128

  adjoining rooms for comfort of faithful,
    GI 280
  artistic, GI 254
  church should be designed according
    to liturgical acts that congregation
    will perform, GI 259
  consecrated, especially cathedral, GI
    255
  role of diocesan commission on liturgy
    and sacred art in building and
    remodeling churches, GI 256

normal place for celebration of
  eucharist, GI 253
ornamentation simple and genuine, GI
  279
other places for certain times, GI 253
symbolic and functional, GI 253
  cf. FURNISHINGS, LITURGICAL SPACE

CHURCH YEAR
  cf. LITURGICAL YEAR

CIBORIUM
  on credence table, GI 80
  material for making, GI 292
  cf. VESSELS

CIVIL AUTHORITIES
  honors shown to, CSL 32

CLERGY
  liturgical education of, CSL 15–18, 128

COLLECT
  rite, GI 32, 88

COLLECTION
GI 101
  cf. PROCESSIONS

COLLEGIATE CHAPTERS
CSL 95

COLORS
  of Mass vestments, GI 307–310

COMMENTARIES, LITURGICAL
CSL 35

COMMENTATORS
CSL 29
GI 68

  in liturgy of the word, LMIn 57

COMMINGLING
GI 56, 113

COMMISSION ON LITURGY AND ART
CSL 44–46, 126

  advises in building and remodeling
    churches, GI 256

COMMISSION ON SACRED LITURGY
CSL 44–46

COMMISSION ON SACRED MUSIC
CSL 44–46

COMMONALITY OF LITURGY
EAW 17, 32

COMMUNAL CELEBRATION
CSL 27

COMMUNION
at Masses of dead, GI 339
ceremony, GI 56, 115, 119
in the hand, GIapp 240
on the tongue, GIapp 240
plates and cups, EAW 96
silence after, GI 23
song after, MCW 72
under both species, GIapp 242
under one kind; minimizing of symbol,
EAW 96
with both species:
a) faithful should be instructed for it,
GI 241
b) intinction, GI 246
c) more complete symbol, GI 240
d) preparations, GI 243
e) use of spoon, GI 251f
f) use of tube, GI 248–250
g) when faithful may drink from
chalice, GI 244, GIapp 242
h) when permitted, GI 242

COMMUNION ANTIPHON
recited if not sung, GI 56, 119

COMMUNION RITE
GI 56
MCW 48
in concelebrated Mass, GI 192–206
in Mass with congregation, priest's
role, GI 111–122; deacon's role, GI
136–138; acolyte's role, GI 146–147
in Mass without congregation, GI
224–230
in Masses with children, DMC 54

COMMUNION SONG
GI 56
GIapp 56i
MCW 62

COMMUNION UNDER BOTH SPECIES
CSL 55
additional times when permitted, GI
app 240
on Sunday, GIapp 242

COMMUNITY
and liturgical formation, DMC 11

COMMUNITY ASPECT OF MASS
GI 14

COMMUNITY MASS
GI 76

COMPETENCE, RESPECT FOR
EAW 45

COMPETITIONS FOR BUILDING
DESIGNS
EAW 44

COMPLINE
CSL 89

COMPOSERS
CSL 121
MCW 78
to create scriptural settings, LMT 26

CONCELEBRANTS: ALTAR DESIGN
EAW 72

CONCELEBRATION
CSL 57–58
GIapp 153
binating, GI 158
bishop makes rules, GI 155
breaking bread, GI 195
embolism, GI 193
entrance procession, GI 162
eucharistic prayer, GI 167
eucharistic prayer II, GI 179, 182
eucharistic prayer III, GI 183, 186
eucharistic prayer IV, GI 187, 191
final acclamation, GI 193
follow form of typical Mass, GI 159
giving peace, GI 194
how to use Roman canon, GI 171, 178
in religious communities, GI 76
liturgy of word, GI 164f
offertory, GI 166
Our Father, GI 192
priest may not enter late, GI 156
principal celebrant's voice should be
heard, GI 170
receiving from the cup
a) at altar, GI 205
b) after receiving, GI 207
c) from chalice, GI 201
d) with spoon, GI 203
e) with tube, GI 202
f) veneration of altar, GI 208
receiving body of Christ, GI 197–199
several times a day, GI 154
superior judges whether opportune, GI
155
those of special significance, GI 157
veneration of altar, GI 163

vestments, GI 161
when permitted, GI 153
without servers, GI 160

CONCLUDING RITE
GI 57
MCW 49

in concelebrated Mass, GI 207–208
in Mass without congregation, GI 231
in Masses with children, DMC 54

CONCLUSIONS TO PRAYERS
GI 32

CONCOURSE
cf. FOYER

CONFERENCE OF BISHOPS
cf. BISHOPS

CONFESSION
cf. RITE OF RECONCILIATION

CONFIRMATION
revision of, CSL 71

CONGREGATION
its music role, MCW 15–18, 34
role in building design, EAW 45
cf. ASSEMBLY

CONSECRATION
of altars, GI 265
of churches, especially cathedral, GI 255
of sacred vessels, GI 296

CONSECRATION OF VIRGINS
CSL 80

CONSULTATION
for building design, EAW 44
on furnishings, EAW 67
on images, EAW 98
value to architect, EAW 48

CONTEMPORARY
new church building should be, GI 280

CONVENTUAL MASS
GI 76

CONVERTS
validly baptized and rite of reception into full communion with church, CSL 69

COPE
may be used for processions and other functions, GI 303

COPYRIGHT
MCW 78
LMT 71–72

CORPORAL
brought to altar at offertory, GI 100
on credence table, GI 80

COUNCIL
Vatican II, intention of, CSL 1

CREDENCE TABLE
candlesticks may be put there, GI 84
preparations for Mass with congregation, GI 80c
vessels may be put there after Mass without congregation, GI 229
washing sacred vessels, GI 120, 139, 238

CREED
cf. PROFESSION OF FAITH

CROSS
entrance procession, GI 82
how to incense it, GI 236
location in sanctuary, GI 84, 270

CROSSES
location, EAW 88
multiplication of, EAW 86
processional, EAW 88

CRUETS
EAW 97
faithful bring them forward at offertory; otherwise, on credence table, GI 80

CULTURE(S)
EAW 16, 101

CULTURE OF PEOPLES
and liturgy, CSL 37
and music, LMT 54–55

CUSTOMS
and adaptations, CSL 40
and cultures of peoples, CSL 37
and initiation rites, CSL 65
and Lent, CSL 110
and liturgical books, CSL 38
and liturgical year, CSL 107

and music, CSL 119
and popular devotions, CSL 13
and rite of Christian burial, CSL 81
and sacred furnishings, CSL 128

DALMATIC
deacon's vestments, GI 300

DANCE
EAW 59

DAYS OF PRAYER
GI app 331

DEACON
and word of God, CSL 35
at concelebration, GI 204, 206
at preparation of gifts, GI 133
at reading of gospel, GI 132
ceremony of peace, GI 136
dismisses people, GI 140
during eucharistic prayer, GI 134
final doxology, GI 135
first among ministers, GI 61
functions, GI 61, 127–141
gives communion to people, GI 137
his communion, GI 137
in entrance procession, GI 128
in liturgy of the word, LMIn 49–50,
  53–54
in preparatory ceremony, GI 129
may make concluding announcements,
  GI 139
musical role, LMT 67
several deacons present for liturgical
  celebrations, GIapp 127
venerates altar with priest, GI 141
washes sacred vessels, GI 141
wears dalmatic, GI 300
wears stole crossed, GI 302

DEAD
cf. MASS FOR THE DEAD, RITE OF
  CHRISTIAN BURIAL

DECORATIONS OF CHURCH BUILDINGS
EAW 100–103
GI 253–280

DESIGN
cf. LITURGICAL SPACE

DEVOTIONS
popular, CSL 13

DIALOGUES
imporatance as sign of community act,
  GI 14

DIDACTIC CHARACTER
of liturgy, CSL 33–36, DMC 12
not to be excessive, DMC 13

DIOCESE
liturgical life of, CSL 41–42

DIRECTORY FOR MASSES WITH
CHILDREN
purpose, DMC 1–7; 54

DISMISSAL OF PEOPLE
GI 57, 124

DISPENSATIONS
from liturgy of the hours, CSL 97

DIVINE OFFICE
cf. LITURGY OF THE HOURS

DOXOLOGY
element of eucharistic prayer, GI 55

DOXOLOGY TO THE LORD'S PRAYER
MCW 59

EASTER
CSL 102
date of, CSL Appendix

EASTER CANDLE
EAW 89

EASTER FAST
GNLY 20

EASTER SEASON
GNLY 22–26

EASTER TRIDUUM
GNLY 18–21
readings, LMIn 95–96

EASTER VIGIL
EAW 77
GNLY 19, 21

ELEMENTS OF MASS
GI 7–57

EMBER DAYS
GNLY 45–47

EMBOLISM OF OUR FATHER
GI 111, 193

ENTRANCE SONG
GI 25–26
GI app 26
MCW 61

ENVIRONMENT
beauty, EAW 34
challenge: return of Christ in glory,
  EAW 107
meaning, EAW 24

ENVIRONMENT AND ART IN CATHOLIC
WORSHIP
purpose, EAW 6

EPICLESIS
element of eucharistic prayer, GI 55

EPISCOPAL CONFERENCES
cf. BISHOPS

EUCHARIST
action of Christ, GI 1
action of the church, GI 2
and children, DMC 8–15
celebration GI 9–6
its nature, CSL 47
its revision and celebration, CSL 48–56
mysteries of Christ present, CSL 6
relation to word of God, LMIn 10
reservation, EAW 78–80
thanksgiving, CSL 6
cf. MASS

EUCHARISTIC CHAPEL
EAW 78–79

EUCHARISTIC PRAYER
MCW 47
at concelebrated Masses, GI 170–191
high point of entire celebration, GI 10,
  54
in masses with children, DMC 52
meaning, GI 54
parts, GI 55
prayer of thanksgiving and
  sanctification, GI 54
Prayer I, GI 322
Prayer II, GI 322
Prayer III, GI 322
Prayer IV, GI 322
with Roman canon should be selected,
  GI 211

EUCHARISTIC SACRIFICE
cf. MASS

EVENING MASS OF THE LORD'S SUPPER
GNLY 19, 28

EXHORTATIONS
by commentator, GI 68
introduction to Mass by priest or one
  of ministers, GI 29, 85
presiding priests, GI 11
to achieve uniformity of movement and
  postures, GI 21

EXPERIMENTS, LITURGICAL
CSL 40

EXTREME UNCTION
cf. ANOINTING OF THE SICK

EYE CONTACT
EAW 58

FABRICS
EAW 95

FACADES
EAW 95

FAITH
nourished, strengthened and
  manifested in eucharist, GI 5
tension, EAW 1

FAITHFUL
ability to participate, GI 2, 58
active participation of, CSL 10–12;
  30–31
and liturgical instruction, CSL 18–19
and liturgical year, CSL 105
and liturgy of the hours, CSL 100
and participation in the Mass, CSL 48
and sacramental signs, CSL 59
and the liturgy, CSL 9–12
choice of eucharistic prayers, GI 322
choice of readings, GI 319
choice of Mass formulary, GI 316
good location in church, GI 273
love of eucharist, GI 66
movements and postures, GI 21
prayers, GI 319–323
sacred vessels, GI 287
should work for spiritual good of all,
  GI 313, 316
their activity, GI 19
they should honor cathedral and
  parish church, GI 255
cf. PEOPLE OF GOD

FAMILY
role in liturgical formation, DMC 10

FAST
eucharistic, FGI 25

FAST, PASCHAL
CSL 110

FEAST
GI 315
description, GNLY 13

FEAST OF THE BAPTISM OF THE LORD
GNLY 6, 38

FEAST OF THE HOLY FAMILY
GNLY 6

FEAST OF THE HOLY INNOCENTS
GNLY 35

FEAST OF SAINT JOHN
GNLY 35

FEAST OF SAINT STEPHEN
GNLY 35

FEASTS
of Mary, CSL 103
of our Lord, CSL 108
of saints, CSL 108, 111
vigils of, CSL 35

FEELINGS
in liturgical celebrations, EAW 35

FILMS
EAW 25, 104

FIRST COMMUNION
catechesis, DMC 12

FLOWERS
EAW 102

FOYER
EAW 54

FRONTAL
EAW 95

FRUITS OF MASS
certain fruits from celebration itself,
GI 4
condition of assembly, GI 3
obtained by ministers and faithful, GI 2

FUNERAL
cf. RITE OF CHRISTIAN BURIAL, MASS FOR
THE DEAD

FUNERAL MASS
cf. RITE OF CHRISTIAN BURIAL

FURNISHINGS
EAW 63–83
adaptation of, CSL 128
care in making and maintaining even
small objects, GI 312
design and care, EAW 65
disposal or preservation of, CSL 126
materials, GI app 288
materials that may be used, GI 288
purpose should be kept in mind, GI 311
sacred, CSL 122–130
unity and harmony, EAW 67
use of all arts in making them, GI 287
cf. VESSELS, VESTMENTS

FURNITURE
EAW 62, 67

GENERAL INTERCESSIONS
GI app 45
description and rite, GI 45–47

GENUFLECTION
if tabernacle is in sanctuary, GI 233
three remain in Mass, GI 233
to tabernacle at beginning of Mass, GI
84

GESTURES
CSL 30
EAW 56
in Masses with children, DMC 33–34

GIFTS
altar, offerings in kind and money,
meaning GI 49
may be incensed, GI 51
procession, GI 50, 101
prayer over gifts concludes
preparatory ceremony, GI 53

GLORY TO GOD
MCW 66
ceremony in itself, GI 17
intoned by priest or cantors, GI 87
meaning GI 30
musical text in Masses with children,
DMC 31

GODPARENTS
CSL 67

GOOD FRIDAY
GNLY 20

GOSPEL BOOK
in entrance procession, GI 82, 128, 143
location at beginning of Mass, GI 84,
129, 144
venerated with kiss, GI 232

GRADUAL
cf. RESPONSORIAL PSALM

GRADUALE ROMANUM
GI 26, 36, 56

GRADUALE SIMPLEX
GI 26, 36, 56

GREAT AMEN
MCW 58

GREETING
greeting before collect omitted, GI 32
priest representing Christ greets
people, GI 28, 86

GREGORIAN CHANT
CSL 116–117

HANDICAPPED, THE
EAW 57

HANDS
concelebrants impose hands over
offerings, GI 174, 180, 184, 188

HANGINGS
EAW 100

HIERARCHY
cf. BISHOPS

HIGH MASS
MCW 52

HOLIDAYS
symbols of, EAW 101

HOLY DAYS
and evening prayer, CSL 100
and homily, CSL 52
and prayer of the faithful, CSL 53

HOLY, HOLY, HOLY
MCW 56
ceremony in itself, GI 17

musical text in Masses with children,
DMC 31

HOMILY
CSL 35, 52
LMIn 24–27
dialogue, DMC 48
during Masses of dead, GI 338
efficacy at readings, GI 9
from lectern or chair, GI 97
given by layperson in Masses with
children, DMC 24
highly recommended part of
celebration, GI 41
in Masses with children, DMC 48
obligatory on certain days, GI 42
silence after, GI 23
who delivers it, GI 42

HONESTY
EAW 36

HONORS
to civil authorities in liturgy, CSL 32

HOSPITALITY
EAW 11, 12, 24, 57

HOSTS
consecrated at some celebration, GI 56
cf. OFFERING

HOURS
cf. OFFICE, DIVINE

HOUSE
for church's liturgical celebrations,
EAW 39–62

HYMNS
liturgy of the hours, CSL 93, LMT 45
metrical for processions, LMT 19

IMAGES
EAW 98
GI 278
sacred, CSL 125, 128

INCENSATION
at gospel, GI 93, 95
how to use incense, GI 236
of altar at beginning of Mass, GI 85
of cross, GI 236
of offering, GI 105
times for incensing, GI 235

INDIVIDUALITY
EAW 16

LECTERN
in liturgy of the word, LMIn 32–34
cf. AMBO

LECTIONARY
EAW 91
adaptations and translations, LMIn
111–118
description of order, Advent, LMIn
93–94; Christmas, LMIn 95–96; Lent,
LMIn 97–98; Easter Triduum and
season, LMIn 99–102; Ordinary
Time, LMIn 103–110
how readings were selected, LMIn
58–88
cf. READINGS

LECTORS
cf. READER

LENT
CSL 109–110
GNLY 27–31
readings in, LMIn 97–98
vestment colors, GI 308

LIGHT
EAW 50

LITANIES
MCW 74
at Lamb of God, LMT 20
penitential rite, LMT 20

LITTLE OFFICE
CSL 98

LITURGICAL ACTIONS
excellence of, CSL 7

LITURGICAL APOSTOLATE
CSL 14, 43–44

LITURGICAL BOOKS
adaptations, CSL 38
held by assistant, EAW 92
qualities; treatment, EAW 91
revision of, CSL 25
rubrics for peoples' parts, CSL 31

LITURGICAL COMMISSION
cf. COMMISSION ON SACRED LITURGY

LITURGICAL DAY
in detail, GNLY 4–16
in general, GNLY 3

LITURGICAL LAW
CSL 22, 40, 128

LITURGICAL LIFE
CSL 41

LITURGICAL ROLES
GI 2–3
their distribution, 70–72

LITURGICAL SPACE
area of presiding, EAW 60
cover or "skin", EAW 42
design: inspire and serve, EAW 46
design: prior requirements of liturgy,
EAW 4
designing norm, EAW 42
ease of movement, EAW 62
major design for eucharistic liturgy,
EAW 78
multi-functional use, EAW 65
necessity; functions, EAW 39
orientation point for believers, EAW 41
pathways to, EAW 54
physical location, EAW 42
primary demands by liturgy, EAW 40
renovations, EAW 43
sacredness, EAW 41
scale; aim, EAW 52
the serving environment, EAW 24
unity; integrity, EAW 53
variety of celebrations, EAW 64
cf. ALSO BUILDING(S)

LITURGICAL STRUCTURE
music within, LMT 6–7
of Mass, MCW 42–49
cf. READINGS

LITURGICAL YEAR
contemporary culture opposes, LMT 48
description, GNLY 1–2
in detail, GNLY 17–44
music and, LMT 46–48
nature of and its revision, CSL 102–111
seasonal table of principal celebrations
of, LMIn Table I

LITURGY
action of the Christian assembly, EAW
9
central place in Christian assembly,
EAW 9
central place in Christian life, EAW 32
climate of, EAW 34
communal nature of, CSL 26–32
didactic nature of, CSL 33–36

hierarchical nature of, CSL 26–32
inherently musical, LMT 5
nature of, CSL 2, 5–11
needed by people, EAW 4
past tradition; contemporary assembly,
 EAW 33
pastoral nature of, CSL 32–36
personal-communal experience, EAW
 16–17
promotion of, CSL 14–20
reform of, CSL 21–25

LITURGY COMMITTEE
GI 73
MCW 10–14

LITURGY OF THE EUCHARIST
in concelebrated Mass, GI 166–191
in Mass with congregation, priest's
 role, GI 100–122; deacon's role, GI
 133–138; acolyte's role, GI 145–147
memorial of Lord's sacrifice and
 supper, GI 48
parts are preparation, prayer,
 breaking of bread and communion,
 GI 48
preparation, GI 100
presided over by bishop or priest, GI
 59

LITURGY OF THE HOURS
CSL 83–101
mixing musical idioms, LMT 44–45
psalm-singing methods, LMT 34–43

LITURGY OF THE WORD
MCW 45
aids to proper celebration, LMIn 32–37
elements of, LMIn 11–31
in concelebrated Mass, GI 164–165
in Mass with congregation, priest's
 role, GI 89–99; presider's function,
 LMIn 38–43; faithful's role, LMIn
 44–48
in Mass without congregation, GI
 217–220
in Masses with children, DMC 41–49
meaning and parts, GI 33
offices and ministries in, LMIn 38–57
music in, LMT 7
separate, for children, DMC 17
cf. LECTERN, READINGS

LITURGY PLANNING
GI 69, 73

LORD HAVE MERCY
MCW 65
meaning, GI 30
rite, GI 30, 87

LORD'S PRAYER
MCW 67
liturgical meaning, GI 56
participation, GI 16
rite, GI 110

LORD'S SUPPER
GI 7

LOW MASS
MCW 52

MARRIAGE
cf. RITE OF CHRISTIAN MARRIAGE

MARTYRS
memorials of, CSL 104

MARY
CSL 103

MASS
CSL 47–57
ablutions, GI 229
adapting parts to assembly increases its
 fruits, GI 313
breaking of bread, commingling, GI
 226
celebrated in connection with
 sacraments and sacramentals, GI 326
celebrated without acolyte only for
 grave reason, GI 211
center of Christian life, GI 1
choice of readings, GI 310, 317, (cf.
 READINGS)
choice of prayers, GI 321, 323. (C.f.
 EUCHARISTIC PRAYER)
communion, GI 227
community aspect, GI 14
concelebrated, GI 153–208
conventual, GI 76
days when there is choice of Masses,
 GI 315b, 316
days when there is no choice of
 Masses, GI 314, 315
eucharistic prayer, GI 223
follows rubrics of Mass with
 congregation, GI 210
for special occasions:
a) any Mass except ritual Masses may
 be celebrated on ferial days or
 commemorations, GI 334

OBJECTS
  used in liturgy, EAW 84–106

OBLIGATORY MEMORIAL
  cf. MEMORIAL

OCCASION (LITURGICAL)
  its music, MCW 19–20

OCTAVE
GNLY 12

OCTAVE OF CHRISTMAS
GNLY 35

OFFERING
  element of eucharistic prayer, GI 55
  in Mass, CSL 48
  cf. GIFTS

OFFERTORY ANTIPHON
  omitted if not sung, GI 50

OFFERTORY CEREMONY
  cf. PREPARATION OF THE GIFTS

OFFERTORY SONG
GI app 50
MCW 71

OFFICE, DIVINE
  cf. LITURGY OF THE HOURS

OFFICES
  in Masses with children, DMC 22–24
  in the Mass, GI 58–73

OPENING CEREMONIES
  list of, GI 24
  procession of ministers, GI 82
  purpose, GI 24

OPENING PRAYER
  description and rite, GI 32

OPTIONAL MEMORIAL
  cf. MEMORIAL

OPTIONAL MEMORIAL OF BVM
GNLY 15

OPTIONS
  in Mass texts, GI 313–325

ORDER OF MASS
CSL 50–56
  cf. MASS, EUCHARIST

ORDER OF READINGS
  cf. READINGS, LECTIONARY

ORDER OF SUPPLYING WHAT WAS
OMITTED IN THE BAPTISM OF AN
INFANT
CSL 69

ORDERS, SACRED
CSL 76

ORDINARIES
CSL 57, 64, 68, 97, 101, 124, 126

ORDINARY CHANTS
MCW 64–69

ORDINARY TIME
GNLY 43–44

ORDINATION
  revisions of rites, CSL 76

ORGAN
CSL 120
EAW 83
  its placement, MCW 38
  its role, MCW 37
  preferred locations, GI 275

OUR FATHER
  cf. LORD'S PRAYER

PAINTINGS
CSL 122–124

PALL
  for use when needed, GI 80

PALM SUNDAY
  cf. PASSION SUNDAY

PAMPHLETS
EAW 91

PARALITURGICAL CELEBRATIONS
  and frequency of Mass with children,
    DMC 27
  their role in liturgical formation of
    children, DMC 27
  word of God in, LMIn 1–10

PARENTS
  role in liturgical formation, DMC 10

PARISH
  and liturgical formation, DMC 11
  liturgical life in, CSL 42

PARISH TEAM
GI 73, 313, 333

PARTICIPATION
acclamations and responses, GI 15
active, of faithful, CSL 11, 14, 19, 30,
    31, 48, 55, 56, 118
and word of God, LMIn 6
arrangement of church building, GI
    253
attentiveness, EAW 58
aware, active, and complete, GI 3, 5, 15
choice of eucharistic prayer, GI 322
communion at Masses of dead, GI 339
communion with two species, GI 240
faithful and ministers participate
    according to their status, GI 2
faithful's role in liturgy of the word,
    LMIn 44-48
greetings and prayers of priest, GI 15
location of altar, GI 262
location of faithful, GI 273
penance ceremony, creed, prayer of
    faithful, Our Father, GI 16
postures, GI 20
procession of gifts, GI 101
ritual lectionaries for better
    participation, GI 320
singing, GI 19

PARTS
of Mass, GI 7-57

PASCHAL MYSTERY
CSL 5-9, 106

PASSION SUNDAY
GNLY 30-31

PASTORAL JUDGMENT
MCW 39-41

PASTORAL LITURGICAL ACTION
CSL 19, 33-36, 44

PASTORAL LITURGY, INSTITUTE OF
CSL 44

PASTORAL PLANNING
MCW 10-14

PASTORS
CSL 11, 14, 19, 100 114
and liturgical instruction of faithful,
    CSL 18
and parish liturgy, CSL 42

PATEN
lifting it at offertory, GI 102
on credence table, GI 80
same one used for celebrant and
    faithful, GI 293

PEACE CEREMONY
a presidential prayer, GI 112
ceremony of giving peace, GI 112
invitation to give peace, GI 112
meaning, GI 56b
wish for assembly, GI 112

PENANCE, SACRAMENT OF
cf. RITE OF RECONCILIATION

PENANCES
CSL 104, 110

PENITENTIAL RITE
participation, GI 16
rite described, GI 29, 87
silence after exhortation, GI 16

PENTECOST
GNLY 22, 26

PEOPLE OF GOD
participation:
a) best location in church, GI 273
b) church should have adjoining rooms
    for their comfort, GI 280
c) elements, GI 14-17
d) especially on Sundays, GI 77
e) priestly character, GI 62
f) single body, GI 62
priest presides, GI 7
cf. PARTICIPATION

PERSONS
distinction of or honor shown in
    liturgy, CSL 32
symbolic function, EAW 16
total approach to, EAW 35

PICTURES
prepared by children, DMC 26

PLACE
of Masses with children, DMC 25

PLANTS
EAW 102

POLYPHONY
CSL 116

PONTIFICALS
  reservation of, CSL 130

POSTURES
EAW 57
GI app 21
  determining postures during Mass, GI
    21
  sign of unity and community, GI 20
  uniformity of movements and postures,
    GI 21
  cf. KNEELING, SITTING, STANDING

PRAY, BROTHERS AND SISTERS
(ORATE FRATRES)
GI 107

PRAYER
CSL 7, 12, 105
  and liturgical formation, DMC 10
  and music, MCW 84
  common prayer and frequency of Mass
    with children, DMC 27
  days of, GI app 331
  personal gestures, EAW 56

PRAYER AFTER COMMUNION
GI 56, 122

PRAYER OF THE FAITHFUL
CSL 53–54
  function and content, GI 45
  may be adapted for special occasions,
    GI 46
  minister and place, GI 47, 99
  participation, GI 16
  cf. ORDER OF MASS

PRAYER OVER GIFTS
GI 53, 107

PRAYER OVER PEOPLE
GI 57

PRAYER, THE COMMON
  cf. PRAYER OF THE FAITHFUL

PRAYERS OF PRESIDING PRIEST
GI 10–13
  choice of collect, prayer over gifts, and
    prayer after communion in
    commemorations and ferial Masses,
    GI 323
  cf. EUCHARISTIC PRAYER, PRESIDENTIAL
    PRAYERS

PRAYERS, PRIVATE
  at offertory, GI 103f
  before communion, GI 113–115
  which they are and how to say them,
    GI 13

PREACHING
  cf. HOMILY

PREPARATION
  for Masses with children, DMC 29

PREPARATION OF THE GIFTS
MCW 46
  description and rite, GI 49–53
  in concelebrated Mass, GI 166
  in Mass with congregation, priest's
    role, GI 100–1007; deacon's role,
    GI 133; acolyte's role GI 145
  in Mass without a congregation,
    GI 221–223

PREPARING FOR CELEBRATION
GI 73

PRESCHOOLS
  and liturgical formation, DMC 11

PRESENCE
  of Christ, CSL 7

PRESIDENTIAL PRAYERS
  in Masses with children, DMC 50–52
  may be adapted in Masses with
    children, DMC 51

PRETENSE
  in liturgical art, EAW 36

PRIEST
CSL 18, 22, 35, 57
  does what Christ did, GI 48
  his music role, MCW 21–22
  may give exhortations, GI 11
  musical role, LMT 67
  presides over congregation in Christ's
    name, GI 60
  represents Christ, GI 48
  says presidential prayer, GI 13
  should be heard when he speaks as
    president, GI 12
  speaks for entire congregation, GI 54

PRIESTHOOD
  of Christ, CSL 5–8

PRIME
CSL 69
  cf. LITURGY OF THE HOURS

PROCESSIONAL SONGS
MCW 60–62
  accompany action, LMT 18–19

PROCESSIONS
EAW 59
  communion, GI 119, 137, 210, 206
  entrance, GI 82, 127, 142, 162
  gospel, GI 94
  in Masses with children, DMC 34
  offertory, GI 49f, 101, (cf. GIFTS) 133,
    147
  songs, MCW 60–62
  vestments for, GI 303

PROCLAMATION OF TEXTS
ACCORDING TO LITERARY FORM
GI 18

PROFESSION OF FAITH
MCW 69
  Apostle's Creed may be used in Masses
    with children, DMC 49
  by priest and people, GI 98
  function, GI 43
  musical text in Masses with children,
    DMC 31
  participation, GI 16
  rite, GI 44
  slowly introduce Nicene Creed, DMC
    39

PROFESSION, RELIGIOUS
  revision of, CSL 80

PROFESSORS OF LITURGY
CSL 15–16

PROPER OF SEASONS
  over particular celebrations, GNLY 50a

PROPERTY, CHURCH
EAW 38

PSALMS
  in liturgy of the hours, CSL 90–91
  how to sing, LMT 34–43

PUBLISHERS
MCW 78

PURIFICATIONS
GI 237–239

PURIFICATOR
  brought to altar at offertory, GI 100
  on credence table, GI 180

QUALITY
  conditions for, EAW 26
  contemplation, EAW 20

RADIO
  transmission of rites by, CSL 20

READER
CSL 29
  function, GI 66, 148, 152
  instituted readers, LMIn 51
  layperson, GI 66
  ordinary reader of various parts, GI 34
  role in liturgy of the word, LMIn 49,
    51–55
  speaking style, LMIn 14
  woman, GI 66, 89, 91

READINGS
  adaptation by conference of bishops
    permitted, GI 325
  adaptations, LMIn 111–118
  any of week for special gatherings, GI
    319
  arrangement of readings in Ordinary
    Time: second reading for Sundays,
    LMIn Table II, first weekday reading,
    LMIn Table III
  at lectern, GI 272
  Christ is present in his word, GI 23
  comments before, DMC 47
  continuous readings on ferial days, GI
    319
  distribution of parts in reading, DMC
    47
  format for proclamation, LMI 119–125
  God's table, GI 34
  how to plan the choice of readings,
    LMIn 78–88
  important element of Mass, GI 9
  in liturgy of the hours, CSL 92
  in Mass, description and rite, GI 34–35
  in the Mass, CSL 35, 51
  lectionaries for Masses during which
    sacrament or sacramental is given,
    GI 320
  number, in Masses with children,
    DMC 42
  on Sundays and Feasts, GIapp 318
  one may be omitted at times, GI 318
  pastoral aim of, LMIn 58–63
  responsorial psalm, LMIn 89

special honor for Gospel, GI 35
three on Sundays and feast days,
  GI 318
who reads, GI 89, 91, 96

RECEPTION OF CONVERT INTO THE
CHURCH
CSL 69

RECESSIONAL SONG
MCW 73

RECONCILIATION CHAPEL
EAW 81

REFORM
  of liturgy, CSL 3, 21–40

RELICS
  of saints, CSL 111
  should be genuine, GI 266
  should be in altar, GI 266

RELIGIOUS
CSL 55, 95

RELIGIOUS PROFESSION
  revision of, CSL 80

RENEWAL
  attention to all human faculties, EAW 5
  recognition of the sacred, EAW 18

RENEWAL OF VOWS
CSL 80

RENOVATION OF BUILDINGS
EAW 43, 44

REPOSITION OF BLESSED SACRAMENT
IEW 65

RESERVATION OF EUCHARIST
EAW 78–79
  kept in burlgar-proof tabernacle,
    GI 277
  other possibilities, GI 276
  should be in special chapel, GI 276

RESERVED BLESSINGS
CSL 79

RESPONSES
CSL 30
  part of liturgy, GI 15

RESPONSORIAL PSALM
GI app 36
MCW 63
  after first reading, GI 90
  ceremony in itself, GI 17
  response to readings, GI 33, 36
  selection of, LMIn 89
  usually from lectionary, GI 36

RESURRECTION
  all things made new, EAW 4
  paschal mystery, EAW 13

RETARDED
  adaptations of DMC to physically or
    mentally handicapped, DMC 6

RITE FOR THE CONSECRATION OF
VIRGINS
CSL 80

RITE OF ANOINTING OF THE SICK
CSL 73–75
  music, MCW 81

RITE OF CHRISTIAN BURIAL
GI app 340
  color of vestments, GIapp 308
  its revision, CSL 81–82
  music, MCW 80, LMT 22–26
  musically overlooked, LMT 30
  progressive solemnity applies, LMT 33

RITE OF CHRISTIAN INITIATION
  music, MCW 80, LMT 22–26
  revision of, CSL 64–66

RITE OF CHRISTIAN MARRIAGE
MCW 82
  diocesan music policy, LMT 28
  revision of, CSL 77–78

RITE OF CONFIRMATION
CSL 71
  music, MCW 82

RITE OF INFANT BAPTISM
CSL 67–69
  music, MCW 80

RITE OF ORDINATION
CSL 76

RITE OF PEACE
GI 56